SWING CITY

Newark Nightlife, 1925–50

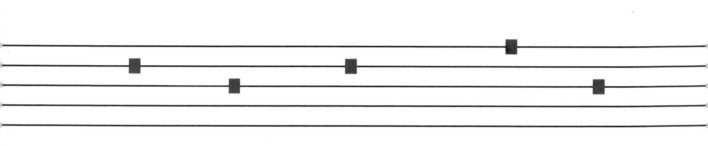

SWING CITY

NEWARK NIGHTLIFE 1925–50

Barbara J. Kukla

Rutgers University Press / New Brunswick, New Jersey

First published in paperback 2002
by Rutgers University Press

First published in hardcover 1991
by Temple University Press
Copyright © 1991 by Barbara J. Kukla

Manufactured in the United States of America

Designed by Arlene Putterman

Library of Congress Cataloging-in-Publication Data
Kukla, Barbara J.
    Swing city : Newark nightlife, 1925–50 / Barbara J. Kukla.
        p. cm.
    Includes bibliographical references and index.
    ISBN 0-8135-3116-0 (pbk. : alk. paper)
    1. Jazz—New Jersey—Newark—History and criticism.
  2. African Americans—New Jersey—Newark—Music.
  3. Newark (N.J.)—History. I. Title.
ML3508.8.N53 K8 2002
781.65'09749'32—dc21   2001048796

Viola Wells (Miss Rhapsody), 1973. From author's collection

*For Miss Rhapsody,
who inspired my life and this work*

Contents

THE CLUBS, 1935–44

TWO INSTITUTIONS, 1939–49

A NEW GROOVE, 1942–50

APPENDIXES

Illustrations

Acknowledgments

This book is dedicated to Viola Wells (Miss Rhapsody), whose love of her hometown, fellow musicians, friends, and neighbors inspired my interest in chronicling Newark's nightlife and provided a firm foundation for my research. After Rhap's death in 1984, I had substantial support, advice, and criticism from Sheldon Harris, author of *Blues Who's Who*, and from my friend Connie (Williams) Woodruff, editor of the *New Jersey Herald News* during the waning days of Newark's nightclub era.

No book on this subject would be anywhere near complete without the input of Bob Queen, whose comments and columns in the *New Jersey Afro-American* over a fifty-year period are among the few written sources of what is largely an oral history. I am deeply indebted also to David Bartlett, director of Temple University Press, my editors, Doris Braendel and Mary Capouya, designer Arlene Putterman, and Edell Grant for truly believing in this venture and bringing it to fruition in such fine fashion.

Four of Newark's elder statesmen, Wesley (Wes) Clark, William (Uncle Willie) Hurt, Bill Roberts, and Charles Sowell, provided much of the material dating to the early 1900s. My heartfelt thanks go also to Charles Cummings, historian for the City of Newark and assistant director of Special Collections at the Newark Public Library, and to Valerie Austin, Bob Blackwell, and Jim Osbourn of the library's New Jersey Division.

The generosity of those who provided an array of heretofore unpublished photographs is sincerely appreciated: James (Billy) Anderson, Clyde Bernhardt, Doryce Bradley, James Churchman Jr., Wes Clark, Lander Coleman, the Reverend Russell Coleman, Meredith Gordon, Billie (Sermond) Hall, Sheldon Harris, Al Henderson, Florence (Williams) Henderson, Marie Jennings, Jimmy (Chops) Jones, William (Willie) Johnson, Floyd Lang, Carl McIntyre, Florence (Hall) McIntyre, Sadie Matthews, Jackson (Flap) McQueen, Harold (Hal) Mitchell, Clem Moorman, Lucille (Dorsey) Morton, Alma Plater, Bob Queen, Eurlee Reeves, Thomas O. (T. O.) Swangin, Flo Thomas, Gertrude (Turman) Brown, Frank R. Wallace, and Cecilia Wilcox. Thanks also to Dick Tashjian and John A. Gibson Jr. for replicating the photos.

Out of a shared concern for documenting this vanishing segment of history, extensive interviews were granted by Howard (Duke) Anderson, Herman Bradley, Wes Clark, Leon Eason, Joe Gregory, Billie (Sermond) Hall, Al Henderson, Thad (Chuck) Howard, Willie Johnson, Audrey (Celeste) Jones, Jimmy (Chops) Jones, Charlie Matthews, Sadie Matthews, Jackson (Flap) McQueen, Lucille (Dorsey) Morton, Hal Mitchell, Grachan (Brother) Moncur, Clem Moorman, Eurlee Reeves, and T. O. Swangin. Several chapters rest largely on their contributions.

For making this work whole, thanks also to Bea Anderson, Estelle Bailey, Robert Banks, Sanford Bell, Clyde Bernhardt, Earline Berry, Nancy Bogar, Humphrey (Teddy) Brannon, Nate Brown, Mary Pitts Jones Cameron, Jimmy Clark, Ada Cole, June (Jay) Cole, Chris Columbus, Rita Costello, Sam Debnam, Frank Driggs, Eddie Durham, Erma Ethridge, Harold Ford, Danny Gibson, Bruce Grossberg, Lois Grossberg, Richard (Dick) Harvest, Kitty and Jack Harvey, Florence Henderson, Jan Jackson, Inez Jennings, Alice Jones, Frank Jones, George Kelly, Frederick H. (Fred) Kukla, Dorothy Latta, Connie Lester, Anna May Lundy Lewis, Billy Lewis, Fred Mendelsohn, Emily Miles and family, James Moody, Dan Morgenstern, James (Chippie) Outcalt, Henrietta Parker, Ernie Phipps, Gene Phipps Sr., Nat Phipps, Jean Pittman, Milton Pittman Jr., Napoleon (Teddy) Powell, Tiny Prince, Bob Queen, Bennie (Red) Robinson, Harold Rollins, Little Jimmy Scott, Hattie Simmons, Grace Smith, Jabbo Smith, Big Ted Smith, Togge Smythe, Jimmy Stanford, Madeline Steffens, Geraldine Surgent, Freddie Toler, Geneva Turman, Bobby Williams, Luther (Gates) Willis, Harold (Chink) Wing, and Eddie Wright. Lastly, I am indebted to Bill Cosby for his kind and generous support of this effort.

Given the magnitude of this effort, I am forever grateful for the patience and understanding shown by those who wished to see their ever-vanishing history preserved. The information herein is as up to date as could be. My only regret is that so many performers did not live to see it published. It would be impossible to capture all of the flavor of Newark nightlife during this period. I hope this effort will be well received by those who were such a vital part of this era, and I pray that these pages will serve as a fitting tribute to them and to the institutions that made Newark swing.

Barbara J. Kukla
March 1, 1991

Preface to the Paperback Edition

This paperback publication of *Swing City: Newark Nightlife, 1925–50* by Rutgers University Press comes at a most appropriate time. Foremost, the year 2002 marks the 100th birthday of Viola Wells Evans to whom the book is dedicated. Known as "Miss Rhapsody," she was one of Newark's earliest and most beloved entertainers. This publication also coincides with Newark's resurgence as a major force in our country's cultural history. As a black history book, *Swing City* speaks as well to the indomitable spirit of African-Americans everywhere.

Since the completion of the manuscript of *Swing City*, many of Newark's most famous musicians passed away. Death dates for several others subsequently were discovered:

Howard (Duke) Anderson, January 24, 1999
Doryce Bradley, September 24, 1996
Herman Bradley, July 24, 1998
Humphrey (Teddy) Brannon, February 24, 1989
Wesley (Wes) Clark, February 20, 1994
Lander Coleman, May 3, 2001
Russell Coleman, July 20, 1999
Leon Eason, March 2, 1993
Harold Ford, April 22, 1999
Clarence (Mouse) Fulford, March 1966
Amelia (Ame) Garrison, August 22, 1997
Danny Gibson, February 20, 2000
Fortune (Fats) Jennings, September 1982
Milton (Prince) Jones, March 10, 1999
Baron Lester, December 10, 2000

Jackie Mandeville, December 26, 1989
Charlie Matthews, March 30, 1990
Sadie (Little Poopsie) Matthews, March 27, 1995
Carl McIntyre, February 23, 1995
Harold (Hal) Mitchell, November 3, 1998
Grachan Moncur, October 31, 1996
James (Chippie, Mr. Chips) Outcalt, February 1988
Alamae Plater, January 5, 1997
Arthur Prysock, June 21, 1997
Ernie (Skeets) Ransom, January 15, 1994
Eurlee Reeves, February 1, 1990
Satchel Robinson, March 11, 1997
Johnny Rogers, May 16, 1998
Billie Sermond, May 14, 1994
Horace Sims, April 23, 1994

Chester (Chet) Slater, March 5, 1998
Ted (Big Ted) Smith, October 2, 1998
Ann Standard, May 20, 1998
James (Jimmy) Stanford, March 14, 1999
Thomas O. (T.O.) Swangin, April 23, 1990
Freddie Toler, July 1987
Charles (Gene) Tolson, January 1, 1990

Gertrude Turman, November 17, 1991
Sarah Vaughan, April 3, 1990
Harry Webber, June 21, 1991
Melvin (Slappy) White, November 7, 1995
Harold (Chink) Wing, December 17, 1993
Connie Williams Woodruff, October 19, 1996
Eddie Wright, May 8, 2000

SWING CITY

Newark Nightlife, 1925–50

Introduction

When Broad Street was only a lonely pasture,
And Market Street was nothing but a lane
Where I used to milk the cows;
Where Hahne's is standing now,
And Bamberger's wasn't even a site to be found
And on old Augusta Street there wasn't a pimp around;
Everybody was your friend,
But things have changed a lot since then;
Broad Street's no pasture now.
(A favorite recitation of Uncle Willie Hurt, a Kinney Club patron)

This book is a broad social history of night-life in Newark, New Jersey, a thriving mecca of entertainment from 1925 to 1950. It focuses on black life during the days of vaudeville and the Swing Era and the instruments of economic and social survival employed by African-Americans at a time when every aspect of American life was strictly segregated. The theme is entertainment and music, but *Swing City* is just as much about the vicissitudes of life in urban black America.

Music historians of this era generally have concentrated on the traditional cradles of black music: New Orleans, Chicago, New York, and Kansas City with the emergence of the Basie band. Yet places like Newark, Baltimore, and Philadelphia were swinging, too, Newark especially because it was just ten miles from New York and was New Jersey's largest city.

Rising gradually from the west bank of the Passaic River, Newark in the first half of the twentieth century was a mosaic of ethnic groups and neighborhoods dominated by enclaves of Irish, Germans, Jews, Italians, middle Europeans, and blacks who emigrated from southern states.

The eastern part of the city, closest to the river, was a combination of heavy industry and older residential areas made up for the most part of working-class homes, close together and fronting narrow streets. The most well-known area was the Ironbound section (also known as "Down Neck"), separated from the downtown business and commercial district on the west by the elevated Pennsylvania railroad line (hence "bound by iron"). This was home, for the most part, to poorer Italians, middle Europeans, and blacks who had come north at the turn of the century.

The city's commercial area was spread north and south along Broad Street (the main artery) to the west, with large department stores like Kresge's and Hahne's on the north and City Hall toward the south. A few blocks west of Broad Street was the Hill area, part of the old Third Ward, which became home to the city's burgeoning black population in the 1930s and 1940s. Here, poor and working-class blacks lived in tree-shaded tenements, interspersed among Jewish merchants who did business along Prince Street and lived in railroad flats above their shops. The Barbary Coast, as the red-light district was called, was on the fringes of the Third Ward, extending (loosely) westward from Washington Street to High Street and from Branford Place on the north to Lincoln Park on the south.

The southern part of the city was entirely residential, composed mostly of single and two-family homes set back amid gracious lawns and gardens on tree-lined streets. By the mid 1930s, and until riots ravaged the city in 1967, most of the area was predominantly Jewish.

In the western sector of the city, toward Irvington and other suburban Essex County municipalities, lived a mix of Irish, Ukrainians, and other Slavic ethnic groups. For the most part they lived in one-, two-, and three-family frame houses off major arteries like South Orange Avenue, where shops and light industry prevailed.

The northern part of the city was a mix of estate-like homes like the old Clark Mansion, built by the founder of the Clark Thread Company in the 1800s, 1920s brick apartment houses, and various configurations of frame houses. It was populated largely by Italians, tenaciously tied to their property.

Since its founding in 1666 as a Puritan village, Newark has had a vibrant and versatile history. In 1746, it became home to the College of New Jersey, founded just a few months earlier in nearby Elizabethtown. The college—New Jersey's first—was the forerunner of Princeton University. When it moved to Newark, Aaron Burr Sr., pastor of Old First Church and father of Aaron Burr Jr., who became vice president of the United States, was named as its second president. The younger Burr was the famous figure who killed Alexander Hamilton in a duel in Weehawken, New Jersey and was tried as a traitor after futilely attempting to get Texas and other southern states to secede from the United States.

From its earliest days, Newark was on its way to becoming a bustling manufacturing town, partly because of its prime location near the river. Initially, tanning was the major industry, spurred by the invention of patent leather by Seth Boyden in 1818. By the late 1800s the city was a thriving industrial center, producing everything from hats and coaches to pottery and drain work pipes. In his history of Newark, historian John Cunningham wrote how visitors to the city's Industrial Exposition of 1872, the first such event of its kind nationwide, saw "a glittering array of Newark products. They saw harnesses valued at $10,000, gold-plated sleigh bells worth up to $200 a set, one hundred styles of table oilcloth, books printed in Newark, pearl buttons, ribbons, and a hundred varieties of paint. They saw buggies, walnut bird cages, ink, rosettes, steam fire engines, gold pens, chalk, tools, toys, malleable iron castings, telegraph instruments, and clocks."

By 1925, Newark had 1,668 factories and a payroll of $90 million. By the beginning of the twentieth century, it had emerged as New Jersey's financial hub, serving as home to major banks and insurance companies like Prudential, which remains headquartered in Newark. It also was the state's center of commerce, connected to the suburbs by its streetcars and railways and to the world by its busy seaport.

A thorough examination of Newark's importance as a great entertainment center, however, has escaped the pages of history. As for black history in general, this is so for two related reasons: because societal restrictions forced a continuing dependence on an oral tradition passed from one generation to another

A Newark nightclub scene, circa 1940: drummer Gus Young and dancer/emcee Satchel Robinson (shaking hands); clockwise, from left side of table, Ella Moncur, wife of bassist Grachan (Brother) Moncur (holding glass); pianist Vernon Biddle; Theresa Rheubina Jackson, wife of bandleader Johnny Jackson; Ruby Robinson (wide-brimmed hat); Ralph Smith, stepbrother of Willie (The Lion) Smith; unidentified; Elijah (Mr. Big) Coleman; next three unidentified; Kinney Club waitress Lucille Dorsey. Courtesy of Lucille (Dorsey) Morton

and because black people's accomplishments were not considered important enough to document. But Newark was important, and a special debt is owed to the hundreds of performers who made it one of the nation's prominent entertainment capitals.

As authors Charles Nanry and Ed Berger—among the few to acknowledge Newark as a jazz center—have concluded, jazz is city music: "Jazz musicians came from all over, but they made their reputations in cities." Along Broad Street, downtown Newark's major thoroughfare, clubs that catered to "whites only" and theaters where blacks were welcome only in the balconies abounded during the Jazz Age and the Swing Era. Shows headed for New

York played Newark on the way in or out. Week in, week out in the 1920s, the marquees of the Shubert, Proctor's, and other opulent downtown theaters advertised appearances by top entertainers of the day—Eddie Cantor, Ed Wynn, Fanny Brice, and black stars like the talented Florence Mills. A decade later the headliners included singers Ella Fitzgerald and Billy Eckstine, along with every major band of the Swing Era, from Count Basie and Duke Ellington to Jimmie Lunceford and Louis Jordan and His Tympany Five.

Nightlife flourished, in part because Newark was a beer town, the nation's third leading brewer in the 1920s, home of the "Big Five"—Ballantine, Hensler, Krueger, Feigen-

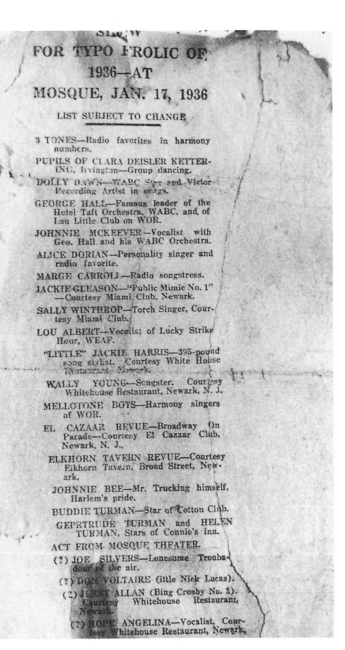

Showbill for the 1936 all-star show at the Mosque Theater. Comedian Jackie Gleason was eighth on the bill. Courtesy of Gertrude Turman

span and Weidenmeyer. During Prohibition Newark was wide open, its speakeasies accessible for the price of a membership card. Although the Volstead Act, energized by illegal rum and whiskey running, took a toll on the beer trade, Newark still had nearly a thousand saloons in 1938, one for every 429 residents, the most per capita of any American city. Many small neighborhood establishments attracted customers by offering live entertainment, often a band, sometimes a singer or an entire revue.

Because there were so many clubs, Newark was a great place to launch a show business career in the 1930s and 1940s. Jackie Gleason got his start at the Club Miami on Clinton Avenue, "borrowing" catchy material from his black counterparts who performed in the neighborhood taverns. Red Foxx, who came from Baltimore, played some of his first club dates in Newark's old Third Ward, the heart of the Hill area that was home to thousands of poor and working-class blacks.

The biggest and most important star from Newark was Sarah Vaughan. As an innovative jazz soloist, Vaughan—along with singer Billy Eckstine, who discovered her, and Dizzy Gillespie—was on the cutting edge of a new form of music called bebop. While Vaughan was stamping her imprimatur on popular music and jazz, her friend and fellow Newarker Ike Quebec rapidly was gaining recognition as one of the world's foremost tenor saxophonists. Hailed by his peers and critics as a jazz legend, Quebec was also a key figure in the shift from swing to bop.

Newark also spawned a rich crop of hometown entertainers who brought their specialties to public attention in the downtown theaters and the maze of Third Ward nightclubs. Newark's grand dame of song was Viola Wells (Miss Rhapsody), whose commanding way with a song has been described as a blend of Billie Holiday and Ella Fitzgerald. Both she and Leon Eason, whose trumpet playing often was compared to Louis Armstrong's, spent their entire working lives in music, performing into their eighties. In his prime, Harold (Hal) Mitchell was revered by his peers— viewed as one of Newark's musical giants, a stalwart of the Swing Era bands of Tiny Bradshaw and Benny Carter. Another veteran, pianist Clem Moorman, still tours in shows starring singers like Della Reese and Eartha

Redd Foxx, mid 1940s. Courtesy of Doryce Bradley

Sarah Vaughan, early 1950s. Courtesy of Florence (Williams) Henderson

Kitt. Howard (Duke) Anderson, who filled in for Count Basie in Basie's later years, continues to perform locally.

In the 1930s and 1940s, a successful career often meant traveling the road night after night, year after year. Newark's roving musical ambassadors included saxophonist Bobby Plater, arranger and pianist Walter (Gil) Fuller, and pianist Bobby Tucker. Plater gained recognition as an instrumentalist with Lionel Hampton's orchestra, then became the backup leader of the Count Basie Orchestra. Fuller, a

Hollywood arranger for many years, was the driving force behind Gillespie's first orchestra. Tucker has been singer Billy Eckstine's accompanist for more than thirty years.

Literally hundreds of performers and musicians made their livelihoods performing in nightclubs in Newark and its environs, rotating their engagements from nondescript spots like Dodger's Bar and Grill, the Boston Plaza, and the Nest Club to the Picadilly, the Alcazar, and, occasionally, the infamous Kinney Club on Arlington Street in the heart of the Barbary

Viola Wells (Miss Rhapsody) with actor Canada Lee, left, promoter Bill Cash, and Dr. Otto Hilton, an old Third Ward physician whose patients included many entertainers, before a program at Graham Auditorium in Newark, early 1940s. From author's collection

Coast, the city's tenderloin district. At clubs like the Nest and Dodger's, full-scale revues were staged, featuring an array of versatile singers, dancers, chorus girls, comedians, and emcees. In retrospect, almost any oldtimer from Newark can rattle off a litany of friends or neighbors who were entertainers.

As an economic force, the city's nightlife, as in most urban areas, was the source of hundreds of jobs throughout the black community when other forms of work were impossible to obtain because of racism and segregation. With the black church, it was at the core of black social life. For the performers, show business, despite its pitfalls and perils, added a touch of glamour and importance to their lives. Generally, it also gave them the chance to travel and explore new horizons. For their fans, going to a show or club offered escape from their dreary, thankless, routine jobs as laborers and servants.

For entertainers who traveled, however, it soon became evident that life on the road was tough, so grueling that those who traversed the Theater Owners Booking Association (TOBA), an eastern seaboard circuit, renamed it Tough on Black Acts, or, more contemptuously, Tough on Black Asses. Often, these performers had to hassle for their pay. Often, they weren't paid at all. Sometimes they got stranded. Most times they had to hustle simply to find a place to stay since blacks were unwelcome at white hotels and rooming houses.

In a broad sense, swing and jazz form part of a continuum of African-American music that began in this country with the field hollers and spirituals of bondage and shifted progressively to ragtime, Dixieland, blues, jazz, swing, bop, rhythm and blues, soul, and hiphop. Its distinctive rhythms and emotionalism is embedded, too, in the hymns, anthems, and gospel music of the church. In slavery, black people often were expected to entertain their white owners, derided and denigrated for their efforts. Despite the Jubilee (Emancipation Proclamation), the "color line" remained legally in force for nearly another century. Not until the mid twentieth century would a black man be "allowed" to drive a garbage truck. In Newark, the hiring of the government's first black postal clerk in the 1940s was tantamount to an historic breakthrough.

As a survival tool, music and other forms of entertainment traditionally have provided black Americans with powerful communicative outlets. From the earliest times, African chants and dances were incorporated into black life. In southern fields, enslaved Africans, forbidden to talk together, sent messages by singing spirituals. "Steal Away to Jesus" had little to do with dying. It was a coded message, sending forth the word that valiant slaves would attempt to escape their shackles by traveling the Underground Railroad to freedom in the North. On slave row, impromptu entertainers provided the masses relief from the miseries of the fields, fiddling, dancing, and singing as a way of making life more bearable one day at a time.

By the 1890s, the black marching bands of New Orleans and ragtime music written by Scott Joplin and other black composers gave rise to a distinctly black musical idiom known as jazz. Like most things original, it was copied and imitated furiously by whites. By the 1920s, Paul Whiteman, a white bandleader, ironically was considered the "King of Jazz." In the early twenties, another form of black music, "the blues," was seized upon by record companies like Columbia and Okeh. Beginning with Mamie Smith's Okeh recording of "Crazy Blues" in 1920, sales were directed toward black audiences. Smith's recordings,

along with those of her contemporaries, Bessie Smith, Trixie Smith, Ida Cox, and Sara Martin, were huge sellers. "Race records" became a rage.

With jobs in the South limited almost entirely to farming, waves of blacks began heading north to the nation's industrial centers (first in the 1880s and 1890s, then at the turn of the century and just before World War I). They were looking for work with the hope of improving the quality of their lives. Jazz headed north with them, first to St. Louis, then to Chicago and New York. Soon, black artists like Louis Armstrong, Zutty Singleton, and Sidney Bechet were at the center of a vibrant new era, the Jazz Age. Whole shows sprang up around their music, a tradition pioneered by Bert Williams, the black star of Broadway's Ziegfeld Follies.

John Cunningham has traced Negro history in Newark to the early 1700s, concluding: "When the first Negroes arrived is not known, but Newark had a few slaves by the 1730s. Most of them lived on large plantations across the Passaic River, where the Schuyler copper mine operated." By the 1930s, Newark's black population, fueled by the teaming migration from the South, had climbed from 16,977 in 1920 to 38,880, and continued to escalate until it reached 45,760 in 1940 (slightly more than one-tenth of the city's 429,760 population).

By and large, life remained segregated for most blacks until the mid 1900s. New York's Cotton Club had a "whites only" policy. Blacks in Newark had to sit in theater balconies. Restaurants and public accommodations also remained off limits. That was the law, a demeaning state of affairs perpetuated until 1949, when, at the behest of attorney and civil rights leader Herbert Tate Sr., Essex County legislator Grace Freeman convinced her colleagues in the Trenton State House to change it.

Until Tate and Freeman joined forces, black lives were ruled by boundaries both real and imaginary. Downtown essentially was off limits. "You could go into a club and sit in with the band or sing if you wanted," recounted Bill Roberts, a well-known bartender at colored spots during the Swing Era. "But downtown was for whites. The few blacks who had money were in the rackets. The masses did like I did on my twenty-first birthday by going over to Harlem. There was no such thing as socializing among blacks and whites. That was out." So blacks climbed into the balcony seats when shows like Eubie Blake and Noble Sissle's *Chocolate Dandies* played the Shubert in April 1925, even though one of their own, Josephine Baker, was cast as the comedienne, or when Bill (Bojangles) Robinson came tapping into Proctor's a few months later.

No wonder black people invented their own forms of entertainment. In the South, minstrel and carnival shows featuring Ma Rainey, Bessie Smith, and Princess White attracted thousands of rural fans. Or they played "for colored only" theaters. In the North, taverns and nightclubs abounded in black neighborhoods in the 1930s and 1940s. So did after-hours joints and brothels.

Despite its large population and prominence as an industrial center, entertainers considered Newark a friendly place in which to live and work. It was a city, as one oldtimer put it, where "ya could get a meal even if ya didn' know no one," more a cluster of neighborhoods than a fearsome metropolis like New York. This was especially true in the sprawling Hill area of the Third Ward, where the black masses congregated in the wooden tenements of the post-World I Jazz Age, living side by side with poor Jews and Germans.

During the Depression, Newark's Negro population was no more homogeneous than the much larger numbers of Italians, Russians, Germans, Poles, and Irish, the city's largest immigrant groups (in that order). There were four distinct black social classes: a small, elite band of professionals who entertained lavishly at home and rarely ventured into the taverns and clubs; working people whose lives centered around the church; clubgoers (a mix of ordinary working people, servants of the well-to-do, and lithe young lovelies and handsome men about town looking for a good time); and the sporting life whose survival hinged on il-

licit activities including numbers running, hootch, prostitution, and, to some extent, music and entertainment. Sacred and secular were the dividing lines, blurred whenever church members forayed into the taverns to socialize after Sunday services and see a show. Often, the distinction was as close as the neighbor next door.

"I can still hear my grandmother talking about Anna Pease, who lived across the street from her," said Connie (Williams) Woodruff, who covered the 1940s nightclub scene for the *New Jersey Herald News*, a defunct black weekly. 'Hussy!' she'd say. 'Sportin' woman!' For my grandmother, who was a pillar of old Mt. Zion Church with Sarah Vaughan's parents, that was the closest you could get to swearing. It was because Anna Pease, a beautiful woman with a figure to match, made her livelihood singing in local nightclubs and sold liquor right out of her house. To make matters worse, she was the wife of a bandleader [Morty Pease] my grandmother said played nothing but the devil's music."

"No group was as hard hit by the Depression as the slowly rising Negro population," Cunningham found. "They had always been hurt by the 'last hired, first fired' policy of employers." In the 1920s and 1930s many black people who lived in Newark worked "in service," in the employ of wealthy Jewish merchants who resided in what is presently the South Ward of the city and rich Protestants who lived in the Essex County suburbs. In retrospect, their jobs as chauffeurs and domestics may appear mundane, but to the black masses of their day—mostly factory workers and longshoremen—they were admired because they came in daily touch with life's luxuries through their interaction with wealthy whites. Often their homes and closets boasted fine furniture and clothing, castoffs from their employers. Because so many people were illiterate or ill educated, even the mailman had status because he could read and write.

With the advent of the Great Depression, emphasis on employment in the black community shifted to the factories. Women often

The Eddie Wells Orchestra, circa 1929: Norman Wilcox, banjo/guitar; George Cooper, drums; Clarence (Mouse) Fulford, trumpet; Joe Holley, piano; Eddie Wells, saxophone. Courtesy of Cecilia Wilcox

worked in the garment trade, making apparel such as women's coats and dresses and related items like zippers and buttons. Men worked in the hundreds of factories in and around the city, mostly in the meat packing, tanning, and tool and dye making trades. Because they were black, they held the least desirable jobs. Often, cleaning up was the only work available.

During the Depression, Newark's Third Ward was run by crooked politicians and gangsters like Abner (Longie) Zwillman and Joseph (Doc) Stacher. In the guise of legitimate businessmen and public servants, they ran the larger, more profitable nightclubs and many of the smaller ones, too, fueling their operations with the homemade hootch of the Prohibition Era, paying off the cops when necessary. Music often was the vehicle that made it all work. Though the area was predominantly black,

Jews controlled the ward's economy. When Mom and Pop Anderson, a black couple who owned the Golden Inn Bar on Charlton Street, were denied a liquor license in the early 1940s, Prosper Brewer, the ward's leading black politician, threatened "to boycott every Jewish tavern and store" in the neighborhood.

During World War II, defense plant jobs were plentiful, giving workers the chance to work double shifts and, for the first time, afford a few luxuries. With the economy booming, Newark's downtown stores and restaurants also began hiring more blacks. At Bamberger's, a major downtown department store, black men and women manned banks of elevators and were hired as general cleanup persons. Along Broad Street, large restaurants like Child's, Simon and Davis, and W. F. Day and Company employed an increasing number of blacks as chefs, cooks, and waiters. Ironically, they could work in these places or, if they weren't shooed along, they might peer in the windows to look at the customers. But they couldn't sit down and be served.

Despite changing times and expanding job opportunities, money generally was scarce. Making it from one day to the next often was a matter of what black folks commonly called "motherwit"—using inborn instincts to get by. The Third Ward's few black entrepreneurs primarily were female beauty parlor owners and proprietors of the neighborhood grocery and candy stores. There also was a smattering of tavern owners. As always, social activity in black neighborhoods revolved around the church and neighborhood clubs and taverns. For men, the clubs offered a relaxing respite from the workaday world of the factories and docks. For women, this swirl of merriment provided a chance to dress up, meet friends, or, maybe, go looking for a man.

Although the local entertainers often were their friends and neighbors, they were role models, too, admired and revered as celebri-ties. Author/playright Amiri Baraka, who lived across the street from Miss Rhapsody in the 1940s, for example, fondly remembered her in his autobiography as "getting ready for evening so she could put on her purple flower and go out and sing the blues."

The starting point for *Swing City: Newark Nightlife, 1925–50* is one of the stops on the TOBA, Newark's Orpheum Theater, now the site of *The Star-Ledger*, one of the nation's largest newspapers (and my employer). From there, it courses through the house rent parties of the 1930s, where scores of Newark musicians got their start, on to the Swing Era and the beginnings of bebop, examining also institutions like Savoy Records and the Coleman Hotel, which singers like Billie Holiday, Big Maybelle, and Ruth Brown considered a second home. It winds down with the beginning of television and the early strains of rhythm and blues in the late 1940s, which brought oldtime live entertainment in the city to a virtual standstill. Once again, blacks were forced to find alternate routes to survival.

FOUNDATIONS

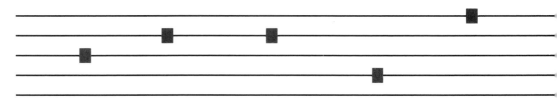

1925-35

A Jazzy Age
—1925 and Beyond
Chapter 1

With the Jazz Age in full throttle and the city's economy thriving, competition was stiff among Newark theater owners to attract top entertainers to their stages in the years following World War I. By mid decade, the downtown vaudeville theaters and burlesque houses were vying madly for the quarter or half-dollar folks were willing to pay to see "continuous vaudeville featuring all-star acts" or, perhaps, a "black and white" revue. All things considered, 1925 was an extremely profitable year.

Downtown at the Shubert, Ed Wynn plied his comedy on the same stage where Houdini's death-defying feats were the headline attraction a few weeks later. At the movie theaters (Loew's and the Capital), Marion Davies' and Mary Pickford's names splashed across the marquees. At the Newark Theatre (later the Paramount), Lippel's Kutie Kids, sixty tiny performers from a local dance school, were the stars, assuring a weekly quota of quarters spent by doting relatives.

This continuous shower of stars and attractions also brought to town many of the top black entertainers and acts of the day. In early February 1925, Buck and Bubbles, the famous dance and comedy team, was on the bill at the Newark. That July, Florence Mills and her "21 colored entertainers" paraded across the stage at Proctor's in a condensed version of *Dixie to Broadway.*

Colored acts were a novelty, intended to amuse white audiences. Hence, some exotic, albeit demeaning advertising heralded shows at places like Miner's Theater at Branford Place and Washington Street, where frequent "black and white" performances were staged. In all probability, the "70 Brownskin Shebas" featured in one show were simply a flock of local teenagers recruited for the week's revue, not some sensuous bevy of imports. The supposedly comical attraction for another 1925 show was "A Real Live Colored Wedding on Stage."

Buck and Bubbles in the traveling show Harlem on Parade, *1934. Courtesy of Doryce Bradley*

The Columbia Theater at Washington and Marshall streets, which became the Orpheum in 1910, at the turn of the century. Courtesy of Newark Public Library

Along with the Lyric, Miner's was one of the city's major burlesque houses, offering huge productions of all-white and mixed revues on alternate weeks. Because of racist attitudes, whites in the cast always outnumbered blacks: one 1925 production featured "38 whites and 37½ blacks."

One of the most popular revues presented at Miner's that year was the *7-11* show that brought the musical Durham brothers—Joe, Eddie, and Roosevelt—to town and starred Sam Cook, Mae Brown, and Speedy Smith. Another was *Lucky Sambo*. Because of the business the show generated, Miner's manager, A. Johnny Mack, added a midnight show following the regular performance. Night after night, *Lucky Sambo* continued to pack the house, making it and the *7-11* the Columbia circuit's leaders in gross receipts.

Meanwhile, Jack's Reid's *Black and White Revue* boasted the talents of Will Ferry, "The Human Knot," whose specialties included impersonating a frog. Also featured were Sambo Reid, Mildred Austin, who did a yodeling number, and Henry Drake, who dispensed "contagious comedy." Presented by producers Drake and Walker, Reid's extravaganza was backed by a jazz orchestra whose featured soloist was trumpeter Gus Aiken. A product of the Jenkins Orphanage of Charleston, South Carolina, Aiken got his big break when he joined Louis Armstrong's orchestra. A review of the show at Miner's described him as "making the air ring with his music." Over at the Shubert, Joe Sheftell's *Southland Revue*, a "colored musical comedy" starring Minta Cato and Bob Williams, was yet another sellout.

Despite this plethora of black entertainers and productions, blacks who came to see the shows had to sit in the balconies. Conditions were entirely different over at the Orpheum Theater at Washington and Court streets, which catered to all-black audiences. Shabby and a bit run down by comparison to downtown theaters, the Orpheum nevertheless was the showplace of the black community. Because it was an important stop on the black theater circuit, all the top black acts of the day came to town: Bojangles, Butterbeans and Susie, the Whitman Sisters, Ethel Waters, even the legendary blues singer Bessie Smith.

The classic description of the Orpheum is the one in *Vanity Fair* by Carl Van Vechten, a wealthy New York writer/photographer of the 1920s fascinated by the lifestyles of ordinary black people. Accompanied by an entourage that included humorist/actor Robert Benchley and the NAACP's Arthur Spingarn, he attended one of Bessie Smith's shows on Thanksgiving night 1925. Even though the price of admission had been doubled for Smith's week-long stay at the Orpheum (fifty cents for a matinee, a dollar at night), the place was packed. For the week, Smith, known by that time as "The Empress of the Blues," was paid $1,000. In his critique, Van Vechten likened Smith to a sorcerer whose "crude and primitive music" evoked "hysterical shrieks of sorrow and lamentations" from the black masses, who had sold out the theater. The fact was Van Vechten, too, came away mesmerized by the power of Bessie's blues.

One of the most popular performers at the Orpheum was Wilton Crawley, an all-round entertainer who could make a clarinet "talk like a chicken." Another was Jesse Cryor, who plucked his nose with his hand and emitted ukelele sounds to the strains of "My Blue Heaven" and "Muddy Water."

The Orpheum was built in 1872 as a home for the nation's first industrial exhibition. At the Newark Industrial Institute, as the huge property was known, Newark's wares were showcased to emphasize the city's importance as an East Coast manufacturing city. More than 130,000 people toured the exhibit, including President Ulysses S. Grant and Horace Greeley, the newspaper editor who was op-

posing Grant for the presidency. But the hall was not so successful as its sponsors had hoped. By 1878 the building was converted into the Grand Opera House. Near the turn of the century it became the Columbia Theater, although it was used occasionally for exhibitions under a new name, Machinery Hall.

In 1910, the building was reconstructed and reopened as the Orpheum, featuring dramatic productions staged by the Corse Payton Stock Company. Payton attracted crowds by billing himself as "the world's worst actor."

By 1915, the Orpheum—its orchestra pit concealed by foliage and a Japanese garden in front of a newly installed screen—had become a silent movie house. A pipe organ provided the musical background for films with dramatic titles like *The Scarlet Sin*. Between the films, a fifteen-piece band and singers entertained. Two three-hour shows were offered daily. Matinee prices were ten cents and fifteen cents with a top admission of twenty-five cents for evening performances. Variety and burlesque shows attracted headliners including Sam Rice and His Daffodil Girls and Gus Arnold and His U.S.A. Girls.

As Newark's black population grew, the Orpheum began offering "colored entertainment," interspersing food and home expositions with boxing matches, vaudeville, movie shows, and dramatic presentations. By the 1920s, top black acts were the Orpheum's staple. Bartender Jimmy Clark recalled the thrill when his father took him to see heavyweight boxing champion Jack Johnson engage in an onstage tug-o-war. Naturally, Johnson won.

Shows at the Orpheum changed frequently. Often, there were no rehearsals. The musicians had to be the best. "Each guy in the pit, and there were about ten, I think, had to play the shows as they came in," noted guitarist Willie Johnson, who landed a job at the theater as a candy boy in 1928 at age thirteen. Floyd Hickman, who played violin, was the bandleader. Clarence Adams, another talented musician, doubled on clarinet and saxophone. Clarence Sinkford played trombone and the trumpet player was named Quallo.

Because the pit musicians could "read" whatever was put in front of them, they had a tremendous influence on the musical development of local youngsters like Johnson and Al Henderson who were just learning to play, youths who were envisioning the day when they, too, would be "starring" at the Orpheum. "Before I took up bass, my father bought me this Keifer–Williams trumpet, and I took it down to Mr. Hickman," said Henderson. "That was my first music lesson. In those days, musicians had to know their instruments and learn their craft. Mr. Hickman was a fine leader."

During the Depression, Hickman doubled as leader of the Works Progress Administration (WPA) Music Project (for blacks only), a guaranteed source of income for musicians like Henderson, who by that time was playing bass and tuba. The band, which also included Johnson and pianist Clem Moorman, staged local shows and entertained at hospitals and Army camps.

Clarence Adams was another Orpheum pit musician the youngsters admired. Adams had been in the band that accompanied Bessie Smith. His wife, the ribald comedienne Carrie Adams, had starred in tent and carnival shows with Gertude (Ma) Rainey, the famous blues singer, before they moved to Newark. "I remember seeing Carrie Adams in 1919 with Ma Rainey in Winston-Salem, North Carolina," said trombonist Clyde Bernhardt. "She was singin' the blues and doing comedy. She was a showstopper. After she settled in Newark, she useta sell home-cooked meals to the performers that was playin' the Orpheum."

To their friends, the Adamses made an odd couple. She was bawdy and adventuresome—learning to drive when she was well into her seventies. Her specialty was telling risque jokes, costumed like Aunt Jemima. Conversely, he was quiet and reserved, a schooled musician who enjoyed teaching youngsters the rudiments of music in his off hours. "Clarence was a gentleman. Carrie was a hustler," said song and dance man Charlie Matthews, who became one of Newark's first black elected officials. "She could always get some money. She

knew every trick there was. He was a gentleman—very inconspicuous. But they had a thing, and they stayed together down through the years."

Among the many careers launched at the Orpheum was that of the Alabams, a group of Newark-area musicians who toured the East Coast in the early 1930s in a show called *Harlem on Parade*. Bill (Bojangles) Robinson, the famous tap dancer, was the star. The Alabams started out as the Melmore Stompers, taking their name from the street in the East Orange neighborhood where most of the boys lived. Sonny Murray, who played banjo and guitar, was their leader.

Bobby Williams, a member of the band who went on to play with Benny Carter and Fats Waller, recalled: "When I first started playing with Sonny I was the only one wearing short pants. I was about fifteen. We played a lot of basketball games and got a few jobs at clubs. Then we formed the Alabams. We traveled through the South, then up through Canada with *Harlem on Parade*. Leon Eason was featured like Louis Armstrong and I played second trumpet."

Also in the band were Williams' brothers, Edward (E. J.) on saxophone and Varis (Vay) on bass. Gene Holder played piano and Clarence Coates, drums. Rounding out the ensemble were the Hayes brothers, Marvin on sax and Gus on trumpet. "We played clubs, theaters, campaign rallies, horse stalls, toilets—everywhere," said Eason, who remained on the road with the show from 1931 until 1936, when the cast broke up. "But there was no money in it."

In the same troupe were four Newark girls who were barely into their teens when they auditioned at the Orpheum as dancers for the show. At the time, they were under the tutelage of Johnny B. Gardner, one of Newark's premiere comics. "Johnny B. was looking for chorus girls for a show at Daddy Grossman's in Singac," recalled Florence McIntyre. "Johnny B. would teach us the routines and we'd practice them in Hazel Hannah's kitchen. Her mother's house was at the corner of West Street and Springfield Avenue. We saw an advertise-

Helena Turman and Florence McIntyre in the traveling show Harlem on Parade, *early 1930s. Courtesy of Florence McIntyre*

The Danny Smalls Revue, 1934. Courtesy of Florence McIntyre

ment that they were looking for new talent at the Orpheum, so we all went down—Geneva and Helena Turman, Myrtle Hutchinson, Billie Sermond, Sally McCarter, Doryce Bradley, and Claudine, whose last name I can't recall. Four of us got picked—Myrtle, Doryce, Claudine, and myself.

"We went back and forth to New York for weeks—many months—to rehearse. My specialty was doing fancy steps and high kicks. Then we took the show out on the road—as far as Baltimore. Buck and Bubbles were in it, and so was Bill Robinson, Ada Brown, Adelaide Hall, and a fan dancer who did a strip tease.

Danny Smalls was the head of it. I was just a chorus girl. We had the Alabams behind us—Vay Williams, Leon, and all of them. I traveled with them two years. Then I came home to get married."

When the show ran its course, Bobby Williams headed to New York to play with Luis Russell's band. Eason began fronting a five-piece band at white spots in Newark. By that time (the late 1930s), tastes in live entertainment had turned to the more intimate environs of the city's bars and nightclubs. The Swing Era was dawning. The halcyon days of the Orpheum were drawing to a close.

Pigsfeet and Beer –Paying the Rent
Chapter 2

By the height of the Depression, the house rent party had become an institution in the tenements, railroad flats, and bawdy houses of urban black America. The aim, as the name implies, was to pay the rent, and when it came due, you could find a couple of good ones almost any night in any neighborhood, given by ordinary people, hustlers—whoever had the inclination and needed a buck.

For the man or woman who worked all day as a factory worker or "in service" as a domestic and was struggling to make ends meet, the rent party was a painless way to meet expenses. The motive was economic, but the by-product was fun, a major venue of black socialization.

More often than not, music was an essential ingredient of the parties. In the homes of the working class, they were relatively simple affairs, offering food, drink, and a bit of music for the price of admission, generally a quarter.

Among the lower classes, gambling, prostitution, and other vices were a possibility, too.

At a time when wealthy whites were plunging out of windows because of their financial losses, blacks, who had nothing to lose, were doing what they always did—struggling to survive. The likelihood in poor black neighborhoods in cities like Newark was that a neighbor was having a party to pay the rent. Or, perhaps in the red-light district, a provocative woman, leaning out a window, was shouting: "We're having a party, darlin'. Why don't y'all come up?"

More than fifty years have passed, but Bill Roberts, once the popular bartender (or, as the black press described him, "mixologist") at the Boston Plaza, a popular night spot in Newark's tenderloin district, still recalls the sights, sounds, and smells of the Prohibition era parties as vividly as last night's hangover: "The windows would be closed and sweat would be

Street musicians "playing for the hat" at the start of the Great Depression. Courtesy of Newark Public Library

Bobby Plater, early 1930s. Courtesy of Alma Plater

Realizing that there was money to be made at such social events, Jesse Jones, a mechanic by trade, started Jones's Hot Music, playing 78 rpm recordings on a portable machine he invented in the kitchen of his home on Warren Street. Jones, who was born in 1892, had ten children to support. By the time they were teenagers, he had five machines, waist-high boxes that resembled today's "rack" systems, with record turntables on top, available for house rent parties and other social gatherings. He charged five dollars for three or four hours of music.

"It helped us out a lot during the 1930s and '40s," said Alice Jones, one of his five surviving children. "We all took part. My father and my brothers played the rougher affairs, while my sisters and I played the machines at the nice parties—weddings and graduations."

At one point, a competitor tried to replicate Jones's machines. But he failed. If there was a party, Jones's Hot Music was the business that invariably got the nod.

There was plenty of live music, too.

For young musicians like Clem Moorman, the parties provided the opportunity to make money to supplement the family income while learning their craft from older, more experienced musicians. Moorman was barely into his teens when his brother Mixie began taking him to neighborhood homes to play piano: "Mostly, I had to sit and be quiet because I really wasn't supposed to be there until my mother gave the O.K. The first one was at the Jacksons, our neighbors across the street. I think I knew three songs—'Margie,' 'Please Don't Talk About Me When I'm Gone,' and one other one—so I had to play them the whole night. Just me and Mixie. I think I got about a dollar fifty for the job, and I think Mixie must have palmed some of it. The people just had to get the money together for the rent. They had what my mother used to call 'collation,' some jive food, nothing heavy."

Playing a party was also a chance for young musicians to get a glimpse into the bawdier side of life, particularly if they got to play an after-hours joint like Marie Houston's, which Roberts said "went all night down on Vine

pourin' down the piano player's face. Some of the girls had high-powered perfume, and if somebody didn't take a bath in the morning, body odor filled the air. When the perfume and the body odor got together, ya knew ya had a party!"

No party was complete without music, whether that meant spinning records or providing a piano player and/or other musicians.

Street," or Angeline Williams' on Washington Street, where stride pianist Donald Lambert was an attraction. Black Beauty was another enterprising woman who catered to the sporting life. Still another was Anna Pease, who operated for years on Washington Street. She also sang. "Anna was a good-looking lady," Roberts recalled, "I think from Orange, and she got in tight with law enforcement. We called her 'Mom' Pease, 'cause she was older than most of us."

Bobby Plater, who became Count Basie's straw boss, and Al Henderson, who played bass with the Savoy Dictators, were still in high school when they first played a rent party. Henderson, who was "foolin' around on trumpet" at the time, noted: "I remember when we were playin' this red-light house on Orchard Street. A cop came in and told the lady, 'Get those kids outta here.' Robby [Plater was 'Robby' to his friends and family and 'Bobby' to the rest of the world] and I would have played for nothin' if we just coulda stayed for that party. That was a wild one—really a wild party. Some women were supposed to come and put on a show, but we never got to see it, 'cause we looked so young."

For older players, black men whose means of employment was harshly restricted by the divisiveness of racism, the rent parties were a key source of economic survival. Floyd Lang, who came north to Newark from his home state of Florida in 1928, was one of them. Fortunately, it didn't take him long to find work: "I was just walking along Railroad Avenue one day when a woman named Lottie was havin' a party and invited me up.

"So I went up, and she asked: 'Do ya drink?'

"I said, No, ma'am.

"'Do ya shoot dice?'

"No, ma'am. Just wanna listen to the music.

"'Wanna pump some?' she asked.

"So, I pumped for a while [on a player piano] and then I started playin' and they all came into the room. That went on and on. Every Friday and Saturday I'd be at one house or another."

The general concept of rent parties, especially those where illegal activities took place,

Floyd Lang, late 1940s. Courtesy of Lucille (Dorsey) Morton

was to keep profits high and overhead low as immortalized in the words of Bessie Smith's rowdy blues song "Gimme a Pigfoot." Pigsfeet, which then cost a couple of cents a pound, and chicken generally were on the menu. But most of the profits came from liquor—illegal until Prohibition came to a halt in 1933—and gambling.

Broome Street, off West Kinney, was Newark's unofficial red-light district, an area where after-hours spots stayed open long after the taverns and night clubs officially closed, often all night. Whatever there was to sell was for sale—barrelhouse music, gambling, sometimes sex.

"During the Depression, everybody was having rent parties all over," said Jimmy Clark, who tended bar at the Howdy Club on Washington Street. "Most of the time they'd have a piano player. You'd dance all night and eat and drink. Once in a while they had singers. It was very cheap. A dinner was somethin' like fifty cents, seventy-five cents at most.

"You could just walk down the street and hear a piano playin'. You didn't have to know anyone. Everybody would have a red light when they were havin' a house rent party. People used to come in whenever they finished work. All of them were fun, but it wasn't a success 'til somebody'd start a fight. It didn't matter over what."

"Black people didn't have any money; that's why they had rent parties," explained Willie Johnson. "It was an economic thing. The rent was due, so they'd give a house rent party. They'd say, 'Hey, so and so is having a house party and he's got Willie Johnson and Alphonso Burford. Be there!' Our very names drew the crowd. Bub Clark would be there, and everyone knew Clark would bring a guy named 'Mouse' [Clarence Fulford], who played sax and clarinet."

Johnson, who started playing ukelele as a teenager, progressed so fast he soon was invited to play a party at 140 Boyd Street with his friend Myles Trent and Trent's uncle, Connie Cabell: "I heard Mr. Cabell and a fellow named Hughie playin' in a pool room where all the musicians used to hang out, and that was it for me. I had been exposed to music at the Orpheum Theater where I worked as a candy boy to help support my sick father. At first, I was scared. I was just seventeen, so I had to ask my mother. She let me and I got paid two dollars and fifty cents. Mr. Cabell tutored me and soon we got so many Saturday night functions and Sunday matinees we could hardly keep up."

Johnson soon got to meet and work with most of the piano players on the scene, most of whom were older—"in their twenties or thirties." There was Broome Street Slim, "a real character who got all the functions," and Harry Payton and "Sparrow, who could play like hell and drink like a fish. By eleven P.M., he was soused." Sam Porter, who never completed a song and "was always tryin' to sound like someone else," was another house party man. "And there was a fellow named Schef-

field, who got all the gigs. He played harmonica. Everyone had to go through him."

The Shaw brothers, Lacey and Mike, were popular party men who "played in crazy keys" to the dismay of the other musicians, especially the horn players, who had great difficulty keeping up with all the changes. Since most of the musicians were amateurs with no formal training, the music tended to consist of chords strung together as facsimiles of popular tunes like "Dinah" and "Japanese Sandman." "The musicians made tunes up as they went along," Johnson said. "They had pretty good ears, but they didn't get the chords in the right places. Still, it sounded pretty good. The people generally knew the melody."

Another of Johnson's teachers was Collins Murphy, "a fairly good piano player, not an artist, but he had the right chords in the right place. He wasn't a fast reader. It might take him a day to learn a piece, but the guys had respect for him." Also on the scene was Kid Noisy (real name, Mr. Douglas), who played four-string banjo and kazoo and had "gigs on top of gigs" to the point where he was "booked for two months."

Bub Clark often played two or three house rent parties and a matinee on Sunday. "Then he'd have his regular thing [job] on Monday," Johnson noted. "Whenever there was a financial need, we'd tell everybody and put out the fliers. There was a lady over on Boston Street, and we'd go over there and say, 'Alphonso and Willie are playin' at such 'n such a place,' and she'd print them up.

"Broome Street Slim had his crowd, and Harry Payton would draw his crowd and the Shaws would draw their crowd. Everybody had their own inducement and they brought people in."

Donald Lambert, Newark's legendary stride pianist, "lived in the nightclubs, but once in a while, 'round three o'clock or four [in the morning], the door would open and in would come the Lamb or in would come Fats Waller," Johnson recalled. "When you had that, Holy Christ the house was full."

The four-room apartment on Rutgers Street

Little Sadie Matthews, Grace Smith, and Sadie's sister, Mandy Matthews, late 1930s. Courtesy of Sadie Matthews

shared by Sadie (Little Poopsie) Matthews, a dancer at the Nest Club on Warren Street, and her chorus line chum, Mary (Sugar) Payne, was the site of many 1930s parties. Said Sadie: "The rent was twenty-five dollars, so we'd give a party to pay it. I used to buy a quart of whiskey and put water in it to make two quarts. One time I left Sugar and Joe Cooke there taking care of the party and Sugar came runnin' down to the Nest Club to tell me my sister Mandy was puttin' water in the whiskey, too, and sellin' it. 'It ain't nothin' but water,' Sugar said. 'You can't get no fifty cents for water,' so I used to hide it [from Mandy]. I had this tub I hid my whiskey in.

"Another time the cops came up there when I was goin' with Blackie, this Italian guy, and we got mad at each other. We was supposed to give a party together, so I gave it anyway and he sent the cops up there. There wasn't many people there, just my sister cookin' chickens. The cop said, 'You sure got a whole lotta chickens here,' so Mandy said to the cop, 'Yeah. You

want some?'" When the officer accepted, all else was forgotten. Whether he considered the meal Mandy set before him a payoff, or was simply too famished to give the impending house rent party additional thought, didn't really matter to the relieved hostesses.

"I thought the cops would catch us gamblin'," Sadie said. "We cut the game—ten cents on the dollar. We used to make out pretty good, around seventy or eighty dollars. There was no music—just the radio. Mostly, we tried to keep it quiet or the cops would come. Sometimes I had a skin game [a card game] in the bedroom and a poker game in the kitchen."

Up in Orange in the mid 1930s, Duke Anderson had just about cornered the market on piano playing at house rent parties: "By my last year at Orange High I was good enough to play them even though I only knew a few chords and two tunes—'Nagasaki' and the boogie blues. I could always play the blues. I picked that up by ear. I didn't have no competition—nobody. I was workin' three or four nights a week and makin' a dollar and a half. My father at that time was makin' seven dollars a week."

With experience, Anderson began branching out, playing parties in Newark when the opportunity arose: "But in order for me to play with the Newark guys, I had to tell them I lived in Newark. The Orange guys weren't allowed across the border."

One night, Anderson unwittingly tangled with gangsters: "It was around 1936 and I was playin' a party where this white guy who was goin' with a black chick had the nerve to come. I found out he was a gangster, but I didn't know it at the time. I thought he was a policeman. He said to me: 'My niece is gettin' married, and I want you to play for the reception.' So I said, O.K. It was supposed to be a month later, and he gave me the address—up in West Orange somewhere."

To Anderson, it was no big deal, one of several job offers he received that night without any money up front. As quick as he agreed to take the job, he promptly forgot about it. Unfortunately for him, the gangster didn't, dispatching two of his henchmen to "take care of" the young upstart who had insulted him and his family.

"One night [soon after] I was comin' out of a house party on South 17th Street in Newark to get the trolley home for five cents when these guys pulled up in a big limousine," Anderson recalled. "I'll never forget the car. It was a LaSalle. I thought they were goin' to give me a ride or somethin'.

"They asked. 'Are you so 'n so?'

"And I said, Yeah [unaware of why they had approached him].

"'Do you know you were supposed to be at such and such a place?'

"And I said, Oh, yeah. I forgot about it.

"Right then and there, I got the worst whippin' I ever got in my life. They broke my jaw and wrist. Eventually, I went back to playin', but from then on, I was scared stiff of anyone who looked like a gangster."

With the advent of World War II and a sudden wealth of manufacturing jobs for blacks created by the war economy, economic reliance on the house rent party diminished. In Newark and other cities, many laborers worked double shifts. After work, with more money to spend for entertainment, many of them went looking for a good time in urban nightclubs, creating a burgeoning demand for live music and entertainment in a more formalized commercial setting. For a brief period—until many of the musicians were called to serve in the military—Newark nightlife reached its pinnacle.

The Kid and Miss Corprew
–Hal Gets a Horn
Chapter 3

In the 1920s and 1930s, Newark was a veritable maze of thriving theaters, clubs, and after-hours joints where sporting folks rambled through the night. There were plenty of jobs for musicians and entertainers, so the city was teaming with musical talent. Often, the older musicians who lived in Newark or were passing through were idols of black youngsters growing up in the throes of a segregated society, inspiring new generations to make music their livelihoods.

Harold (Hal) Mitchell, whose lyrical trumpet playing rang out from the 1940s bands of Tiny Bradshaw and Benny Carter, was barely into his teens when he came under the wings of two of the giants of stride piano: Willie (The Lion) Smith and Donald (The Lamb) Lambert. But it was Miss Corprew, who ran the neighborhood house, who gave him his start in music.

Like many Newark musicians of his era, Mitchell came from a poor home, poorer than most: "Up until I was eight, we lived at 28 Clayton Street. Then my mother decided to get married again. My stepfather didn't believe in paying rent, so we moved—many times.

"At that time, Bamberger's [the department store] was involved in putting up a new neighborhood house on the corner of Morton and Howard. A local band of maybe nine or ten pieces played there. I don't remember who the leader was, but the trumpet player's name was Blue Dawn. I always thought that was an odd name. I used to sit and watch him. I guess the man thought I was crazy. I'd never take my eyes offa him. I'd watch his fingers.

"This was at night. Most of the guys in the band worked during the day. During that time, you couldn't even have a weekend trio unless you rehearsed. They played the stock songs of the day like 'Prisoner of Love.' None of 'em could read or had much style. These guys would fight a stock song like they was carryin' bricks.

Hal Mitchell, circa 1935. Courtesy of Meredith Gordon

"Whatever night it was, I had gotten permission from Miss Corprew—she ran the place—to come by and watch them. I was hittin' around fifteen, so it musta been 1930. I had worked the street carnivals once they got the building up. The carnivals took up a whole block—from Baldwin to Morton. I'd got permission to come and watch the band 'cause it was after hours. Miss Corprew knew my mother was workin', doin' day's work.

"She'd say, 'Harold, your mother's working?'

"I'd say, Yeah. Not yeah. Yes, ma'am.

" 'Would you like a horn like that?' she asked

one night as my eyes remained glued on Blue Dawn.

"Yes, ma'am.

"The year was coming around [1931] when I'd be fifteen. I came into the neighborhood house one night and Miss Corprew said, 'Harold, come in my office.' She had this stern look on her face. 'I got something for you,' she said, opening this sad-looking case. I knew what kind of case it was 'cause I'd been watching him.

" 'If you can't practice at home, I'll let you come around here,' Miss Corprew said.

"I immediately said, Can I go, now?

"I went back home and, boy, when I opened that case up and I tackled that horn it was the worst thing you ever heard. When my mother came home, I showed it to her. 'Boy, I can't afford no lessons,' she told me.

"I played around with that thing about three months or so, trying to get something out of it. People like Larry Ringold, Mr. Chips [Chippie Outcalt], and Clarence Adams gave me some pointers and there was a music store around the corner on Branford Place, where Frank Gibbs [who became a bandleader] used to work. They sold books for twenty-five cents."

Mitchell turned to his mother for help:

"I said, Ma, I need a quarter.

" 'What? Boy, you crazy? A quarter's for things like rice. A book! For what?'

"To learn how to play this trumpet.

"So, she counted out twenty-five cents and I walked from Baldwin Street, where we lived then, over to Branford Place and got a book. I carried that book with me everywhere, tucked between my school books so I could sneak a look during class. I never listened to what the teachers were sayin'.

"Finally, I got into Robert Treat School. One night during my first term somebody called me, maybe Larry [Ringold], to go up to Freeman's Hall around the bend on Charlton Street between Spruce Street and the next block. They needed a trumpet player, which I was not. But I went. It was the Schenck boys from up around Paterson, Bill and his brother.

"Meanwhile, in this little bit of time I had

Hal Mitchell playing at the Villa Maurice on Washington Street in Newark in the late 1930s: from left, unidentified security guard; dancer Gertrude Turman; Danny Gibson, drums; Mitchell, trumpet; Joe Crump, piano; Cornelius Chinn, saxophone; singer Elsie Paige; emcee Abe (Snakehips) Moore. Courtesy of Gertrude (Turman) Brown

worked my ass off. I took that horn to bed. I took it to the toilet. I'm about sixteen and no one ain't gonna tell me nothin'. I made the night, working from about nine 'til three in the morning. I think they paid me either fifty cents or a dollar fifty. I think Buster Stothoff was on piano. I looked at that dollar and a half, stuffed it in my pocket, packed up my horn, and waited for my mother to come for me.

"I said, Ma! Look what I got!

'Boy, where'd you get that money?' she asked. 'You didn't do nothin'?'

"I got it playing.

'You ain't lying to me, boy! I'll crucify you. How could you make a dollar fifty playing?'

"In those days, my mother had to work all day to make a dollar and a half. She left home at eight o'clock on the trolley and came back home at ten or eleven o'clock. I guess she figured I was on the way to success. That's what led her to go around to see Miss Corprew and thank her for what she had done for me.

"From then on, I played around, not connected to nobody. But everybody knew about this kid with the horn. I was nosin' into everything that came close to the business. About two years later, I came in contact with Duke Richardson's band, which had Duke on trombone, Herbie Lee Williamson on trumpet, Bobby Plater on saxophone, and Dee Richardson on drums. The piano player was gay, a real thin guy who looked like someone had beaten him in the face. Al Henderson was on tuba. I know because I used to have to carry the top of it.

"Duke's band started operatin' out of the neighborhood house. They'd rehearse and then would play on Saturdays—all kinds of fundraising stuff. I did that for quite a while, maybe a year, year and a half.

"During this time we had lots of piano players. Most places had a piano in it—what you'd call a gatherin' place. If you didn't have a piano you'd be by yourself. One of the spots was the Democratic Club or what was a disguise for bein' a Democratic Club. You'd buy whiskey or send across the street to get a pint of corn whiskey or whatever they were making downstairs.

"No one had a piano at home. The odd thing about it was most of the players played in the keys of E natural, F sharp, and C sharp. All of these people played by ear. I used to wonder how they could play in such hard-ass keys when there were so many people who'd study them for hours and couldn't play.

"There were plenty of piano players—Morty Pease, who I never worked with, Joe Holley, Joe Crump, Buster Stothoff, George Gordon, Larue Jordan, and Ike Quebec—long before he started playin' sax. Plenty of them played in these strange keys. In order to come in to play with these guys, you had to know a little bit about what instrument you played or else you would just sit there. I went through a good year of that shit until Melvin Smith took me over [to New York] to see his brother, the Lion. We grew up with the Smiths. They were our neighbors on Clayton Street.

"One day, Melvin said, 'C'mere, you little bastard. I'm gonna take you over to see the Lion.' I knew he [Willie Smith] was something I shouldn't be goin' to see. Melvin took me and

the Lion said, 'Hey, kid. Play somethin'.' I was so god-damned scared I don't remember what I did. He said, 'You sound alright, but you gotta keep playin'.' He told Melvin to take me back home to Newark to see the Lamb.

"So Melvin took me over to 95 Prince Street, where they had a club upstairs over a curtain store. Who did they have playin' but Donald Lambert. By this time, even though I was around eighteen and thought I was grown, I was alert enough to know that me and a thousand more like me had no business bein' nowhere near Donald Lambert. He gave me a nod of recognition and told me to sit down damn near behind the piano.

"He said, 'What do you know, kid?' and went into a verse of 'Stardust,' which is in the key of E or B flat. I started, but I couldn't go no further. He just looked up and said, 'Sit down.' I started to pack up, but he said, 'Smitty says you can play. Sit your ass down.' So, I sat and sat. Finally, he said, 'Maybe, I'll see you tomorrow night, boy. Get your ass in here tomorrow night.'

"I said, Yes, sir, and for six months we worked up there, just him and me. All the piano players who had a name at that time came there lookin' for the Lamb. Claude Hopkins. Art Tatum. The Lion. So many of them. I've never seen so many of them in one room since. Everybody but Ellington and Basie. Most of the single stride players. The piano never stopped. That's when I began to get a little maturity, when I began learning how to make music. All because of Miss Corprew."

Mitchell went on to play with the Savoy Dictators, then spent the next fourteen years on the road with bands led by Tiny Bradshaw, Benny Carter, Jimmie Lunceford, and Louis Jordan. Although his playing often was heralded by critics and name musicians who considered him one of the finest trumpeters of his time, greater recognition eluded him.

Money (more precisely, a lack of it) finally drove Mitchell off the road—not just money to pay his bills and enjoy a few of life's luxuries, but the fact that what he made never measured up to his talents. Understandably, it made him feel cheated. "The top echelon al-

The Al Henderson Orchestra, forerunner of the Savoy Dictators, circa 1936: from left, front, Baron Lester, vocals, seated; Danford (Larue) Jordan, baton, standing; Bobby Plater and Lowell (Count) Hastings, saxophone; Howard Scott, trombone; center, Clem Moorman, piano; Mitchell and unidentified, trumpet; rear, Al Henderson, bass; Earl Nelson, drums. There is no known existing photograph of the Dictators. Courtesy of Al Henderson

ways finds a way to put the squeeze on the peasants," he lamented to writer Gary Carner in 1989.

One of the few honors to come Mitchell's way occurred in 1985, when a musical tribute to him was given at Essex County College in Newark. For the occasion, he led a combo, accompanied by Duke Anderson, Grover Mitchell, and Danny Gibson. Little Jimmy Scott sang. Troubled in recent years by ill health, Mitchell remained a musician at heart. But the mortgage had to be paid, so he continued to work-part time in the mail room of a downtown Newark bank. Ever the artist, Mitchell in

1990 put his heart into a new venture, managing his wife Helen's career as an aspiring actress and in commercials demanding "a mature woman."

Among veteran musicians, even after all these years, his name evokes fond memories of a master at work. "Newark was swinging and Hal Mitchell was my favorite Newark musician," said veteran drummer Chris Columbus. "He was a great trumpet player and a great arranger." In his memoirs, Dizzy Gillespie agreed: "Hal Mitchell was a trumpet player, a marvelous trumpet player."

The Lion and the Lamb
—Two Newark Legends
Chapter 4

Two of the world's top stride pianists were from Newark, the flamboyant, fast-talking, cigar-smoking Willie (The Lion) Smith and the equally gifted Donald Lambert, whose legend as a loner has tended to obscure the acclaim warranted by his tremendous talent.

Smith was the better known, a celebrity by comparison. With Jersey-born James P. Johnson and Johnson's wide-bodied protege Fats Waller, he was one of the kings of Harlem hangouts during the late 1920s and early 1930s, gregariously ruling over Leroy's, the Rhythm Club, and other uptown lairs. He recorded extensively and influenced many musicians, including his protege, the young Duke Ellington.

Lambert, conversely, kept to himself and Newark. Except for a few forays into the limelight, including a heralded appearance at the 1960 Newport Jazz Festival, he preferred playing in near obscurity in taverns in and around Newark. He remains a "name" only among

musicians who still regard him as one of stride's all-time masters.

To Newarkers, Smith and Lambert were known as the Lion and the Lamb, two braggadocious oddballs whose talents somehow managed to match or surpass the audaciousness of their claims. With Johnson, Waller, Art Tatum, and Stephen (The Beetle) Henderson, they were part of a musical clique of highly competitive stride piano players. When they went looking for each other, which they often did, it was "cuttin' time," a term used to determine who could outplay the other.

By far, Smith was the cockier of the two, stylistically an earlier version of the loquacious Waller. Like Waller, his tilted derby and ever-present stogie were his trademarks. In *The Jazz Story*, Dave Dexter Jr. paints a vivid image of Smith as "a cigar-smoking, big-talkin' pianist who could hold his own with Jelly Roll [Morton] in musicianship, boasting, humor, lying, drinking, eating, swearing,

Willie (The Lion) Smith in his later years. Courtesy of Newark Public Library

sleeping, and possibly everything else but wielding a pool cue."

William Henry Joseph Bonaparte Bertholoff Smith was born in Goshen, New York in 1897, supposedly of Negro and Mohawk Indian heritage blended with a few Spanish, French, and Jewish genes. Bonaparte was his father's name; Bertholoff and Smith came from his mother's two subsequent marriages. After his mother married John Smith, a packing plant worker, the family moved to Newark. The union gave him four stepbrothers: Robert, Melvin, Norman, and Ralph Smith. In the mid 1940s, three of them also were involved in show business. Bob Smith was the manager of Newark's Welcome Inn. Melvin was the drummer at the Howdy Club. Ralph recruited and booked talent.

Smith's interest in music was nurtured by his mother, who taught him the rudiments of organ and piano, and by an uncle who taught him "a decent buck 'n wing." As he noted in his autobiography, he started "to roam the joints" of the tenderloin area in 1911. Barely into his teens, Smith was hired to play piano at a saloon at Arlington Street and Branford Place. For his efforts, he got three or four dollars to play piano from two to six on Thursday afternoons, the traditional day off for colored folks who worked for whites. By the time he entered Newark High (now Barringer), he'd played at most of the clubs along the Coast (the red-light district). Next, he moved downtown to a white spot: "Johnson's Cafe in Newark was one of the best spots in town. It had the reputation of being a real dicty [high-class], cabaretlike place with tables of good food. You weren't anything in show business around Newark unless you played Johnson's or the Hotel Navarro. I played both, but my first job away from the Coast was Johnson's."

At Johnson's, Smith met many of the city's top entertainers, including guitarist Nick (The Troubador) Lucas, Tess Gardella, who played Aunt Jemima, and comedian Joe (Wanna Buy a Duck) Penner.

In those days, his chief rivals were Dick Huff, a fellow "who could sing, dance, and play a lot of piano," and Harold (Bon-Bon) Gardner, who played "all types of piano, and was an ace showman besides." About the same time he met his stride contemporaries Lucky Roberts and James P. Johnson, who "showed up one night in 1914 at Randolph's on the Coast," where Smith was playing regularly.

During the summer of 1915, Smith replaced Eubie Blake at Kelly's in Atlantic City, then got his first job in New York City with a band led by Wilbur Hegemin. Before long he began playing at clubs in Greenwich Village and Harlem. When World War I erupted, Smith joined the army and was sent to France with the 350th Field Artillery. He apparently won a citation for heroism under fire.

After the war, he became a fixture at Leroy Wilkins' cabaret at 135th Street and Fifth Avenue in Harlem, one of a growing number of small cellars where stride pianists like Johnson and Roberts were the draw: "The bosses expected you to stay at your stool from night until dawn," Smith told biographer Ed Kirkeby. "Man, if you got up to go to the men's room, those guys would scream. Leroy would come up wailing, 'What are you trying to do, put me out of business?' And in those days you worked seven nights. You'd rather piss in your pants than leave the piano when a rival was in the house. That was the best way to lose your gig."

Smith's style was an odd mix: lacey and airy on one hand, driving double-fisted powerful ragtime on the other, fueled by both the energetic forcefulness of his personality and his musical savvy. An able accompanist, he was a member of the quintet that accompanied blues singer Mamie Smith in 1920 on "Crazy Blues." Blues experts consider it to be the first "race" record—music aimed directly at the black masses. Within a year, a million records were sold.

Duke Ellington was new to New York's music scene when his drummer, Sonny Greer, introduced him to the Lion. As he later noted: "Anybody who had a reputation as a piano player had to prove it right there and then by sitting down to the piano and displaying his artistic wares. And when a cat thought that he was something special, he usually fell into that trap (or, you might say, into the jaws of the

Lion). . . . Like if the player was weak with the left hand, the Lion would say, 'What's the matter, are you a cripple?' Or, 'When did you break your left arm?' Or, 'Get up. I will show you how it is supposed to go.'"

Ellington was struck, too, by Smith's versatility as an accompanist: "I never heard anybody accompany a singer like the Lion (they used to swing twenty or thirty choruses, each one different) and every supporting phrase that Willie played fit like a glove and drove her [the singer] into the next melodic statement."

Like Waller, Smith often accompanied himself on piano, grunting and groaning through witty little tunes like those he recorded on Bluebird in 1936 with Mezz Mezzrow and His Swing Band: "I'se a-Muggin'" and "The Panic Is On." He led his own groups like Willie (The Lion) Smith and His Cubs and played with bands led by early jazz giants like Sidney Bechet. In 1939, in a tribute to his friend Lambert, he recorded "The Lion and the Lamb" on Commodore.

When stride gave way to swing, Smith returned to Newark to play. For a while he led a band at the Casa Blanca on Broad Street near Kinney. In 1941, he took a trio into the Picadilly with vocalist Inez Lester (then the wife of bandleader Benny Carter), Joe Watson on bass, and Ernie Perfido on alto sax and clarinet.

Smith remained musically active into his seventies, playing what critic Dave Dexter described as "a refreshingly original piano style which mixes ragtime with harmonic ideas." In 1969, at age seventy-two, he was invited to the White House by President Nixon to play for a celebration marking Duke Ellington's seventieth birthday. He died in 1973 at age seventy-five.

While Smith was making musical history in Harlem, Lambert, seven years his junior, dominated the stride scene in Newark. There were some very fine players around, but none, with the possible exception of Roosevelt Durham (brother of Basie trombonist/arranger Eddie Durham), approached a talent anything like Lambert's. By all accounts, the Lamb had one of the hottest left hands in the business. And he could play two songs at once, intertwining them while quickening the pace to a frenzy.

Donald Lambert was born in Princeton in 1904. His mother, a piano teacher and bandleader, gave him his keyboard groundwork when he was about five. Yet he never learned to read or write music. At ten, he got his first job, playing in a movie pit. At sixteen, he quit school to become a jazz musician.

"Donald played entirely by ear," said Miss Rhapsody, who worked with him regularly at Angeline's, an after-hours joint on Washington Street in Newark. "As a child, he told me he sat under the piano while his mother gave lessons. He absorbed everything he heard. He could play anything—stride, classical, anything you ever heard. If you'd hum it, he'd play it. And he could play stone drunk or sober."

Lambert was a teenager when he met the Lion. They both were working spots in Newark. Soon after, while Lambert was playing at a Harlem nightclub, Johnson and Waller dropped in to hear what he "had." They began hanging around together and influencing each other's music. Among his peers, Lambert was known as "Muffin," a nickname bestowed by Smith.

"He used to come up to the Rhythm Club around 1936 or 1937 and ask for Art Tatum," Clyde Bernhardt recalled. "None of the other musicians gave him credit 'cause he came from Newark, and that was supposed to be country. But one night he came over and he blasted those cats. Then they had more respect for him. Willie Smith was good, too, but he couldn't do nothin' with Lambert. The Lamb would boast, but he could back it up." As Fats Waller noted in his memoirs: "Donald Lambert remained until his death a tough man to beat on the piano. Donald was one of James P.'s favorites and could cut anybody on a good night." Ellington, a protege of Smith's, also acknowledged Lambert's genius: " 'The Lamb' came to the [Harlem] battlefield once or twice a year. He astounded everyone and then returned to New Jersey again." Eubie Blake, who lived to be one hundred years old and was stride's senior practitioner, recalled: "Me and Willie the Lion played a concert with Don Lambert once. We didn't know him at the time,

Donald Lambert at the baby grand at Wallace's, circa 1950. Courtesy of Frank R. Wallace

and Willie made fun of him before he started to play. Lambert wiped us both out."

Lambert was just coming into his own when his wife died in 1936. Grief-stricken, he decided to leave New York for good. The bars in Newark and at the Jersey shore became his haunts. As Newark's ace of the ivories in the late 1930s, he held forth at Fisher's Tavern, the Howdy Club, and other bars around town. Whenever a struggling musician or singer stopped in, "Donald was always willing to lend a hand," said writer/editor Bob Queen.

Clem Moorman was a boy when Lambert started coming to his house to make music with his brother Mixie and drink whiskey: "Donald was a friend of Larry Ringold and Ringold was a friend of Mixie's. One day someone said for Lambert to come up to our apartment—our railroad flat. Larry said we'd have to get some whiskey. I think Mixie arranged it. My mother was out. I still remember my first impression of Lambert. He sat down at the piano and said, 'Get up, kid.' So I got up and he sat down. I didn't know if what he had was good or not. If Larry Ringold thought it was good, we all thought it was good. Personally, his playing never got to me. It sounded like the same thing over and over again. He'd play, then Larry'd take five thousand chords."

On the flip side, pianist June Cole was an admiring fan who recalled: "Donald Lambert was a tremendous influence on all of us. We'd hang around with Donald all night to try to learn something new."

Because of his preference for small clubs and after-hours joints, Lambert could dress and act as he pleased. And he could play as much for his own pleasure as for the patrons'. Except for occasional jaunts to Harlem, he remained uninterested in playing in New York. He proved that by balking when Miss Rhapsody took him to Kelly's Stable on 52nd Street to play for the bosses. "He went and got hired on the spot, but when I went with him to buy a tuxedo he backed out," she remembered. "He didn't like New York or anything fancy. He just wanted to play." Lambert ventured into New York again in 1946 to play at Jock's Music Room on Seventh Avenue at 138th Street.

Maxine Sullivan was the headliner. But that was it. Before long, the hot drifts of his piano could be heard back at the Howdy Club at Washington and Marshall streets.

Bartender Jimmy Clark was his daily companion: "Every morning while I was polishing the glasses and getting things ready, we'd have a contest. The Lamb would play a tune. If I could name it, he'd buy me a drink. If I couldn't, I had to buy him a drink."

Because so many musicians played Newark, Lambert still had plenty of company. One time, for instance, trombonist Jack Teagarden was leading his band at Newark's Adams Theater and noticed a newspaper item about Lambert enlivening the Star Bar on Halsey Street. Teagarden went to hear him play, requesting encores of a tune (it's unclear which one) Lambert had written. Enchanted by it, Teagarden orchestrated it and added it to his book.

Lambert finally found his niche in 1948: the baby grand at Wallace's, a corner tavern in West Orange, a stone's throw from Newark. He played there for the final fourteen years of his life. "Who needs New York?" he asked years later in a *Newark News* interview. "Here [at Wallace's] I can play what I want and the life is peaceful."

Owner Frank J. Wallace had hired Lambert for a Sunday gig after hearing him play at the Town House, across from the police headquarters in suburban Montclair. When the Town House closed for renovations, Wallace invited him back, and he decided to stay.

"Don was a genius, but he was tough and temperamental," said Wallace's son, Frank R., whose job it was to settle up with Lambert on pay day. By that time the seldom-sober Lambert had downed enough gin to owe the boss, the younger Wallace remembered. "What have I got coming?" Lambert generally would ask, bellowing that he was "The Lamb of God" when Wallace gave him the bad news.

But no one could deny his talent. Eubie Blake came to see him twice. And when Mary Lou Williams stopped by, Lambert moved over on the piano bench to let her play "Handy Eyes," a tribute to W. C. Handy, the Father of the Blues. Another regular visitor was Marshall Stearns, who founded the Institute of Jazz Studies.

"Don could take 'The Bells of St. Mary' and make it sound like he was playing in St. Patrick's Cathedral," said Wallace (the son). "And then he'd rag it, going ninety-eight miles an hour. He could make 'Chopsticks' sound like a concerto."

Lambert remained at Wallace's until he became ill in early 1962. While he was in the hospital, he chose Big Ted Smith, a longshoreman who played piano part time, to fill in for him. "But he never, never came out," said a still-astounded Smith.

The essence of Lambert's giftedness is aptly captured in Dan Morgenstern's 1960 Newport (Rhode Island) Jazz Festival critique of a rainy day program that also featured the Lion and Eubie Blake: "It was Lambert's day. He had a good piano, he was at Newport, and there were a couple of good piano players [Smith and Blake] in the house. Only the ear can define greatness in music. In Lambert's case, it is a matter of touch, of authority, of conception—a sense of form of the highest order which infuses everything he plays—and perhaps more importantly, of beauty." Lambert's *pièce de résistance* was his ability to superimpose counter melodies. As Morgenstern noted that day, " 'Tea for Two' goes on in one hand while the other plays a medley of standards ranging from 'April Showers' to 'Because of You,' all done with excellent taste, subtle humor and outstanding technique."

Despite such acclaim, Lambert recorded infrequently. For Bluebird in 1941, he demonstrated his tremendous virtuosity by jazzing up an array of classics by Wagner, Grieg, Massenet, and Donizetti. "I've got something I'd like the world to hear," he said at the time. Who could doubt him?

Tales of a Runaway
–Duke Hits the Road
Chapter 5

When Duke Anderson ran away from home in 1927, he had no idea it would be the start of a nomadic life on the road, playing piano for a jumble of one-nighters up and down the chittlin' circuit with some of the Swing Era's most famous bands.

In the 1940s, Anderson played and arranged for Tiny Bradshaw and Ike Quebec, then joined Dizzy Gillespie's first band. In the 1960s and 1970s, he filled in for Basie whenever the Count was too sick or tired to play. Then he turned to teaching piano, perfecting a simplified system of playing to support his family between gigs. Like many of his contemporaries, Anderson has written scores of songs, most of them stolen or lost in some crap game: "When I joined Tiny, I was doin' a lot of arranging. He paid me twenty-four dollars a night. Everyone else was getting fourteen. I'd get in a crap game and send four or five thousand dollars home. One week I sent twelve thousand. Then, for two or three months, I'd be broke and didn't send

nothin'. It all hinged on the dice. But my wife stayed with me—all these years."

Anderson was wearing knee pants when he began playing at house rent parties in the late 1920s. When he started playing gigs at the Orange Y, he had to "sit on a stack of telephone books" to reach the keys. At the time, his idol was Clem Moorman, the Savoy Dictators' piano player/arranger.

At twelve, he hopped a freight train headed for Baltimore, fearing his grandmother would blame him after a pretty young roomer seduced him. He had never been farther than Newark, but he got lucky. A band of white hoboes looked after him and he landed a job for fifty cents a day with Ida Cox, the famous blues singer. Officially, his job was to walk Cox's two afghans. As a by-product, he became a man of the world, learning about music, show business, and the theatrics of carnival life: "Everywhere Ida Cox went, I went. I stayed with her for a year and a month. We had a carnival

Duke Anderson, foreground, with the Billy Ford Orchestra, circa 1950: from left, Charli(e) Persip, drums; Howard Buchanan, bass; Billy Ford, trumpet; Earl Watson, saxophone. Courtesy of Jackson (Flap) McQueen

show. She made sure none of the girls—the shake dancers—bothered me. I was like an adopted son. That's how nice she was. This was in 1928–29.

"Ida Cox was a terrific blues singer, but she was frustrated 'cause she was in competition with all the oldtimers, like Bessie Smith. She came from Georgia. She was what you called an octaroon—very light-skinned with lots of freckles. White people thought she was white, so we had a lot of trouble when we got to Mississippi and Alabama.

"She could dance her ass off, and she was beautiful, but she was slick. She was the first entertainer that started pickin' up a dollar with her pussy [a practice known as "ups"]. She really did it with her thighs. And she had a way she'd hit her hips at the end of a number that made the people scream. She was a heavy woman and she wore gowns that was very revealing. She never wore a bra.

"We traveled south from Baltimore into Virginia, North Carolina, and South Carolina by trailer. Some of the trailers were horse-drawn and some were motorized. We didn't do the big towns—just the rural places. One time we played this big plantation in South Hill, Virginia. The man must of had two or three thousand [workers]. He had the show for them. When we came to town we had to see the sheriff. We always came to town on the border of the black section. All the black people would know we were there by word of mouth. Then the sheriff would come. The sheriff was 'The Man.' You had to pay him ten dollars a day or maybe five and one of the girls. That was part of the deal, and she better be good! If she ain't good, then we don't have no carnival. This was prevalent all over the South.

"My job was to take care of the dogs and keep an eye out for the sheriff, 'cause we sold near-beer and corn whiskey. The corn whiskey was Ida Cox's private stock. I think it cost twenty-five cents a glass, but you got half a water glass and it was good stuff. It'd make you burn, baby. You couldn't smoke a cigarette after it.

"Ida Cox had everything. She had one woman who was supposed to be the alligator lady and a big black woman who was supposed to weigh five hundred pounds, but she only weighed two-eighty. She was short and dumpy, and it made her look big. She had a little midget and a tall man who was about six foot seven or eight, not seven feet like they said. Then she had the strong man [boxer]. You paid a dollar, and if you could hit this big guy you got your dollar back. He was good, but he got appendicitis and I had to take his place. That's where I got my nickname, by using my dukes, not from Duke Ellington like most people think. Nobody hit me 'cause I was fast and I could run.

"This was strictly a carnival atmosphere. Ida Cox had a candy booth, card games, and a crap game. She must of made two or three hundred dollars a day, and that was big, big money at that time. I was one of the best crap-shooters, and I made a lot of money. I could pad roll—make 'em stop where I wanted."

The show featured more than a dozen dancing girls who did the "hoochie coochie," two black-face comedians, and a minstrel act in which nine men called stereotypical names like Sambo and Rastus sat on stage in a line of chairs, bantering comically with a straight man known as an interlocutor. Cox clearly was the star, but she occasionally created new interest by hiring top-flight entertainers like Buck and Bubbles, who were on their way to becoming vaudeville headliners. That generally happened when she had the money and the carnival played a city like Baltimore, Norfolk, or Raleigh.

"We usually stayed in a town about three weeks," Anderson recounted. "Mainly, it was a minstrel show. It was free, but after you got in you had to pay ten cents to see the attractions in two smaller tents. We always played outdoors under a tent, and the show was always in the daytime, usually at two, sometimes at five, 'cause there were no lights.

"The dancers would go out on the edge of the tent and shake their tambourines to attract attention. They wore costumes with tassels, but they didn't show no flesh. That wasn't allowed. The band usually played on a flatbed truck with the minstrel show on the ground in

Bandleader James (Billy) Anderson, circa 1950. Courtesy of James (Billy) Anderson

front. In another tent you could see the shake dancers do their thing. They didn't have much music, just a conga drum."

For some unknown reason, possibly for lack of money, the band had no piano player. Yet a broken-down piano without hammers was hauled from town to town with a man seated at it who went through the motions. According to Anderson, he acted just like he was playing, but it was all an illusion. The band had five pieces—a drummer, a tuba player, two banjo players, and a saxophonist, Baltimore Red, who was from Newark. For a time, Humpy Williams, whose brother Rudy was with the Savoy Sultans, also was in it.

On the road with Cox, Anderson picked up a gimmick that earned him "a lot of extra bread"

over the years: "I learned how to play the piano with a sheet over the keys. The audience loved it. When I was with the big bands, I got paid extra to do it. Ida Cox used to tell me that you had to have something different. If you're normal, you'll never make it! That's why she was such a crowd pleaser!"

By 1929, Anderson grew tired of the road and decided to return home: "When I got home, everybody was glad to see me, but my father whipped me, my grandmother whipped me, and just about everyone in the family gave me a whippin' all over. I went back to school and finished high school. I graduated in 1936, though I should've graduated in 1934. Then I got into music full time. I always had a band 'cause I played funny and couldn't always get gigs.

"In 1937 or '38 I had seven pieces—the Duke Anderson band. I had Brother Kelly on drums; Al King, who also was quite a piano player, on bass; a guy named Johnny from New York on guitar; and Mouse [Clarence Fulford] and Geech [Julius Smalls] on trumpet. Geech couldn't read a note, but he could play his ass off. I had Ike Quebec on tenor and Johnny B. Gardner was out front as the leader. We played upstairs at the Wideway Ballroom on Broad Street and a place up in Orange called the New World. Then we had a gig in Belleville right near where I live now. Forgot the name.

"At that time, a lot of piano players from New York went out on the road 'cause they could make more money. I had three weeks with Cab Calloway, two weeks with Teddy Hill, and a short time with Vernon Andrade and Erskine Hawkins. Then I worked with Mildred Bailey for three or four months in 1938 or '39, around the time she married Red Norvo. In 1939, I went with the Savoy Sultans. I took the place of a West Indian guy named Elliott. When the Sultans broke up in 1943, Rudy [Williams], Sonny Stitt, and I joined Tiny Bradshaw. I came in the week after Mitch [Harold Mitchell] left. Bobby Plater, who was in [the] service, got me in that band. I couldn't read a note, but Tiny didn't say nothin' 'cause I had New York experience."

Eventually, Anderson learned to read music

A segregated World War II Army dance for blacks at Fort Lee, Virginia, circa 1943. Newark trumpeter Jimmy (Chops) Jones is second from the left in the band. Courtesy of Jimmy (Chops) Jones

and became a talented arranger: "For Louis Armstrong, I wrote the tune 'Let's Put One On.' It was about pot. And I wrote for Conway and Parks. They sang and danced and I wrote their whole act for them." In 1950, Anderson teamed with his younger brother, James (Billy), to form the Billy and Duke Anderson Orchestra.

Life on the road was tough on musicians, especially black musicians. Virtually every night, night after night, gig after gig, they had to struggle to find a place to sleep or eat. "There were no young men [in the towns]. They were all in the service. So the women were wild. With a travelin' band, the best thing you could do was find you a woman so you could get a free night's action—a place to stay and a free meal. You didn't get no nice lookin' woman, 'cause she'd want to show you off. So you had to look for the ugliest woman out there—find one with a cockeye and no shape—and say, 'Hey, baby. What's happening?' If you got with a girl that was pretty sharp, she'd want to show you off to her friends, and you might end up not gettin' no pussy, or she'd want a few bucks for stockings."

In Orlando, Florida, Anderson ran into trouble when he went home for breakfast with two fans: "One of them invited me to her house for breakfast after the show. They were pleasant, and to me it was a free meal. I'll never forget it. We played at the Blue Paradise Inn. I had bacon and eggs, brains, and cornbread and coffee. When I asked for my hat and started to leave, the lady who lived there said she forgot where she put it. Then she said she remembered my hat was in the bedroom, and the other one pulled this switchblade knife.

"I said, Sweetheart, I got thirty dollars on me. It's yours.

"She said, 'That ain't what I want.'

"Then she took that knife and cut my shirt.

"She said, 'Before you leave, I want you to fuck me and my girlfriend.'

"So, I'm laying up between these two broads, and I can't get a hard on 'cause I'm under duress. So I did the best I could. For a while after that I didn't bother with no chicks."

The affairs the band played were replete with racism: "During the war, to get gas for the bus, you had to play an affair at an Army camp. We had to play two dances—one for the whites where there was no blacks; then you played for the blacks with the whites up in the balcony. Every place you went they had cops. If a [white] fella wanted an autograph, he had to tell the cop and the cop would come up on the stage and say, 'There's a fella who wants your autograph.' With the black folks, there was no problem."

While traveling with Bradshaw's band in the South (1943–45), Anderson encountered harrowing racial experiences: "In one southern town, one of the boys almost got beat to death by the sheriff's men 'cause he had a picture of a white woman in his wallet. All it was was a picture of a movie star that came with the wallet when he bought it. In most southern towns there was a law against 'reckless eyeballin'.' For black men that meant running the risk of arrest simply for looking at a white woman. In New Orleans, you couldn't buy vanilla ice cream 'cause it was white."

The most painful experience occurred near Natchez, Mississippi: "In the South when you'd rent a bus, it had to have a white man drivin'. Comin' into Natchez, we saw what we thought was a carnival. One guy was sellin' candy and balloons. On the other side of the road, they were sellin' hot dogs and ice cream. When we got halfway to where all these people were, a state trooper stopped the bus driver and told him, 'Don't stop. Take your time. Then keep goin' and get the hell outta here.' I was wonderin' what was goin' on. When I looked out, the white kids were waving at us. About two hundred yards to the left I looked and saw two black guys hanging. It was a lynching party."

THE PERFORMERS

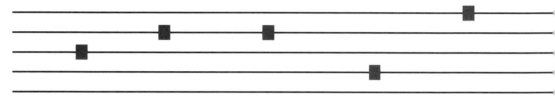

1935-45

Ballads and Blues
—The City's Singing Sensations
Chapter 6

In the halcyon days of the Swing Era, Ethel Waters, Billie Holiday, Dinah Washington, Ella Fitzgerald, and an array of lesser-known singers, including Lil Green, Una Mae Carlisle, and Bea Morton, were the headliners at Newark theaters or at dances or band battles. Occasionally, they also played the city's colored clubs, attracting throngs of admirers.

The biggest and brightest star to come out of Newark was Sarah Vaughan, the only child of the Asbury Vaughans of Avon Avenue. But Newark also produced many vocalists who had just as much standing with their audiences, sometimes even more than the bigger names brought in to liven things up. Besides Miss Rhapsody, whose career spanned more than sixty years, key among them were "Newark's own Miss Grace Smith," Geneva Turman, Billie Sermond (who married man-about-town Eldridge Hall), Emma Hawkins, and Audrey (Celeste) Jones. Among the popular male troubadours were Marshall Haley and Man-

hattan Paul and romantic balladeers like Bob Taylor, Joe Timmons, Thad (Chuck) Howard, and Lawrence Miller. Ballads and blues were their staples with jump tunes tossed in to show versatility.

In later years, Grace Smith turned her attention to church singing. But in the 1930s she was a worldly young girl singing torch songs at spots like the Rin Tin Inn and Fisher's Tavern. "Easy Livin'" was her big number, sung with such a bluesy compassion that the whole place would rock. After a tour of the Bahamas in the early 1940s with a group of entertainers from Newark, Gracie became "Bahama Mama," a nickname that stuck. Another tour took her to Canada in 1944 with Arthur Terry, emcee at the Nest Club.

"Mostly, I played Dodger's, the Nest, the Pic [Picadilly], Fisher's, the Rin Tin Inn, and Tyler's [Chicken Shack in Avenel]," Smith said. "My other big numbers were 'I Cried for You' and 'Them There Eyes.' I also played Small's

Grace Smith, circa 1940. Courtesy of Meredith Gordon

Paradise, the Baby Grand, and Kelly's Stable in New York, and I was on the road for a while with Wynonie Harris."

In 1945, Smith traveled with a USO show as far as Bangor, Maine, teaming with Johnny Berry as a dance and song duo. With Berry decked out in a zoot suit and Smith pleading in song for "a two-fisted, double-jointed, rough 'n ready man," they were the hit of the show.

Handling the sweet songs at Newark's top night spots was another Newarker, Geneva Turman, whose endearing renditions of "Call Me Darling" and "I Let a Song Go Out of

My Heart" reportedly "held the soldiers spellbound" during the war years. One of four talented Turman children, Geneva got her show business start entertaining with her sister Helena and brother Buddy. Soon after, their sister Gertrude joined the act. As a soloist in the late 1930s, Geneva sang, and sometimes danced, at Dave and Maney's in Orange, then was booked regularly for several years at Dodger's Bar and Grill on Bedford Street in Newark.

Another popular sweet singer, Billie Sermond, a light-skinned beauty, became Geneva's best friend. "They called me 'Smoke Ring Billie,'" she recalled. "I must have sang that number thousands of times over the years, starting in Asbury Park. I sang mostly in white clubs, like the Palm House in Newark, three blocks south of Lincoln Park. I was the first colored girl to work Broad Street. It never dawned on me that no colored girl had worked Broad Street before. From then on, everybody told me the ice was broken."

"Billie could really swing," said soprano Celeste Jones, whose specialty was "Trees." "She could sing a sweet number, too, if she had to. She's what I'd call an all-round singer."

Sermond's light, mulatto coloring proved to be a mixed blessing: On one hand, she had no trouble finding work at white clubs; on the other, like Lena Horne, she often was discriminated against and subjected to unfair treatment. Still, her good looks won her an offer to go to Hollywood (if, indeed, the offer was on the level), but she was fearful and "too stupid to go," she recalled wistfully. Instead, she married Hall and continued to sing at local clubs and affairs into the early 1960s.

To her audiences, Emma Hawkins simply was "Queen of the Nightclubs," reigning at Dodger's Bar and Grill for so long that a reporter noted in 1939, "Once she opens a place, she can't let it go." One of the numbers that pleased the crowds most was her delineation of Duke Ellington's "I Let a Song Go Out of My Heart."

"Emma had a whole lot of personality. She was very attractive and a good singer and dancer, too," said bartender Bill Roberts. "People would throw quarters when she sang

Billie Sermond, left, and Geneva Turman relaxing during Sermond's break at the Silver Ball, a white nightclub on Broad Street, circa 1940. Courtesy of Billie (Sermond) Hall

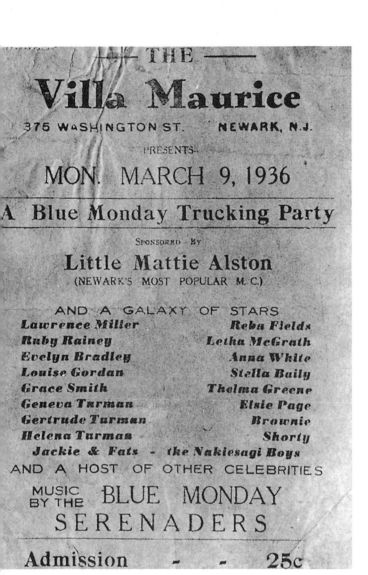

Ad for a 1936 show at the Villa Maurice. Grace Smith, Geneva Turman, and Lawrence Miller shared the spotlight. Courtesy of Gertrude (Turman) Brown

and she'd scoop 'em up. She had a magnet under her gown. She took me in her dressing room one time and showed me." Added trombonist Clyde Bernhardt: "Emma could swing it, baby."

Circa 1935, Sermond, Hawkins, and another young and attractive singer, Louise Gordon, joined forces and formed the Three Regular Girls. They put out posters around town to promote their shows, which were sold out. In the late 1930s, Gordon fell ill and faded from the Newark scene.

Celeste Jones, born in New York in 1908, was raised in show business. Her mother and stepfather, Ethel and Thomas Robinson, ran the Riverlette between 136th Street and 137th Street on Seventh Avenue in New York, a club that featured "live music, generally a piano or three-piece band."

By 1937, when she arrived in Newark, Jones already knew "a lot of people from Jersey who used to come over to the Riverlette. The first place I worked in Newark was Dodger's—jam sessions on Monday nights. Everybody got a chance to get up and do something. For a while I couldn't get work and I got disgusted. I'd get up and sing and tear up the place, but I couldn't get hired. Then one night at Dodger's I got up and I guess I sang like I felt. Ma and Pa Frazier [the owners] hired me that night and told me to come to work Thursday night. I stayed for a year. I guess I got nine or ten dollars [a week]."

Jones's specialties, "Trees" and "Marie," showcased her high soprano. Because of it, she was called "The Girl with the Mockingbird Voice." Her male counterpart was Marshall Haley, who sang at the Kinney Club around the same time, employing a light opera-like style. "Marshall used to do all the big numbers like 'Ah, Sweet Mystery of Life,' not exactly the kind of thing you'd expect to hear in a nightclub," said Connie (Williams) Woodruff, former editor of the *New Jersey Herald News*.

"Marshall was trained in opera," Al Henderson noted. "He could sing Pagliacci and make you cry. He had a crying sound in his voice. Supposedly, it was too classy for a black man. A black man ain't supposta sing that."

Another troubador type was Manhattan Paul, a smooth peddler of sentimental wares. Booked out of New York, he entertained in the Newark area for more than two decades, starting in 1939 at Dave and Maney's in Orange. "He was a class act with tails and top hat, a cosmopolitan kind of guy," Woodruff said. "He reminded me a lot of [bandleader] Lucky Millinder, but he was bigger. He wore a big, high pompadour and a big diamond, and he was always dapper. He was one of the first people I ever heard of who was gay. That seemed to be the reason he was so fascinating."

Bob Taylor was one of Newark's most popular band singers and nightclub emcees in the late 1930s. "Trees" was one of the songs that won him legions of female fans. "Let Me Dream," "Marie," "Dark Eyes," and trumpeter Leon Eason's "Beverly" were his other big numbers. Taylor eventually became more interested in acting. In 1945 he was cast in the Broadway production of *Anna Lucasta*. Although he still sang occasionally at dances or social soirees, Taylor's career had taken a new turn. He changed his first name to Lance and began making movies. Eventually, he found his way into television, popping up occasionally on the tube in the 1960s and 1970s as a detective or in other supporting roles.

When it came to stopping hearts, Lawrence Miller was king, possessing a tenor so fine he could make even the rowdiest of patrons at the Waverly Tavern, Nest Club, or Cotton Club, a few steps off Kinney Street, "hold their breath with rapture." Miller's repertoire included tunes like "Outside of Paradise" and "Call Me Darling." But his showstopper, the one he used most to charm Newark's womenfolk and make his money, was "My Mother's Eyes." "He made a lot of money going around to tables on that one," recalled bassist Wes Clark. "A whole lot of money."

"Lawrence just took all the women's hearts," said Leon Eason. "He just took 'em—like magic." Added Billie Sermond: "Lawrence was on the trim side, and he had eyes that could say something to a woman, although they never said anything to me. He was the cutest thing. We all loved everything he sang, mostly love songs. And he had a whole lot of personality."

Miller was a man of many talents. An airy dancer and debonair emcee, he supposedly was the first black to perform with an all-white band at Newark's Branford Theater, appearing with Ted Lewis of "Me and My Shadow" fame. Although he was a very polished singer, in the vein of Billy Eckstine, he never reaped the recognition his colleagues thought he deserved.

Joe Timmons, whose lush tenor made him the vocal star of the Golden Gate Quartet in the early 1940s, was another heart-stopper. After gaining a group of faithful fans at the Al-

Singer Joe Timmons, left, with two unidentified friends, late 1930s. Courtesy of Lucille (Dorsey) Morton

cazar in 1942, he moved over to the Nest Club, where he had one of the biggest followings in town. In 1946, Timmons suddenly gave up singing. Supposedly, he moved to Nashville, went into business, and was never heard from again.

Singer/emcee Thad (Chuck) Howard's first

job was at the old Shady Rest Country Club near Plainfield, New Jersey in the early 1930s: "Lucky Louie [Anderson] had booked the job but couldn't make it, so he asked me," Howard related. "I had never emceed or sang anywhere before. Prince Hall, Joe Gregory, and a bunch of lindyhoppers from Newark were on the same show. I had to sing eight songs before I could leave the stage. My pay was two dollars and fifty cents. They called me a singing emcee, but I couldn't sing a stroke without a mike. I was a crooner, and I had tremendous range then, a lot of falsetto. I could reach G above high C. Then, in 1940, I caught a cold and my voice dropped down to a baritone. I had to change my style."

By that time, Howard was working at the Club Miami on Clinton Avenue, where Jackie Gleason got his start. His longest "gig" was at Dodger's, where he worked two years. In 1940, he left Newark "with a band and show," settling eventually in Latham, New York, his home until his death in 1990. "All we did in Newark was entertain people," Howard once said. "We were pioneers. In a way, it's our heritage. If you came to Newark and you didn't have a cent, somebody would take you in. If you were hungry, somebody would give you a meal. It was the neighborly thing. Compared to New York or some other big city, Newark was a neighborly place."

Miss Rhapsody
—Newark's Number One Brown Gal
Chapter 7

When Miss Rhapsody stopped the show at Harlem's Apollo Theater in 1939, the *New Jersey Herald News*, a black weekly, described her as "the perfect example of a local girl making good." She had made such a "decided hit" that Claude Hopkins, with whom she appeared, was "expected to sign her to a long-term contract." That didn't happen, possibly because of an exaggerated expectation by the hometown press, possibly because she had just returned home to Newark and was tired of traveling. More likely it was because she didn't fit the image of the "band singer": young, pretty, and light-skinned (high yellow in black terminology). To the contrary, Rhap was almost thirty-eight, handsome but heavyset, and brown-skinned. Nor was she suited to serving as window dressing for a band. Small intimate settings were her bailiwick, taverns and clubs where she could command her audiences backed by a trio and maybe a horn or two.

The name "Miss Rhapsody" was bestowed by a Pittsburgh newsman in the early 1930s. Sometimes—her performances at the Apollo are examples—she was billed as "Viola Underhill" or "Rhapsody Underhill." By the time Rhap played the Apollo, she'd spent more than a decade traveling the East Coast with a band led by Banjo Bernie Robinson and touring the South with blues singer Ida Cox. She'd just completed a fourteen-month stint at the famous Sunset Crystal Place in Kansas City, where she scouted the talent for amateur shows, sang, and served as emcee. She spent her spare time hanging out with the better-known blues singer Julia Lee. "Hold all the women, 'cause we've got the men," Julia would call out when Rhap arrived. Not that Rhapsody was looking for a man. Her "husband," guitarist Harold Underhill, was always nearby, generally accompanying her on a gig or playing at a nearby club.

Like her contemporaries, Rhap went where

Miss Rhapsody, circa 1944. From author's collection

her work took her. The prolonged stop in Kansas City was just one of many unplanned legs in her journey. Ultimately, she viewed that experience as a highlight of the six decades she spent in show business, for it put her in contact with musicians in the national limelight. Kansas City, at that time—just after critic John Hammond discovered Count Basie playing there at the Reno Club—was teeming with "name" musicians. The city was "wide open." Illegal activities like prostitution and numbers running abounded. The downtown was a maze of clubs and after-hours joints.

Ironically, Rhap landed in Kansas City because of the jealousy of Ida Cox: "I joined Ida

Cox in Oklahoma after working a carnival show in Toledo. The morning after the first show she called me to her room and fired me. She was mad, screamin' 'cause the newspaper said 'a certain buxom young lady stole the show. Ida Cox can't sing no more.' She said she couldn't have two singers in the show. I said, You knew I was a singer when you hired me.

"A man named Jack Schenck drove me and my guy [Underhill] and my baby [her daughter, Yvonne, then a toddler] through a storm to Kansas City. I went straight to the union office. They had two spots, the Sunset Crystal Palace, a big spot, and the Spinning Wheel, a white spot. I automatically took the colored spot. The owner, Felix Payne—he was a newspaper publisher—gave me two weeks. I stayed fourteen months.

"The big bands always had a night. Another night we had the amateur shows. Several of them became stars. Walter Brown, whose hit was 'Confessin' the Blues,' was one. When Joe Turner'd get drunk, I'd hold him up to the microphone. He was the 'Father of the Blues,' no doubt about it. Couldn't read his name, but if you played the blues, he'd give you a lyric."

After a disagreement with a tenor player who refused to accompany her on "Dear Old Southland," Rhap quit the Sunset and went to work across the street at the Spinning Wheel: "Pete Johnson was the attraction there with five of Benny Moten's boys. I was the only straight thing in the place. I worked there until Basie came back to Kansas City. I was makin' enough tips for two or three salaries."

Toward the end of 1938, she decided to head home to Newark, taking the bus with her daughter, who had just turned three. Soon, she once again was rivaling singers Emma Hawkins and Grace Smith as the queen of Newark nightclubs, dubbed "Newark's Number One Brown Gal" because of her theme song, "Brown Gal." If anyone loved Newark, it was Rhap. No matter where she went she never failed to mention the city where she was born. At eighty, two years before her death in 1984, she was called on by Newark radio station WBGO (Jazz 88) to record a ten-second spot welcoming listeners to "my hometown."

Born at 21 Scott Street in the city's East Ward in 1902, Miss Rhapsody (real name, Viola Wells) was the daughter of Earle and Roberta Wells, who had come north from Surry County, Virginia at the turn of the century. (Newark then had just 6,700 Negro residents, about 3 percent of the population.) In later life, she referred to herself as a "motherless child," having been raised by her father after her beautiful young mother died giving birth to her sister, Estelle, when she was just four. Soon after, her father sent her and the baby south to Surry to live with their maternal grandparents.

"I guess you could say my grandparents were well off," she recalled, "because they had three hundred acres of land and lived in the Big House—that's what they called it. In the living room, my grandmother had an organ and a player piano, too. When I told my cousins I wanted to be in show business, they just laughed and said, 'Sure, Viola.' But I knew I would be. I've been a singer all my life. I guess I was born with it."

Almost immediately, she came face to face with diametrically opposed worlds—sacred and secular. Her grandfather, the Reverend Morgan Simmons, was a stern Baptist minister, taken to preaching brimstone and fire and enamored of church music only. Yet her Uncle Charlie, his oldest son, was a terrific song and dance man, surrounded by a flock of nieces and nephews eager to learn his latest routines in a household where such fun ordinarily would be forbidden. "Uncle Charlie would dance, and I'd imitate every step. Then I'd gather all the children into a chorus and stage shows out in the barn. One of the first tunes I ever learned was 'Sweet Man'" (recorded by her idol Ethel Waters).

When she was nine, her father remarried and brought his daughters back to Newark. By then he was a lay leader at Thirteenth Avenue Presbyterian Church and a prominent figure in the growing Negro community. At her father's insistence, she joined the church's Salika Johnson Choir (named for the great opera singer Madame Salika) under the direction of Ruth Reid, a gifted music teacher. By twelve, she

Comedian Fortune (Fats) Jennings and Harold Underhill, circa 1940. Courtesy of Lucille (Dorsey) Morton

had traveled with the choir as far as Philadelphia and Baltimore and was invited to sing on WOR radio at the Westinghouse Building in Newark to raise money for the city's first black YMCA.

"As a young girl," she said, "I was observing everything. I wanted to be a singer so I'd go to these different parties to hear people sing. Still, I respected my father and the church too much to do anything professionally until I got married. A lot of church people believe popular music is the Devil in you. But my father wasn't like that. He had respect for everyone and everything. I say God's music and the blues are related. They have the same mother and father. When I sing His music, I'm down on my knees, praying to Him. When I sing about troubles with my man to other folks, it's on this [gesturing horizontally] level. It's an earthly thing."

Like other young girls, she was attracted to the shows at the Orpheum, where top vaudevillians performed. She was attracted, too, by the Orpheum's amateur contests. Finally, she entered and "just walked away" with the prize money, five dollars or so: "T. W. Walker was the manager. If anybody came from New York for an amateur contest, he'd come and get me and say, 'Go get this money, child,' and I'd walk out there and just take it. Later, I came into the Orpheum with Sunshine Sammy. Jerome Carrington [a singer from Baltimore] spied me and took me over to Charlie Roberts' Plantation Club [in Newark]. He sat me at the rail and had me sing when he played piano. It was quite an encouragement."

At nineteen, she married Howard Nicholas, the son of a New York policeman she'd met at a dance hall—primarily "to get out from underneath" her stepmother. They were "just kids" and the marriage didn't last long. But it gave her the independence she needed to pursue a career in show business.

One of her first jobs was at the Elks Home (next door to Little Blue Heaven on Broome Street): "There was a woman who sang there by the name of Lucille Atkins. Her husband was a musician. They called her 'Black Beauty.' She musta been forty or fifty years old. I was just a kid, maybe nineteen. Billy Atkins played there with Bam Holman on clarinet and sax."

Rhap worked next "out at the Kingsland Hut in Nutley," about ten miles from Newark: "It was my show. I had a singer [Lawrence Miller] and five chorus girls. We played there about six months. In those days, Lawrence

used to wear tails every night, and he could dance—really dance. Frankie Young was in the show. Quallo, too. He played trumpet at the Orpheum. The Kingsland Hut was strictly white. It was like a local, family place. Everybody'd come out at the end. We'd do a dance step and sing a song, maybe 'I Found a New Baby' or 'Papa De Da Da.'

"Then I worked Miner's downtown. It was the first big thing I did—a black and white show. They had seen me singing and they got me and Cora LaRedd, who was quite a popular performer at the time [and later appeared in several Broadway shows], and Geneva and Helena Turman. Alex Lovejoy put the show together. It was burlesque. We worked the Empire, then put it on in Baltimore, but it didn't go no further. I was only twenty-one years old and afraid of being stranded. I had heard about being stranded. Later, in Sumter, South Carolina, I had to sell my fox stole to get the band [Banjo Bernie's] through."

That was about the time she met the famous Durham Brothers—Roosevelt, Earl, Joe, and Eddie—who had come north from San Marcos, Texas, with the popular 7-11 traveling show starring blues singer Mamie Smith. "Mamie couldn't do the last two shows, so Miss Rhapsody did them," Eddie Durham recounted. "She was just a young girl, maybe still in her teens." Nonetheless, one reviewer noticed, "Unlike many great singers, she knows her notes, can hum any tune after hearing it a vague once, knows her arrangements, and, most important, knows how to sell a song."

One summer, while she was still in her twenties, she got a job in an Atlantic City night club where her boyfriend, a trumpet player nicknamed "Mouse" (Clarence Fulford), was playing: "Ethel Waters and Mattie Hite [another singer] heard about this kid singin' and came to hear me. I guess I shoulda been thrilled, but my biggest interest was playin' the twenty-five-cent machines. Atlantic City was wide open then. The boardwalk was nothin' but a casino."

That fall she got a job in Chester, Pennsylvania, where Waters was born, playing nightclubs there and in South Chester until the next summer. Then she played Scranton, where Pearl Bailey was in the chorus and sang in a trio with her and another girl. Next came another summer in Atlantic City, where she spent the summer singing at Dan's Tavern on Arctic Avenue, awaiting a break that could propel her career: "In those days, they didn't pay much attention to brown-skinned women unless they were extraordinarily beautiful or had all these gowns. No one showed me nothin'. Makeup. Nothin'. But I knew I had something."

That winter she went to live in Harlem with her Aunt Rebecca, her mother's twin sister. She worked as an elevator operator and sang on weekends at after-hours joints. Gradually, the partygoers began taking notice of her talent. Other entertainers, including Newark's Eloise Coffee, whom she'd met at the Plantation Club in Newark, began stopping by just to hear her sing: "The tips started rollin' in. One night six guys came in and asked the boss for me to do a certain number. I did two and went home with sixty dollars. Then Eloise came by. By that time, everyone in the joint had introduced themselves to me. She realized who I was from Newark. She'd mention my name here and there. After that, the road was easy. I never looked back for a job. Never!"

First came more than a year on the road with Banjo Bernie, traveling back and forth from New York to Florida, playing clubs including Ike Dixon's in Baltimore and the beautiful Hollywood Casino in Savannah, Georgia, and Palatka, Florida, an all-black town: "In the South, we worked black audiences one night and white audiences tomorrow night—two nights each stop. Bernie invariably didn't pay his musicians, so they voted me financial secretary. I saw the guys had three meals a day. Never thought nothin' of it; just did it. Bernie was big and fat and black as coal. But he could play any instrument. One night I was wearin' a plain white form-fitting gown studded with rhinestones. I did the splits at the end of a number and lost my shoe. A white man retrieved it and put it back on. Bernie was yellin', 'God damn, Rhap. You're gonna have us hung.' "

When she returned home from Kansas City in 1938, Rhap was ready for the big time. For a while she played local taverns, including Fisher's and the Picadilly, and appeared at the Apollo. Her appearance with the Claude Hopkins Orchestra at the Apollo was one of three she made at the famous New York theater within a year, next with Erskine Hawkins and then with Bunny Berigan. Berigan, too, supposedly wanted her to travel with his band, a proposition even more preposterous because of its unacceptability to white audiences, especially in the South.

After the Apollo, Rhap hired an agent and got a call to work at Kelly's Stable on 52nd Street in New York. The 1940 billing read: "Art Tatum, Seer of the Keys; Benny Carter and his International Band; Billy Daniels, the Sweetest Voice This Side of Paradise, and (if you had a spyglass) Miss Rhapsody, the Ebony Stick of Dynamite." "I opened up scared to death. I had to look up and say a little prayer. I opened with the blues, and I mean the blues. I said to myself, These people won't understand, but they did. I did 'Brown Gal' and 'Bye, Bye, Baby.' After a while, I was moved to the middle of the show and then to the top to co-star with Tatum. Kelly's Stable belonged to me. It was my kitchen sink. When I got tired, I'd play Washington [the Crystal Caverns] or Detroit [the Three Sixes], or sometimes Cleveland [the Blue Grass]. I was in and out of Kelly's for somethin' like three, maybe four years."

During those years she shared the bill with some of the nation's premiere performers, including Nat King Cole, Coleman Hawkins, and Benny Carter. Although she was older than Carter, she had an unrequited crush on him. One night, on the subway back to Newark, she wrote a song for him, "I Fell for You," which she subsequently recorded on Savoy.

Newark was still home. In between Kelly's and her tours, she was a regular at the Picadilly and at Dodger's Bar and Grill. For weeks, she had the patrons rushing over to Herman Lubinsky's Radio Record Shop on Market Street to plunk down seventy-nine cents for one of her cuts on Savoy records. Twice in 1946 the *Afro-American* reported, "Miss Rhapsody

Miss Rhapsody with piano player Elwood Hardy, left, and William (Bass Byrd) Lindbergh during a radio broadcast for the American Broadcasting Company, mid 1940s. From author's collection

broke all records for a continuous appearance at Dodger's."

"Eventually, I decided to get some of these kids together here in Newark, the ones who really started with me. So I got Jay Cole on piano, Bass Byrd [William Lindbergh], and Harold [Underhill] on guitar. We rehearsed six weeks while we was workin' at Dodger's and went out on the road [as far as Norfolk] as

Miss Rhapsody and Her Three Sportsmen of Rhythm.

In 1950, after her father was murdered by their minister—a sensational case that drew hundreds of spectators to the Essex County Court House in Newark—she went into semi-retirement to spend more time at home with her teenaged daughter. In the 1960s, after four decades as an entertainer, she began singing regularly again at Pitt's Place on West Market Street, where she also ran the kitchen. On information provided by trumpet player Leon Eason, who led the combo at Pitt's, blues author and critic Sheldon Harris found her there and helped revive her career.

In the early 1970s, when she was nearly seventy years old, Rhap became the vocalist for the Harlem Blues and Jazz Band, co-led by June (Jay) Cole and Clyde Bernhardt, and traveled to Europe for the first time, winning legions of new fans. With the band, she toured Sweden, Belgium, the Netherlands, England, and Germany, making annual trips for the next six years. Then tragedy struck. In a rush to get an autograph, a fan in London stepped on her diabetic foot. Seven months later, unable to work and in constant pain, she felt as if her gangrenous foot was "sitting in a bucket of lye." There was no choice. Her left leg had to be amputated below the knee.

But her career was not over. She was determined to walk again, and she fought back ferociously, undertaking a plan of therapy at the Theresa Grotta Rehabilitation Center in West Orange, New Jersey. To strengthen her arms, she did five hundred pushups with weights every day. To strengthen her good leg, she did five hundred more. And to keep the stump of her amputated leg straight to fit into her prosthesis, she did a series of stretching exercises every day for the rest of her life. Within a matter of weeks she became the center's good will ambassador, dispatched by doctors and nurses to cheer up patients who had decided to give up on life. Accompanied on piano by Clem Moorman, who volunteered his time, she gave a concert, the first of three, to the patients' delight. "Music is an international language,"

Miss Rhapsody with her pianist June (Jay) Cole before the start of a concert for the Newark Branch, National Council of Negro Women, 1974. Courtesy of New Jersey Newsphotos

she told her audience from her wheelchair, launching into a program of oldtime favorites, including "Trust in Me" and "You're Nobody 'Til Somebody Loves You."

Three months later Rhap walked out, unaided by a cane. Six months later she was driving. And in less than a year she was back singing with the Harlem Blues band on Sunday nights at the Ginger Man in Manhattan. Because of her age, jazz critics soon dubbed her the "uptown Alberta Hunter." Hunter, then in her eighties and Rhap's longtime friend, was singing the blues at the Cookery in Greenwich Village.

In her later years, Rhap made little money but she reaped many honors. At seventy-two, she made six half-hour programs in Paris for French television. In 1980, after her operation, she was honored by the Board of Concerned Citizens at the University of Medicine and Dentistry of New Jersey as "Citizen of the Year." In 1982, shortly before her eightieth birthday, she was honored for sixty years in show business at Essex County College in Newark and received the key to the city from Mayor Kenneth Gibson. Her final appearance, two weeks before her death in December 1984, was at Sweet Basil's in Greenwich Village as a guest of saxophonist Eddie Chamblee.

To her friends and fellow Newarkers Rhap's influence on Newark nightlife extended far beyond her significance as a singer. She is fondly remembered as a strong and courageous woman who was always willing to reach back and lend others a helping hand. "If you needed a hundred dollars and Rhap had ninety-nine, she'd go out and borrow the other dollar," said Little Sadie Matthews. "She helped a lot of us [entertainers] along the way."

The Comics
—Rollin' 'em in the Aisles
Chapter 8

Comedians were a staple of most vaudeville acts and traveling shows during the 1920s and into the 1930s. Almost every bill on the black theater circuit featured a slapstick comedian, perhaps Dewey (Pigmeat) Markham, Johnny Hudgins, or Tim Moore, or a comedy team like Conway and Parks or Butterbeans and Susie, a touch of minstrelry carried over into New York's famed Apollo Theater and nightclubs where floor shows were presented regularly.

Newark was no different. Jackie Gleason's career, for example, was launched at Newark's Club Miami and in the city's small black clubs, where he'd take to the stage or shoot cracks from the audience to polish his routines. Most of the black musicians and entertainers liked Gleason, and "The Great One," too, appreciated their talent, sometimes helping them get jobs at otherwise off-limits white niteries.

Trumpeter Leon Eason, born in 1910, was one of Gleason's friends: "Jackie was from Brooklyn. He used to come up to the Park Rest [a white spot] on Frelinghuysen Avenue, where I was workin' on Sundays, and tell a few jokes. That was around 1936 or '37. Then he got me into the Club Miami. He was the emcee."

Thad (Chuck) Howard, who played the Club Miami soon after, remembered the "friendly feud" Gleason had with Bummy Rogers, the emcee at the Shady Rest Country Club in nearby Union County, headquarters of North Jersey's black elite. "They used to put each other down," said Howard. "Gleason would say somethin' like 'A thief is in the house,' and Rogers would shoot off some equally derogatory retort. Back and forth it went."

A decade later, Redd Foxx was another young comedian on the rise in Newark, his career propelled by his reliance on the novelty of using foul language in his routines. Foxx's material, unlike the suggestive blues of Ma Rainey and Bessie Smith, was 100 percent explicit, earning him the nickname "Filthy Mouth" among staid locals.

In the mid 1940s, Foxx worked for a while as the emcee at the Picadilly at Peshine and Waverly avenues, when it began importing bigname acts. When Billie Holiday headlined the Pic in September 1946, she was backed by musicians calling themselves the Redd Foxx Sextet.

Of the comedians who came out of Newark, Mantan Moreland probably was best known to modern audiences. A familiar face to theatergoers in the early 1930s, he appeared on Broadway in black musicals including the 1930 version of Lew Leslie's *Blackbirds* with Ethel Waters and Buck and Bubbles, *Blackberries* of 1932, and *Shuffle Along* of 1933. In films, Moreland's work included *Cabin in the Sky,* in which he teamed with Louis Armstrong in the Satan sequence. Author Gary Null saw him as an "excellent character actor" unfairly typecast in roles ranging from "Charlie Chan's bugeyed stooge for several years" to "the classic, foolish servile clown."

Among Newarkers, Moreland is fondly remembered. Pianist Clem Moorman recalled: "He used to have an act where one guy would say something and the other guy would answer. Like, 'I'm going down there.' 'Goin' where?' He'd start a sentence and the other guy would answer. Before he could answer, the other guy would interrupt. He was a scream."

Newark also was a spawning ground for comediennes. In the early 1930s Jackie (Moms) Mabley was on the bill from time to time at the Club Alabam on Arlington Street. Another favorite at the Alabam and Kinney Club was Little Bits Turner, a petite entertainer on the order of Imogene Coca who wore outrageous outfits and painted freckles on her face.

Flo Thomas was another. A fixture at the Kinney Club in the late 1930s, she wore hilarious costumes—set off by hats with feathers and other silly touches—rolling her audiences in the aisles from the moment she stepped on stage. Her big number was "Old Man Mose Is Dead." Although tame by modern standards, the suggestive lyrics of the novelty number were so popular that her patrons never seemed to tire of them. Often, she had to sing the song twice a night.

Madame Porkchops, who entertained at the

Boston Plaza, was another funny lady—in the mold of Phyllis Diller. "She wore big, long shoes and raggedy clothes," bartender Bill Roberts recalled. "I never knew her right name. She told crazy jokes, and she was young, very young."

Newark's top comedians were four funny men: Crackshot Hacksley, who "held the lease" at Dodger's Bar and Grill in the late 1930s, Herbie Pugsley, and the Nacki Sacki Boys: Fats Jennings and Jackie Mandeville.

By the time Hacksley (whose first name has been lost to time) decided to settle in Newark in the late 1920s, Newark nightlifers were long familiar with his antics. As half of the black-faced dancing comedy team of Crackshot and Hunter, he often had headlined Newark's vaudeville theaters.

In Albert Murray's biography of Count Basie, Count explained how he came to appreciate Crackshot's talent while traveling with Gonzelle White's *Big Jazz Jamboree* in 1926: "Crackshot and Hunter were also two very good dancers. They did some skits, and they had their own dance routines and sometimes they used to dance and make jokes at the same time, and there were also some numbers that featured them with the chorus. There wasn't anything out of the ordinary for comedy teams to do things like that in those days. They didn't come out there just to tell jokes. Most of them were all-around entertainers."

According to Basie, Crackshot was the troupe's "top comedian" when Dewey (Pigmeat) Markham joined the company in Macon, Georgia. Also in White's show was Doris Rheubottom, Crackshot's girlfriend, described by Basie as a beautiful young woman who "sang ballads and popular show songs like 'Indian Love Call,' 'Somebody Loves Me,'" and whose "great voice and stage personality" could "break up the house every time." Trombonist Clyde Bernhardt, who arrived in Newark in 1928, when Crackshot and Rheubottom were anchoring shows at the Orpheum Theater, described Rheubottom as "a very, very good soprano singer that was singing in most of the leading black shows in Newark and New York City then. She was very, very good!"

Comedienne Flo Thomas, circa 1939. From author's collection

After years on the road, Crackshot turned to running revues at Dodger's Bar and Grill in the early 1940s, calling on veteran funnymen like Jazzlips Richardson to take Hunter's role as a foil for his madcap antics. Richardson shared the bill for *Crackshot Hacksley and His 1942 Revue* at Dodger's, a New Year's week gala that also featured Skippy Williams, Rubie Smith, and emcee Smokie Coleman.

The following year Hacksley reorganized,

teaming with Monte Hawley as Monte and Crackshot. Their New York opening at the Apollo Theater reportedly "put New Yorkers in the aisles." Hawley was characterized by the black press as "the ideal straight man for Crackshot" and the act was said to have been "heading places if the booking is right."

Hawley, however, faded from the scene. By 1949 Crackshot had a new partner, Roscoe Dyla. Despite decidedly changing tastes in entertainment, they performed regularly at Newark's burlesque palace, the Empire Theater, and at local clubs. In 1952, they toured the South with Wynonie (Mr. Blues) Harris and singer Larry Darnell in a show that also featured Princess Margo, an exotic dancer from Newark.

That year, too, Crack found a new niche at Lloyd's Manor on Beacon Street, where he shared the bill with early proponents of bop including Babs Gonzales and Larue Jordan. That September, after appearing in Manhattan Paul's revue at the Newark Opera House (the old Orpheum), he performed at Lloyd's with Albennie Jones, a blues singer from New York.

Eventually, he faded off the scene, but even today the mere mention of Hacksley's name among oldtimers brings smiles and laughter: "I worked with Crackshot one time in New York at a spot where Becky Harding was the mistress of ceremonies," entertainer Joe Gregory recalled, convulsing at the thought. "I was the straight man, a policeman. I had on this police jacket and a black stocking crammed with a lot of stockings to make it hard, just like a club.

"Crackshot had on all this blackface, all this charcoal. It came to a point where I was supposed to tell him to get off the corner, 'cause he was disturbin' the peace—drunk and talkin' a whole lot of stuff. I said, move on, and he wouldn't, so I was supposed to take my club and hit him. I hit him, and this is true. He kept sayin' under his breath, 'Hit me harder, Joe. Make it look real. Hit me harder.' So I hauled off and really did whack him and he fell into my arms from the force. He kept mumblin', 'You hurt me, Joe,' and while he was rubbin'

his face against mine all the charcoal came off. His face was clean and mine was black. The audience fell out."

Another local favorite, Herbie Pugsley, was the mainstay comedian at Dodger's from 1936 until Crackshot took over. Then he moved his act to the Nest Club on Warren Street. By 1939, Pugsley was in his third year at Dodger's, a lengthy run predicated on the sheer force of his personality. Like Hacksley, he was multitalented, singing a bit when his gift of gab wasn't laying out the patrons. At Dodger's, Pugsley teamed mostly with blues singer Emma Hawkins, crooner Bob Taylor, one of the regular emcees, and the popular little dancer Myrtle Hutchinson.

One of his most popular routines was the side-splitting skit, "The Doctor's Dummy," in which he played the title role, supported by the entire cast. According to a reviewer, the patrons "laughed so heartily one lad fell away in a dead faint and had to be revived by a waitress." Another of Pugsley's routines was an early form of rap music, with lyrics that went something like this: "If everybody stopped knocking on everybody, what a wonderful world this would be." "He'd repeat it, throwing in a lot of funny lines," Gregory recounted. "It was one of his themes. Another thing he used to do was pick a name out of the audience, like 'There sits a man named Joe; knock on Joe; he's gotta go.' He'd rhyme as he'd go along. The people loved it."

By 1945, Pugsley's interest turned to politics. He was elected Democratic chairman of the city's old Third Ward, one of fifteen such political units in the city at the time. All accounts of his career seem to end there.

The most popular comedy team to come out of Newark was the Nacki Sacki Boys—tiny Jackie Mandeville and his towering partner Fortune (Fats) Jennings. Before teaming with Fats, Little Jackie, as he was called, paired with Little Black Jimmy Fairbanks, a dancer who subsequently teamed with Newarker Georgie Rollins as the Two Turbans, a duo that toured England with Cab Calloway and appeared before the king and queen.

Jennings, who died in 1983, was as light on

Nacki Sacki Fats and Jackie (Fortune Jennings and Jackie Mandeville) in a comedy routine, mid 1930s. Courtesy of Marie Jennings

his feet as he was fat. With Mandeville, he formed a stellar act—one most of their fans believe should have taken them much further. "They were a class act," said columnist Connie (Williams) Woodruff. "They were gentleman dancers. They wore top hats and tails and they used to tap their asses off. They took their name from the popular 'Nagasaki' song of the 1930s and danced to tunes like 'Pennies from Heaven.'"

"They were a scream," said singer Celeste Jones, who shared the bill with them at Dodger's and other Newark clubs. "People would just wait for Little Jackie to jump into Fats's arms at the end; then Fats would carry him off like a baby."

Said Gregory: "They were in full swing when I came to Newark. They could have really went somewhere. When they lindy-hopped, Fats wore a dress and took the girl's part, then Little Jackie threw Fats out there and would reel him in. They had a top act. If it were nowadays, they'd be tops on TV."

At times, big things did seem in store for the Nacki Sacki Boys. Yet the furthest they got, according to Jennings' sister, Inez, was Rockhead's Paradise in Montreal: "They kept working for years. They always had jobs. They were outstanding, but for some reason they never got that big break. Finally, my brother got married and began raising a family. He became a longshoreman."

In the 1940s, Jackie went solo, emceeing regularly at the Picadilly and other clubs. In 1947, his comic rendition of "I Can't Get Started with You" still was earning "lots of applause at the Cameo Club," according to a review in the *New Jersey Afro-American*. Until he retired, he played occasional gigs at dances and social affairs.

By 1950, the homespun humor these comedians had so successfully transferred from vaudeville onto the stages of local nightclubs no longer was in demand. For local comedians, the occasional gigs that came along—sorority dances or other social functions—grew fewer and farther apart. Like many other entertainers, they were forced to take "regular" jobs. Until his death in the late 1970s, Hacksley was a porter at an auto dealership on Central Avenue in Newark. Jennings, who died in 1983, was a custodian for the Newark Housing Authority. Mandeville sold costume jewelry part time until his death in 1989.

$\mathcal{J}$oe Gregory
—Song and Dance Man
Chapter 9

Dapper and diminutive song and dance man Joe Gregory was one of Newark's most versatile talents during the Swing Era. Suave and stylish, sometimes zoot-suited, sometimes outfitted in top hat and tails, Gregory had a smooth and polished act. An all-round entertainer, he could play drums and piano, too.

Joe was a hep cat out of the Babs Gonzales school. Like Babs and Larue Jordan, Newark's wheeler dealers supreme, he tuned into the nuances of bebop long before it really caught hold. When he danced, he floated across the stage, every note, every step building on the beat. Whether soft and airy like a drummer's brushes passing over the skins or rat-a-tat crisp like the licks of a snare drum, his presentation was solid, always on the money.

Gregory's introduction to show business began in the living room of his parents' home in Morristown, New Jersey, where he entertained guests by playing the banjo: "I guess I was about eleven years old. I'd make about eight or ten dollars every week. Then I started dancin', tapping on the side of my bed, beating on the walls and on pots and pans and with clothespins on the side of the house. It's all a matter of rhythm. I do believe I was born with rhythm."

In childhood, Gregory and his friend Thomas Collins began dancing in bars and taverns in the Morristown area. Soon they decided to hitchhike to New York to find work. Uptown in Harlem they were hired right off to play a spot called the Harlem Cave. The owner, Bo Bo (Slim) Gaillard, later was part of the popular recording team known as Slim and Slam.

"In those days, performers would give other performers a break," Gregory said. "We told him we wanted a job dancin'. He liked us and started us workin' that night. We came back with two white satin blouses and black pants. That was our little outfit. We were about twelve—at the most—when we started going back and forth each night on the tubes."

Joe Gregory in top hat and tails, circa 1940. Courtesy of Lucille (Dorsey) Morton

As a teenager, Gregory's interest in show business was encouraged by his neighbor and friend Gus Young, a talented drummer who later made Newark his home: "Gus played a big part in my life. He used to tell me, 'You have to get away from Morristown.' Gus was older than me; he was like a man. He was playin' drums in Newark then. One night he took me in his car and carried me out to some place where I'd never been before. He put me out and said I had to dance my way back to Morristown. I actually danced my way back. That gave me the confidence I needed to make some money.

"My next break, you might say, came when I met a carnival performer named Mongol who was workin' in a sideshow in North Summit. Mongol taught me the shim sham shimmy, my first real routine." With his mother's permission, Gregory accepted Mongol's invitation to go to New York and join *Miss Cleo Wilson and Her Mississippi Revue*, a carnival show on 42nd Street at Hubert's Museum: "Miss Cleo Wilson was tall and dark-skinned and had been in show business for years. You could tell. I imagine she was in her thirties. I was about fifteen. In her sideshow was Miss Bell Bonita and her snakes and other attractions. Miss Cleo played the piano and she had a drummer."

To get the job, however, Gregory had to audition: "Miss Cleo said, 'Get up there and dance.' She played 'Nagasaki' and I went through my little routine, closing it with the shim sham shimmy. She gave me the job and laid down the rules. Whatever discipline I had, it came from her to me."

On stage at the museum, Gregory and Mongol were joined by shake dancers, a comedian, and singers: "We had to sit on chairs. When she introduced you, you got up and did your number. You were supposed to be very attentive. I always did laugh a lot, but if we got caught we got fined—fifty cents each time. I was makin' nine dollars a week, but I was always gettin' fined."

In addition to his salary, Gregory and some of the other show people got room and board at Cleo Wilson's apartment at 138th Street and Lenox Avenue: "Her husband was Frankie Newton, the trumpet player. He was a nice lookin' man who looked somethin' like Joe Louis at the time. He was workin' at Small's Paradise [in Harlem] and through him I met Don Redman [the bandleader and arranger] and Jimmy Crawford from [Jimmie] Lunceford's band. Lucky Millinder—all those people—used to come to Miss Cleo Wilson's house. She bought me clothes, fed me, paid me nine dollars a week, and didn't charge rent.

"I began to get better and better and I began to meet other dancers like Honi Coles, Baby Laurence, and George Brooks of the Dominoes. George and I got a room together and he showed me a lot of steps and style. Now, I'm thinkin' about bigger things. They had this Hoofers Club, where all the big dancers would go and rehearse—like Bill Robinson. We'd watch the rehearsals through a little knothole and get the steps. When they'd leave, we'd strip down and dance from twelve at night to eight or nine the next day. That's how we got the style.

"After about six months, I decided to strike out and do my own thing, so I left Miss Cleo Wilson and came back to Jersey. I started hanging out at Saul's Tavern in Newark. They had amateur nights every Tuesday. They let me get in and I won first prize—five dollars. Three Tuesdays straight I won the amateur hour. I told them you might as well give me a job, but Matty Alston, who was workin' there as the emcee, said I wasn't ready. So I went over to Dodger's Grill and Arthur Terry said, 'I'll let you do a number, Joe, and maybe you'll get a job.' So, through Arthur Terry, I got my first legitimate job in Newark and I tap danced at Dodger's for a long time.

"This was in the early part of 1938. I was fresh in Newark and I was packin' them in. The news got around and everyone came to see the new dancer. They had somethin' like a circuit. If you worked one club and did all right, you worked them all. They hired me at Saul's Tavern and I was the emcee there. Then I worked the Kit Kat Club, which later became the Picadilly. Gus [Young] was always my main man. As soon as I got to where he was playing, he would hand me the sticks and I got to be pretty

Joe Gregory in a zoot suit, circa 1940. Courtesy of Lucille (Dorsey) Morton

fast on drums. Back and forth over the years, from 1938 to '41, I went from Saul's to the Waverly Tavern, to the Pic [Picadilly] and the Alcazar. Abe Moore and I were Slip and Slide and Anna May Hall and I were Bread and Butter. We played all the Newark clubs.

"My main thing was 'I Ain't Got Nobody.' I would sing it first; then I'd go into stop time and then I'd go into my arrangement. You could hear the tap. Another little song I used to do was 'Nagasaki,' the one I did for Miss Cleo Wilson. I had a parody on it. Everybody knew

'Nagasaki.' Guys would say, 'Just play a Nagasaki chorus and you could play ten or twenty songs.'

"If you went to New York, you were a star. When you came back to Newark everyone would say, 'That's Joe Gregory,' and buy you drinks. We had no agents. That's why all the entertainers used to help each other. Miss Rhapsody called me her son. She was like a mother to me. She'd been singin' at Kelly's Stable in New York and I wanted to dance in New York, so she said, 'Son, I'm gonna see if I can get you a job.' She took me to New York and introduced me to the boss. Coleman Hawkins' band was playin' and Bunny Briggs had just closed. The boss liked me and hired me for a hundred and twenty-five dollars a week. Even now, it makes me cry just to think about it. It was the most money I had ever made.

"But I was kinda scared. Bunny Briggs was such an accomplished dancer, and I had to follow Jimmy Smith, who had this novelty act dancing on vibes. I felt so small. The first night I danced my heart out, and the boss said, 'You're in the show, Joe.' Coleman Hawkins' drummer was out sick, so I asked Coleman if I could play the drums after I danced. I'd played so much drums and I was pretty fast. I remember they played 'Mop Mop' real fast and all the musicians were lookin' back at me and smilin'.

"Coleman was going to Canada and he wanted me to come, but I didn't have a set of drums and I didn't have a musician's union card. He was going to pull some strings and told me to meet him the next day at the union [Local 802] office. In those days, you had to do a little test to get a union card. As it turned out, the president wasn't there, so I couldn't get a card and Coleman went off to Canada without me. How it might have changed my life!"

After leaving Kelly's Stable, Gregory went into the Yacht Club in New York as a dancer, rounding out a bill that starred Art Tatum, Una Mae Carlisle, and Trummy Young: "My buddy from Newark, Vernon Biddle, was playin' [piano] at the Downbeat next door. Years before, I told him one day at Roscoe's pool room on Broome Street [in Newark] that someday we'd both be playin' 52nd Street.

And it came to pass. Last time I heard he was in California doin' background music for movies."

After that, Gregory returned to Saul's, where he teamed with Slappy White and his partner, Clarence (Red) Scheffey. They became Slip, Slap, and Slide: "We wore green ties with tails and danced around Newark for a while. Then, we went to Philadelphia. We played Columbo's and other places and wound up going to Montreal for nine months in 1942, where we played Rockhead's Paradise. Johnny B. Gardner [the Newark comedian] was there when I played it later."

White, who was from Baltimore, claimed he arrived in Newark accidently. "I came by train, and when the man said 'New-ark,' I got off," he recounted. "I was in Newark six months before I realized it wasn't New York. I did pretty good, so I stayed, maybe four or five years. There was no work for me in New York, anyway. In Newark, I was working three days a week, first at Saul's Tavern, then at the Nest Club, the Kinney Club, the Boston Plaza, then out at Pat and Don's in Harrison."

When he and Red decided to return home from Canada, Gregory stayed on for another week "to make the last payment on an English tweed overcoat." When Gregory got back he learned Red had died, on the dance floor. That was the end of the act. Slappy went with the Big Zephyr and Gregory went solo again.

From there, Gregory worked at Wright's Hotel in Schenectady, New York, where he had his "own TV show." Then he played the Paddock Club in Atlantic City, where he started "messin' around" with the piano for kicks: "Mr. Kravitz, the owner, got me a union card and paid me twenty-five dollars a week. I stayed at the Paddock three years. I made a fortune in tips—sometimes four or five hundred bucks a week. But the most money I ever made steady was with Doles Dickens [who led a quartet]. I wrote a lot of songs and sang 'Route 66' and things like that, 'cause I liked Nat King Cole a lot. But I was limited on piano.

"One day Scotty [Herb Scott, the trumpet player] came by my room while I was playin' Atlantic City. He was playin' with the Doles Dickens Quartet at the Five O'Clock Club. Doles was interested in my rhythm. I turned to drums 'cause I was tired of playin' piano and I joined them in Washington at the Crystal Caverns. I stayed with them for seven years.

"Billy Daniels and Ruth Brown were on the same bill the first night. I was playin' conga drums and doing uptempo specialty numbers. We played the Blue Mirror, the Star Dust, and all the other D.C. clubs and we played a war drive at the Howard Theater. Then we went to Florida with Doles and played at Mother Kelly's and Snooky's Rendezvous on the beach. We broke up in Miami in 1952 over money matters."

Gregory worked next for Irv Berman, who owned Miami's Zanzibar, playing drums in an intimate lounge act with Douglas Duke, "this white fellow who played piano. I was the first black musician to play that side of town. When Douglas went to Georgia, Irv asked me to get up a trio and I got Monk [Harmon] on sax and Ham [?] on bass."

Eventually, Gregory returned to Newark and left show business for steadier employment in the tool and dye trade. Still single, he lives in East Orange, just over the Newark line, in a third-floor apartment in a private home. In recent years, he's taken up guitar. And he teaches tap—to pre-schoolers at a Jersey City dance school.

The Dancers
—Taps and Terpsichore
Chapter 10

In its musical heyday, Newark produced some terrific dancers, entertainers of the caliber of Georgie Rollins, who toured Europe with Cab Calloway; Slappy White of Slip, Slap, and Slide, who became a Las Vegas comedian; Doryce Bradley, who played top clubs in the United States and Canada; and Reese LaRue, an exotic interpretive dancer.

Dancing—alone, as part of a team, or in the chorus—was an integral part of any show, generally a mix of tap, soft shoe, and the more worldly forms of the genre, shake dancing and other interpretive styles. At some of the black clubs, the Nest Club for one, dancing in the chorus was required of female performers. "All of us had to be in the chorus, even Mae Darling, who had that high voice and was the prima donna," said Sadie Matthews, a 1930s Nest Club chorine. "Mae didn't wanna, but Mrs. [Eurlee] Reeves [the owner] made her."

Generally, the so-called exotic dancers were billed in sensational fashion. Shake dancer Belle Williams, for example, was known as "The Gorgeous Huzzy." Pearl Swan, who was in a revue at the Twinlite in 1945, was called "The Atomic Bomb." For a while, too, as a carryover from vaudeville and carnival shows, contortionists like Sheila, the "torso twister" in a 1938 show at the Boston Plaza, and Baby Banks, who appeared occasionally at the Picadilly, were popular attractions. Sometimes, the star dancer of the show had a peculiar physical attraction, like Baby Bush, who was billed as "two hundred pounds of rhythm."

In some instances, starting out in show business as a dancer led to a musical career. Leon Eason and Ike Quebec are prime examples of musicians who got their start as dancers in theatrical productions. As a rule, emcees like Johnny B. Gardner, Charlie Matthews, Buddy Turman, Johnny Fussell, Joe Gregory, and Little Jackie (Mandeville) also were song and dance men or comedians, sometimes both.

So were Lucky Louie Anderson, Demon Turp, Satchel Robinson, and Smokie Coleman.

Among the local dancing favorites were Anna May Hall and her partner, Bill (Robinson) Chapman, Myrtle Hutchinson, whose specialty was high kicks, pert Sugar Payne, and Gertrude Turman, whose brother, Buddy, and two sisters, Helena and Geneva, also were entertainers.

Hall was a beautiful, dark-skinned woman, billed as a "tapologist." With Chapman, a Bojangles dance-alike who acquired the nickname "Bill Robinson," she starred in shows at the Boston Plaza, Nest Club, and Kinney Club. Over the course of a twenty-five-year career that began in the early 1930s, Hall played local clubs exclusively, except for a USO tour at the end of World War II. For a time in the late 1930s, she and a girl named Flora Jones teamed as the Two Brown Dots.

Chapman and Hall also were among the city's best lindyhoppers, competing in contests at local dance halls and at the Shady Rest Country Club in nearby Union County, which catered to "blacks only." "They were part of a group that included Prince Hall, Johnny Mason—a terrific dancer who died in his twenties—and Herbie Wright," said Thad (Chuck) Howard, then a local singer and emcee. "There were about seven or eight couples. Prince was a rhythm dancer. My wife, Annetta, was with Whitey's Lindy Hoppers, a professional troupe whose agent was Herbert White, the bouncer at Harlem's Savoy Ballroom."

Arthur (Prince) Hall, Anna May's husband, was the first among them to get a big-time break, appearing on Broadway in the mid 1940s in *Memphis Bound*. In dancer Joe Gregory's estimation, "Prince was like a little genius dancing, but he died young, soon after I came to Newark. Everybody else was into rhythm and fast dancing, but Prince wanted to dance slow. We'd go by Pete's, where they sold hot dogs on Spruce Street, and we'd go in the back and dance. Prince always had a little step he wanted to show me. By wanting to dance slow, it took a lot of control."

Another popular dance team was the husband-wife duo Billy and Kitty Avant, who

Anna May Hall and Bill (Robinson) Chapman, mid 1930s. From author's collection

were booked into the Boston Plaza in February 1941 "direct from the Club Harlem." What their 125th Street agent failed to say was that Kitty was a native Newarker who lived just a few blocks away from the club. She and her husband were a versatile team. Billy often doubled as emcee at the Kinney Club. Kitty, a former Ray Green vocalist, sometimes worked as a single, too, standing her audiences on their feet with her specialty, "Ol' Man River."

"Billy and Kitty were a dance team like Ike

Comedian/emcee Jimmy (Demon) Anderson and dancer Arthur (Prince) Hall trading quips, a traditional part of any nightclub revue, late 1930s. Courtesy of Gertrude Turman

and Tina Turner," said Lucille (Dorsey) Morton, a waitress at the Kinney Club when the Avants were the headliners. "They use to argue with each other—not really argue; it was challenge dancing. She did somethin', then he'd cut in front of her and do somethin' a little better."

Myrtle Hutchinson, who also was born in Newark, got her start dancing in a New York show with Bill (Bojangles) Robinson. She toured Canada with Noble Sissle and Buck and Bubbles. In the mid 1930s, she also traveled with a show led by bandleader Lucky Millinder. Back home in Newark in 1938 she formed a song and dance team at Dodger's Bar and Grill with Satchel Robinson, a popular

emcee. Billed as "The Queen of Taps," Hutchinson often played New York clubs in the early 1940s. Toward the end of World War II, she also toured with the USO. Shapely, athletic, and always a lady, Hutchie refused to do "ups." She told a local reporter: "Entertainers want to be called performers. Performers perform. Entertainers go table to table."

Gertrude Turman, youngest of the talented Turman siblings, was a child when she got her first taste of show business: "My father made liquor in a little gutbucket place on Broome Street. Donald Lambert used to play the piano there, and my friend Geraldine and I used to dance. The people would throw money on the floor. I was about eight."

Accompanied by her "guardian," Marion Cheeks, Turman began traveling when she was about fourteen: "I mainly worked in Elmira and Montreal, Elmira for ten years. In Elmira, the Green Pastures was like home to me. It was the only place with black entertainment."

During those years, Turman was in and out of the Nest Club, billed as everything from a "sophisticated" to an "Oriental" dancer. "Actually, I was a shake dancer," she explained. Although Turman and her peers were good dancers, there was a tendency toward exaggerating their talents in advertisements in the black press. The proprietor of Saul's Tavern, for example, placed this ad in the *New Jersey Herald News* for the 1937–38 New Year's Eve show: "Appearing will be Lucky Louie Anderson, the tap dancing demon, as emcee, Hazel Hannah, and Gertrude Turman. These girls are the products of Newark, and they always give high class entertainment. Saul's Tavern has gone to extra expense to get these three star entertainers to perform for guests on New Year's Eve night. The performance will continue from early Friday evening, December 31, through breakfast Saturday morning, January 1, 1938."

Anderson's other haunt in the 1930s was the Colony Club on Broome Street, notorious for its reputation as a red-light area of the center city. In the opinion of the locals, it was a "mob joint." Along with Joe Crump and His Band of 1,000 Themes, Anderson was one of its most popular performers, generally appearing in white top hat and tails while doubling as the dancing emcee.

Satchel Robinson was another suave dancer whose good looks and pleasing personality made him all the more attractive to the female patrons at Newark night spots. While he often appeared as a single, Robinson would team, too, with Myrtle Hutchinson. When singer Marva Louis, wife of then heavyweight boxing champion Joe Louis, appeared at the Apollo Theater in New York in March 1945, Robinson was on the bill as tap dancer and emcee. In the mid 1940s, he also was a fixture at the Club Bali in Washington, D.C.

Demon Turp also specialized in tap, doubling as emcee for shows at the Kinney Club in the late 1930s. He was considered a "colorful dancer" by the local press, noted for his witty commentary during the shows.

Of all the entertainers to play Newark, Ruby Rainey was one of the most versatile, a spellbinding entertainer who could dance, sing, and play the piano and drums. In the late 1930s, she often appeared at the Club Del Rio. In the early 1940s, she frequently was on the bill at the Hydeaway.

One of Newark's most popular entertainers and versatile, too, was Johnny B. Gardner, whose talent for packaging shows gave many Newark performers a chance to excel locally, then widen their horizons through travel. In the early 1930s, he encouraged dancers like Florence (Hall) McIntyre and Doryce Bradley to try out for *Harlem on Parade*, which took them on the road for two years. In the early 1940s, he spent summers at Rockhead's Paradise in Montreal, where his friend Buddy Turman and Miss Rhapsody shared the bill. "Johnny B. and my brother Buddy used to work together all the time," said Gertrude Turman. "They were just plain nuts." Recalled Al Henderson: "Johnny B. had a good personality and a face with a little mustache that was always smiling. It was like he was always on stage."

In a class all his own was George Rollins, who could "bring down the house at Dodger's with his furious tapping." He began playing hometown clubs again in the late 1930s after

Myrtle Hutchinson, left, and an unidentified partner, early 1940s. Courtesy of Doryce Bradley

traveling with Duke Ellington and Cab Calloway in a show called the *Cotton Club Revue*. During one overseas venture, he entertained the king and queen of England. Under the aegis of his agent, Nat Nazarro, Rollins and his partner, Little Black Jimmy Fairbanks, were known as the Two Turbans, debonair dancers outfitted in top hats and tails.

Bill Roberts, the bartender at the Boston Plaza, where Rollins danced and sometimes doubled as emcee, recalled him as "a terrific dancer, classified with the boys who went all over Europe." But Rollins "let himself go down," and his career sank.

Gertrude Turman mimicking the Billie Holiday look, late 1930s. Courtesy of Gertrude (Turman) Brown

the Club Bali and Crystal Caverns in Washington, D.C.

The lithe and lovely Doryce was described by a *New York Amsterdam News* reviewer as "a torrid hip tosser." A Washington critic described her as "artfully obeying" while the band plays and sings "Take It Off" "until only a G-string remains."

Reese LaRue—real name Albert Jones—was born in Newark's Ironbound section and "was bitten by the show business bug" when he was about sixteen. Adept at creative dancing, he performed out of New York with the Apollo Theater Male Chorus, which traveled all over the country. LaRue's specialty was interpretive ballet; his trademark, his flamboyant costumes. From the mid 1940s into the early 1950s, he starred in and staged shows at many Newark nightclubs, including the Kinney Club, the Picadilly, Dodger's Bar and Grill, the Cafe Superior, and the Silver Saddle. His themes, to the delight of his audiences, often were as lavish and torrid as his terpsichore: *Gay Paree* and *Tropical Revue* at the Kinney, *Paris to Picadilly* at the Pic.

Another of Newark's dancing sensations was Princess Margo, an exotic dancer whose real name was Yolanda Majors. Her father, Clement Majors, played trombone in a band out of New York in his spare time. "She had a fantastic figure, and, like many dancers of our era, she was self-taught," said writer Connie (Williams) Woodruff. "Sometimes, she tried to sing, but she had a weak voice. Dancing was her real specialty."

After establishing herself locally in the mid 1940s at the Twinlite, Margo joined blues singer Wynonie Harris for an extended tour of the South. Also on the bill were Newark's great comedy team Crackshot Hacksley and Roscoe Dyla. When they returned, they found fewer jobs. Margo eventually retired. At last report, she was employed at Newark City Hall.

Although she was from New York, Audrey Armstrong's ties to Newark began in the early 1930s when she toured with Leon Eason, Doryce Bradley, Florence McIntyre, and other young Newark-area performers in *Harlem on*

As a teenager, Doryce Bradley toured with Buck and Bubbles and Bill Robinson on the RKO circuit in *Harlem on Parade*. After starring as an exotic dancer at Newark's Villa Maurice in 1938, she teamed with Detroit Red (risque entertainer Laura Livingstone), headlining a show that summer at the Paradise Club in Atlantic City. Next they played Montreal. Billed as an exotic dancer, Bradley performed at many of the nation's top clubs during the 1940s, including Dan Montgomery's in Buffalo, the Plantation Club in St. Louis, and

Dancer Doryce Bradley, circa 1943. Courtesy of Doryce Bradley

Parade. In the late 1930s, she frequently performed at the Kinney Club. "Audrey had a good body and a beautiful complexion," said Clem Moorman. "She was quite a good dancer. I think at one point she played the Apollo [Theater in New York]."

Dancing
—Frenzied and Formal
Chapter 11

In barnlike ballrooms and dime-a-dance halls—wherever young people congregated—the whole country seemed to be dancing up a storm during the war years. The Great Depression was winding down. With its end, youngsters of all colors were spilling onto dance floors everywhere, unleashing pent-up energies as they gyrated to a wild new acrobatic dance called the lindyhop.

For the younger set, the early 1940s became an era of big bands, crooners, bobby soxers, jive talk, hepcats, and zoot suits. For their parents, it was a time to waltz around the living room to mellow radio music or—in middle-class homes—go formal for some community social function.

In white America the stage had been set by an age of spectacular Hollywood musicals, well costumed and well choreographed. Fred Astaire, Ginger Rogers, and Eleanor Powell were the epitome of suave sophistication for the older set. The youngsters, meanwhile,

flocked to theaters and gathered around bandstands, going wild over Frank Sinatra.

Black Americans adopted their own forms of dance entertainment. Like their white counterparts, professionals generally entertained at home or within the confines of a segregated country club setting. Among the working class, membership dances sponsored by groups like hairdressers or Masons were common as fundraisers. Often a big-name band was billed to attract the audience. Young people, too, adopted idols of their own: Ella Fitzgerald, Herb Jeffries, Louis Jordan and His Tympany Five, and Dizzy Gillespie.

In Newark the in spot in the late 1930s for black youngsters—often their parents, too—was Skateland on Montgomery Street, a huge dance hall where they swooned to the music of a handsome bandleader named Pancho Diggs and his orchestra. The fans came in droves, two thousand or more, packing the cavernous hall to hear vocalist Emzey Waters croon the

The Pancho Diggs Orchestra, mid 1930s: from left, front, Charlie Shavers (not the famous trumpeter), Luther Smith, and Allen Gibbs, alto saxophone; Alton (Pancho) Diggs, leader/tenor saxophone; Emzey Waters, baton/ vocals; center, Billy (Weasel) Ford, Louis (Slim) Purnell, and Joe James, trumpet; Woodrow (Fats) Williams, trombone; rear, Jackson (Flap) McQueen, bass; Merrille Wortham, guitar; Robert Roebuck, drums; Duke Parham, piano. Courtesy of William (Willie) Johnson

band's signature song, "Swanee River," and do the lindyhop for cash and prizes.

One of the best dancers was a wiry little fellow named Carl Brinson. "They called me 'Tiny Prince' because I only weighed about ninety-eight pounds, and I was a smooth dancer," he recalled. "I was part of a group of about twenty or thirty guys and girls from Newark who often went over to challenge Whitey's Lindy Hoppers [a New York group]. The guys in New York wouldn't let you dance with their girls. When they did, you knew you had arrived. I was a little agitator, always asking to dance with the New York girls. In our group, we had Gladys Slade, Annie West, and Annetta, who married Thad Howard. Twice we formed a Dancers' Appreciation So-

ciety out of the Savoy Ballroom on Springfield Avenue, where the Savoy Dictators played. About the same time, Pancho's band was playing at Skateland on Montgomery Street. He had one of the most popular bands. Everyone went there to dance."

Wavy-haired with movie star good looks, the light-skinned Diggs was still a student at Newark's Central High School when he decided to parlay his saxophone skills into a musical career. In short order he assembled a fourteen-piece aggregation composed of some of the area's top musical talent.

In the trumpet section were Bloomfield's Billy Ford, Louis (Slim) Purnell, a virtuoso of great promise who died before the new decade dawned, and Joe James, who had only one

Trombonist Woodrow (Fats) Williams, bassist Jackson (Flap) McQueen, and trumpeter Louis (Slim) Purnell practicing outdoors, mid 1930s. Courtesy of Jackson (Flap) McQueen

arm. Ford went on to lead several groups over the years, including Billy Ford and the Thunderbirds. In 1957, he and songstress Lillie Bryant teamed to record the rhythm and blues million-seller "La Dee Dah." James became one of New York's top arrangers. Also in the original band were Duke Parham, piano; Jackson (Flap) McQueen (who became the leader of the popular recording group the Ray-O-Vacs), bass; Robert Roebuck, drums; Joe Holloway and Woodrow (Fats) Williams, trombone; and Diggs, Charlie Shavers, and Eddie Ransom, saxophone.

Because of Diggs's shrewd business sense and Waters' smooth tonsils, the band was immensely popular. The crowds came, too, because wherever the band played Diggs gave a

local youngster a chance to perform. "One little girl was always pushed up to do her number," said Bob Queen, who covered the night club scene for the *Afro-American*. "The dancers would always stop and move forward to listen. Her name was Sarah Vaughan."

Among musicians, however, the band got mixed reviews. "Pancho's band wasn't all that good—not as musically sound as our group," bandleader Al Henderson maintained. "It wasn't sayin' nothin', but it was popular. The kids loved it. Only the people who knew music and appreciated it went for us. The crowd went for Pancho."

On the other hand, just the mention of Newark to jazz great Dizzy Gillespie dredges up painful memories of the night fifty years ago

The brass section of the Pancho Diggs Orchestra, early 1940s: from left, top, Joe Holloway and Woodrow (Fats) Williams, trombone; bottom, Willie (Coot) Nelson, Billy (Weasel) Ford, Luther (Gates) Willis, and Little Benny Harris, trumpet. Courtesy of Jackson (Flap) McQueen

when Diggs's group blew away the band with which he played. "We made the mistake of coming over [to Newark] from Philly with Frankie Fairbanks's band and Pancho's band washed us," Gillespie noted in his autobiography.

Over the years, Diggs's orchestra played every major dance in town—for the hairdressers, cosmetologists, Old Timers—organizations that comprised the so-called black elite of Newark and its environs. Like Johnny Jackson's and later Mose Garland's orchestra, it was synonomous with dance music. The difference was that Diggs's guys could jump, which made the band a popular attraction at band battles that attracted the young lindyhoppers.

During one spurt in 1939, the band played the Conservative Club dance at Newark's Hi Spot, a lindyhop contest at Dreamland Academy, another popular hangout for young people, and a "Swing War" at Newark's Essex Theater against drummer Herman Bradley's band and then embarked on a road trip that summer through the Carolinas, Virginia, and Tennessee.

A 1939 review described the group as "a strong favorite with dance lovers at the Greenbriar in Central Jersey, where the boys are packing the place. The band, in fact, is just as good a drawing card as the big name favorites of the jitterbugs in Newark."

Meanwhile, the band's personnel changed. Diggs hired several members of the original Savoy Dictators: Chippie Outcalt, known for his tight arrangements; trombonist Howard Scott, who later went with Billy Eckstine; Count Hastings, who subsequently joined Tiny Bradshaw; and Ike Quebec, destined for stardom as a saxophonist with Cab Calloway.

With this stronger aggregation, Diggs's popularity in the early 1940s shifted across the Hudson, uptown to Harlem, where the fellows jammed weekly at the Renaissance Casino and played some memorable gigs at the Savoy Ballroom, home of the lindyhoppers.

The vocalist was Nina Mae McKinney, the energetic star of black film musicals. Beautiful and a natural talent, she was as well an all-round entertainer, gifted with an appealing singing voice and a natural flair for comedy.

McKinney also had a "name" that could get the band considerably more work than Diggs could secure on his own. So the band's name was changed to the Nina Mae McKinney Orchestra for a cross-country tour.

For Diggs, the deal proved to be a mixed blessing. On one hand, McKinney's name was a drawing card. Black audiences across America knew and idolized her as a beautiful but wacky screen star on the order of Carole Lombard. In New York, she was a favorite at the Apollo Theater, where she teamed with the top male comedians of the day in an act similar to that of the oldtime entertainers Butterbeans and Susie. Yet with McKinney fronting the band, its importance musically was greatly obscured. Rather than viewing McKinney as the vocalist, the patrons saw the musicians as the backdrop for her act. At the time, Queen wrote: "They toured for about a year as Nina Mae McKinney and her Orchestra. That was O.K. for McKinney because roles were sparse. All it did for Pancho's band was to help it lose its identity."

Whatever the case, the association ended in 1943, when Diggs was drafted into the Army for a not-too-taxing three-year hitch as dance band director of the 770th AAP Band and assistant director of the military band. After the war, he returned to Newark and organized a new band that played Monday night sessions at Lloyd's Manor on Beacon Street. For a while it attracted some of the faces seen at the old Skateland, but the days when thousands of fans would gather around the bandstand were long gone. With the advent of bop and rhythm and blues, club dates grew fewer, prompting Diggs to regroup as a dance band available almost exclusively for affairs sponsored by groups such as the Harvest Club, the YMCA, and the National Council of Negro Women.

In 1946, Diggs was elected president of the Newark Musicians' Staff Club and began spending as much time organizing events as playing them. Eventually, he became the union representative for Essex County Local 16 of the American Federation of Musicians, gaining a reputation as the "main man" in any deal involving black musicians. He became the union's business manager in 1977 and

Nina Mae McKinney, mid 1940s. Courtesy of Doryce Bradley

served in that capacity until his death in December 1982 at the Veterans Administration Hospital in East Orange, New Jersey.

While Diggs was "King of Swing" to Newark's jitterbuggers, Mandy Ross and His Walkin' Rhythm, Johnny Jackson, Corporal Brady Hodge, and Bobby Jarrett catered to the musical tastes of an older crowd, men and women who were at the core of the city's black civic and social life in the 1940s. Their successors in the 1950s were Mose Garland and

Bandleader Mandy Ross, circa 1946. Courtesy of Jimmy (Chops) Jones

His Syncopators and the Billy and Duke Anderson Orchestra.

In the 1940s, hardly a week passed in spring or fall without some civic or social group sponsoring a dance, sometimes called "a seasonal frolic." Many of them were sponsored by small groups of prominent men in the black community whose names and the success they had achieved by hosting similar events served as a drawing card.

Lacey Brannic, Major Taylor, and Johnny Jackson, for example, were known as the Captivators, booking Jackson's orchestra for dances, fashion shows, and other social affairs at the Clinton Manor and Graham Auditorium. At the same time, Earl Harris, elected president of the Newark Municipal Council in 1978, and Carl Jones, who later bought the popular Bridge Club on Washington Street, were booking big bands, including Ellington's and Basie's, into Krueger's Auditorium, Clinton Manor, and the hall at Graham's on Belmont Avenue.

These dances were huge affairs, attracting a thousand or more patrons to spacious dance halls like Krueger's, where Noble Sissle and Eubie Blake were as likely to be on the bandstand as a favorite local entourage. By and large, the stars were friendly people who mixed easily with their audiences and were proud to perform for their people. Ethel Waters, who sang at Krueger's with the Eddie Mallory Band for a 1938 dance sponsored by the Newark Eagles, the city's all-black baseball team, made that clear in a *Herald News* interview after the show: "White people are easy to please, but when my own applaud me, I know I am still up there."

Ross's band came onto the scene about 1940, playing swing matinees at Victoria Hall in North Newark. By 1943, the talented young bandleader from Montclair had secured a permanent niche for his musicians at the Campus Terrace, where their solid arrangements alternately were geared to quiet conversation, then had the joint rocking.

Because it could jump so, the band also played jitterbug contests at the Savoy Plaza on Springfield Avenue. By 1945, the fellows were playing six nights a week at the Bluebird Ballroom on Broad Street, where they broadcast from 11:30 to midnight on WAAT radio. The band's primary attraction at the time was Sam Woodyard, a terrific percussionist from Elizabeth who later joined Duke Ellington. Mary Corley and Horace Sims, who doubled on guitar, ably handled the vocals.

Like Diggs, Ross had a coveted engagement at Harlem's Savoy Ballroom, then moved downtown to the Lincoln Center Ballroom, a small dance hall on part of the site that is now Lincoln Center. When his aggregation was invited to tour the South in 1945, Ross jumped at the chance to gain wider exposure among white audiences, but the trip was marred by racism when the band members found themselves being ushered out of a restaurant because of Jim Crow laws. Ross commented angrily in the *Afro:* "The colored are O.K., but the whites ain't nowhere."

Another racial brush occurred that year in

Atlantic City, where the band, according to a report in the black press, had been "accepted to play the city's leading white nightclub, the Cliquot Club," and made headlines when a "Southern white singer refused to sing with the band."

After a brief stint playing with smaller groups, including a gig on trumpet at Diamond Jim's in the North Ward, Ross formed a new nine-piece band in 1946, vying with Corporal Brady Hodge in a swing battle at Graham's. The band foundered, however, and by the following year was reduced to a sextet.

Hodge, whose brother Bob was a drummer with Pancho Diggs, formed his dance band after serving in the Army. Like Ross, he was a trumpet player who concentrated on playing for civic association dances and an occasional swing battle, like one in February 1945 against Gene Phipps at the Graham Auditorium. By 1946, his was the featured dance band at Lloyd's Manor, playing a steady stream of dances around town for groups including the masons, cosmetologists, and cab drivers.

Johnny Jackson's Orchestra, with Clem Moorman on piano, was an offshoot of the old Frank Gibbs Orchestra. Strictly a dance band, it was a favorite of groups that included the Swanksmen, Chauffeurs' Club, Craftsmen's Club, Beauty Shop Owners, and postal employees, playing at dances, scholarship functions, proms, and graduations.

Jarrett, once a member of the Barons of Rhythm, formed his own band in 1945. The following year it was featured at Lloyd's Manor. As live entertainment at clubs and area armories faded, his group also turned its energies to playing for social functions.

Diggs, Ross, Jackson, Jarrett, and their aggregations played many dances at the Terrace Ballroom, which was restored in the 1980s and continues to reverberate on occasion to Swing Era-type functions.

When Frank Foster brought the Count Basie Orchestra to town in January 1991, *Star-Ledger* jazz critic George Kanzler enthused: "During World War II, gas rationing made it impractical for people to drive to such ballrooms as the Meadowbrook in Cedar Grove, and the scene for big band dances shifted to big cities. Here

Miss Rhapsody singing with the Johnny Jackson Orchestra at a social function, late 1940s. Jackson is on saxophone. Courtesy of Sheldon Harris

in New Jersey that meant the Terrace Ballroom in the basement of the Mosque Theater, with its spacious wooden dance floor, became the venue for dances featuring many of the most famous big bands of the Swing Era, including Count Basie's orchestra. The Terrace Ballroom continued to host swinging bands through the '50s and early '60s, but in later years, continuing under its old name in the basement of the newly named Symphony Hall, the dances have featured more contemporary music."

Actually, the shift came in the early 1950s, as the era of bobby soxers and club dances vanished from the scene. New tastes in black music had gripped the nation, fueled by the recording industry and a spate of new labels that produced the rhythmic but bluesy sounds of new artists like Ruth Brown, Wynonie (Mr. Blues) Harris, and Amos Milburn. Increasing interest in a new medium—television—also reshaped the entire entertainment industry, keeping people at home or attracting them to bars or clubs where TV was the main draw. Gradually, swing and pop were replaced by the less danceable sounds of bop and rhythm and blues.

According to rhythm and blues expert Al Pavlow, this new chapter in American music officially began when "*Billboard* changed the name of its 'race' records to the top selling 'rhythm and blues' records" on June 25, 1949. "By 1950, the sounds now known as rhythm 'n' blues had evolved to the degree that the average hit record could not have been mistaken for a mid-forties race or jazz hit," he found. Roughly a dozen small independent labels, including Atlantic, Apollo, Aladdin, Imperial, Specialty, and Regal, dominated the industry from coast to coast, drawing heavily on New Orleans artists like Fats Domino, Paul Gayten, and Larry Darnell and vocal groups like the Dominoes and Ravens to produce what Pavlow describes as "a blend of gospel-tinged vocals and powerhouse instrumentation."

THE BANDS

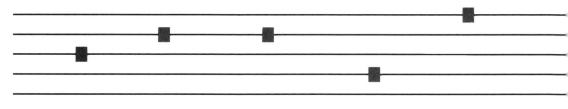

1935-42

Newark's Finest —Sultans and Dictators
Chapter 12

Fifty years have passed, but the debate rages on like a Swing Era band battle in which words have replaced music. Which band was Newark's best during the swing years? Which was the tightest? The toughest? Most musical? With rare exception, conversation narrows to two: the Savoy Sultans and the Savoy Dictators.

Years ago the arguments took place in taverns and pool halls, sometimes in the more intimate setting of some musician's or fan's home. Today, they take place to a lesser degree wherever the city's oldtimers get together, perhaps during a tribute to one of the older musicians, often at a funeral. Pancho Diggs's band generally gets a mention or two. And maybe someone will put in a good word for groups led by Frank Gibbs, Herman Bradley, even Russell Mann. But when it comes to the best, it narrows to the Sultans and the Dictators.

The Sultans—intermission band at the legendary Savoy Ballroom in New York in the late 1930s and early 1940s—by far was the better known of the two bands. All the top bands of the era—Ellington, Basie, Lunceford—along with scores of other good, but lesser-known groups, played the famous Harlem ballroom. As the stories go, the Sultans were just as good, if not better, than most of them.

While the Sultans recorded a number of tunes subsequently reissued on an album, the Dictators made only a couple of seventy-eights on the Savoy label, issued in 1942. Essentially, the Dictators were a hometown band that broke up when Tiny Bradshaw came to town and signed half of them to tour with his band. But they could "cook." While they were together, they were just as solid and at times more musical than the Sultans.

The Sultans were signed to play the Savoy Ballroom as the result of a 1938 appearance at New York's Apollo Theater. From the moment they arrived, they were a hit, sending lindy-hoppers reeling onto the floor at intermission

Drummer Herman Bradley, circa 1950. Courtesy of Al Henderson

to let loose their libidinous energies. Other bands came and went, but the Sultans stayed on for more than a decade, surviving the onslaught of every name band in the business.

Al Cooper, who played saxophone, was their leader and business manager, while his half-brother, Grachan (Brother) Moncur, played bass. Originally from Florida, Cooper came north to Newark first, followed by Moncur. Rounding out the group were fellow Newarkers: Alex (Razz) Mitchell, drums; Sam Massen-berg and Pat Jenkins, trumpet; Rudy Williams and James McNeal, sax; and Oliver Richardson, piano. Jack Chapman, a talented guitarist from Newark who spent every spare minute writing music, handled the arrangements.

As Count Basie recalled in his memoirs, "Unless I'm mistaken, the house band [at the Savoy Ballroom] was those bad Savoy Sultans . . . [with] Mitchell on drums. They had about nine pieces and the leader was Al Cooper, who played alto and clarinet, and they ran the hell out of us. I don't ever want to see them cats no more. Everytime I came down off the bandstand, they were right up there swinging."

Before forming the Sultans, Cooper and most of the band's members played with Herman Bradley's Rhythm Dons at Dodger's Bar and Grill on Bedford Street in Newark and the 101 Ranch in New York.

Bradley, a drummer, was one of Newark's most popular bandleaders in the mid 1930s. Born in Charleston, South Carolina, in June 1908, he began beating on his mother's washtub and stove and "playing behind records" as a teenager while his family was living at 99 West Street in Newark. His inspiration was a fellow named Buster Tyler. Another influence was Joe Crump, who played piano and got Bradley his first job at a club on Twenty-Third Street in Bayonne.

"I was the organizer of the Sultans," Bradley recounted. "We were the Rhythm Dons, with Oliver Richardson on piano, Massenberg on sax, Al Cooper, alto, and myself on drums. As we went along, I added Pat Jenkins, Rudy, Moncur, and McNeal. When I left the group, Razz replaced me.

"The four of us started out working out of the old Pasadena Club [in Newark] at South Fourteenth and Orange streets [circa 1933]. Then we went into Dodger's. Eventually, we had eight pieces and went over to New York to play a big night club, the 101 Ranch. We became quite popular. Jack Chapman did all the arrangements. He was responsible for the band being so good."

As Bradley tells it, "a lot of jealousy set in" around the time he suffered a foot ailment and had to miss work for a while. From then on, he said, Cooper began to "take the band over," making a deal with the boss "to work for less."

Said Bradley: "They couldn't fire me, so they got on the side of the boss. The first week I was back the boss held back a hundred dollars, saying he'd make it up the next week. The next week he wanted to owe me another hundred. Finally, I said, Get yourself another band. If anything, you should offer us more money."

Angrily, Bradley left the group, taking all the arrangements with him: "I burned them up with a can of gasoline, but I was curious. So I went back the next night and listened from outside, and they were just as good. They knew all the arrangements by heart."

Because he was older than the other guys and married with a family, Bradley believes the breakup was rooted in a difference in age and lifestyles. To him, the other musicians were "wild," uninterested in "saving money to pay union dues," as he wanted, or going along with his "old-fashioned" ideas: "They wanted to party and drink, but I had no money for the good times. They kept approaching me about going out, but for me music was a business. I had a family to take care of." Some musicians, however, believe that racial discrimination—the fact that Bradley was jet black and a "geechie" from South Carolina (a reference to people who come from the Charleston area and speak a form of pigeon English known as "gullah")—made him unacceptable as a New York bandleader.

When interviewed by a *Herald News* reporter in 1938, soon after he left the group, Bradley described his future in music as "rather bleak": "Things were so discouraging that I abandoned the band and the boys, and now look at them. Maybe it was the mistake of my life, but we all are glad the boys went on to make the grade."

Moncur, who was born in Miami, was influenced musically by his mother, who "played the concertina and piano," and by his older half-brother, Alphonso (Al) Cooper: "I started playing tuba in a school band. I couldn't really play it, but I took it with me to get into the movies—the Ritz Theater in Miami. One day, they called my bluff and made me go on the stage. I just sat down and made a sound. The fellows in the band decided to chip in and buy me a bass."

The band, Little George Kelly and the Cavaliers, was led by Moncur's friend Kelly. For both of them, the gig at the Ritz was an exciting step up from their previous job—working at a neighborhood grocery store. "Our pay at the Ritz was our ticket to get in," recalled alto saxophonist Kelly, who remains active musi-

Rudy (Bones) Williams, Babs Gonzales, and Grachan (Brother) Moncur, mid 1930s. Courtesy of Florence (Hall) McIntyre

cally. "Then we did midnight shows. We only knew three tunes, 'How Deep Is the Ocean?' 'What Is This Thing Called Love?' and a song called 'That's a-Plenty.' We'd vary the three of them."

By 1933, Cooper had settled in Newark, earning his living playing at local clubs. Soon, he sent to Florida for Moncur, who was then eighteen or nineteen. He and "Brother" began "gigging around Newark" together. Kelly stayed behind until 1941, when he came north to join the Sultans in New York.

"Nothing was formed at first, but we had Al, Pat Jenkins, Larry Ringold, and Joe Crump," Moncur said. "There was no band. We just played clubs Down Neck [in the Ironbound section of the city]. Then my brother sent me to school—the George McHaskell School in New York City."

For the next several years, Moncur played with the Matinee Idols, a Newark group led by banjo player Norman Wilcox. The members wore tuxedos and broadcast every Sunday at 3 P.M. on Newark's WHBI, downtown on Ship-

man Street. "While I was with the Idols, John Hammond [the Columbia record executive and talent scout] discovered me and I made records with Red Norvo and many with Mildred Bailey," Moncur related. "The first one I made was with Billie Holiday.

"At the Savoy, we played against all the bands of the era—Benny Goodman, Jimmy and Tommy Dorsey—all of them. We were the house band, the intermission band. We alternated with whatever group that came in. Our theme song was 'Gettin' in the Groove.' We had eight pieces—Cyril Haynes on piano; Razz on drums; Sam and Pat on trumpets; Rudy, first alto; Al, second alto; McNeal, tenor; and me on bass. We didn't have a guitarist in the beginning. Chapman came in along the way."

Back home in Newark, the band was always a sellout, attracting 2,500 jitterbugs to Krueger's Auditorium for a July 4, 1942 swing battle against Lucky Millinder.

"After we became popular, we began traveling on the road," said Moncur. "We were makin' about ten bucks a week, and that was

The Matinee Idols, early 1930s: from left, Brother Moncur, newly arrived in Newark from Florida, bass; Teddy Cole (holding cymbal), piano; Clarence (Mouse) Fulford, saxophone; Norman Wilcox, guitar. Courtesy of Cecilia Wilcox

plenty of money at that time. You could get a room for two dollars, and there was plenty of bootleg whiskey. Traveling was never a problem. I had never been anywhere or seen anything. With the Sultans, I had a chance to go from coast to coast."

The group stayed together twenty years, twelve of them at the Savoy. "Then, we just drifted apart, got married, et cetera," Moncur explained.

While the Sultans were ensconced at the Savoy Ballroom in Harlem, the Savoy Dictators made their living traveling the road, playing marathons and dances. "Larue Jordan [a local pianist] gave us our name," recounted Harold Mitchell. "He called us 'The Dictators of Music.' We made a little name for ourselves 'cause we could outplay anybody."

"I got the Dictators from Frank Gibbs," said Al Henderson. "It was Frank Gibbs' band.

The Duke Richardson Orchestra, 1932: from left, unidentified; Herbie Lee Williamson, trumpet; Henry Walker, piano; Duke Richardson, trombone; Herman Gibson, guitar/banjo; Al Henderson, tuba/bass; unidentified; Bobby Plater, alto saxophone/clarinet. Richardson's band, launched in 1931, was a progenitor of the Savoy Dictators. Courtesy of Al Henderson

The Frank Gibbs Orchestra, mid 1930s, including the Savoy Sultans' Sam Massenberg and three of the Savoy Dictators, Al Henderson, Clem Moorman, and Lowell (Count) Hastings: from left, Massenberg, Sam Cureton, John Giles, and George Cook, trumpet; Henderson, bass; Moorman, piano; Frank Gibbs, trumpet; Fun Raymond, guitar; Eldridge Hawkins and Allen Gibbs, saxophone; Nathaniel (Fats) Ennis, drums; unidentified; Hastings, saxophone. Courtesy of Jimmy (Chops) Jones

Frank got us a job playing walkathons—working with W. E. Tebbetts and Red Skelton at Convention Hall in Camden. Frank had a day job and couldn't be with the band. He'd just come down on weekends, so the fellows elected me as the leader and it became the Al Henderson Orchestra.

"In that band was Mickey Waters, a helluva arranger and a fine musician, Chippie Outcalt, who played trombone, Count Hastings and Allen Gibbs, Frank's brother, on sax, Earl Nelson on drums, and Arthur (Fergie) Ferguson on trombone. We had a singer [Emma Reeves]—a girl who won a prize at the pier in Long Branch. Tebbetts had a chain out west. He came east to run these marathons. They made thousands of dollars—big money in those days.

"We had been playin' for a marathon in Long Branch. Tebbetts was in Asbury Park and heard about us. He gave me four hundred dollars to put the band in the union. At that time, the dues were about twenty-five dollars a man. He just gave me this check and told me to be in Camden at the appointed time. That impressed me. In those days, four hundred dol-

lars was like two thousand. You could buy a Cadillac convertible for eighteen hundred.

"We played from nine at night to one in the morning every day and then we'd broadcast in the afternoon, playing popular tunes that we got ahold of three or four months before other bands started playing them. Our theme song was 'Sleep,' but we put riffs in it. We had three arrangers—Robby [Plater], Clem [Moorman], and Chippie [Outcalt]. Besides the arrangers, we had a helluva lot of other talent, including Courtney Williams, our first chair trumpet player.

"Robby Plater [later the straw boss of Count Basie's orchestra] came into the band a little later than most of the fellows. I tried to get Robby for years," Henderson said, "but he was a very faithful fellow. He wouldn't leave the band he was playing with. He said the fellows needed him, even when I offered him more money and steadier work. He was working with 'Brownie,' a very fine trumpet player, and Cornelius Chinn in a band called the Heat Waves."

Harold Mitchell, who eventually succeeded Henderson as the Dictators' leader, was play-

The Sultans of Swing, 1939: from left, front, Rolin Bynum, Lloyd Wheeler, Sam Taylor, and Fenton Carey, saxophone; center, George Chapman, leader/saxophone/vocals; Herb Barney, drums; Sam Debnam, bass; sixteen-year-old Bill Bynum, Clarence Hatchett, and Solomon (Moose) Satterwhite, trumpet; rear, Gene Kee, piano. Courtesy of Harold (Hal) Mitchell

ing at the Colony Club on Broome Street with Joe Crump's Band of 1,000 Themes when he got a telegram from Henderson to play a marathon with the orchestra in Hagerstown. "Hagerstown, Maryland, might have been Africa or somewhere," Mitchell recollected, "but I found Maryland and I found Hagerstown," not that it was anything like he imagined. Instead of playing in the clublike atmosphere that he was used to, he found himself playing a tent show: "The first night was a bitch. A big storm came along and blew the tent down."

Soon after, the band returned to Newark and took part in a "Battle of Jazz" at the old Dreamland Academy on Beacon Street, competing with the Barons of Rhythm, the Sultans of Swing out of nearby Montclair, and bands led by Don Linton, Leon Eason, and Pancho

Diggs. Said Henderson: "We were the uninvited guests from out of town, but we came in and upset that joint. By that time, we had been organized two or three years and had our own book. I didn't organize the band, but I took care of it and got the fellows work for seven years. We went from marathon to marathon, from Schenectady, New York to Hagerstown, Maryland. Except for two weeks, we were never out of work."

When the Dictators returned to the road, Ferguson and Nelson left and trombonist Howard Scott, Plater, and Danny Gibson, who replaced Nelson on drums, came in, joining Henderson, Mitchell, Outcalt, and Clem Moorman on piano.

One of the next stops was Rudd's Beach, New York, near Albany, where the band played in a show with Apus and Estrelita, a comedy team, for about eight weeks.

"Around 1938, Pancho Diggs told me about this ballroom over Borok's [furniture store] on Springfield Avenue near Belmont," Henderson said. "I figured I needed a white partner. If my people didn't act right, the storeowners downstairs would put me out—so I got Irving Goldfinger for that reason and because I didn't have enough money for the rent. They wanted four hundred a month with two months in advance, so it was twelve hundred bucks to get the keys. Goldfinger got the place for two hundred a month and soon after we moved in."

For the thousands of dancers who took one flight up at Newark's Savoy Ballroom, the rage was the lindy hop. In keeping with that theme, the backdrop for the band was a mural painted by Larue Jordan and Al Madison of two lindyhoppers in action. Promoter Tiny Prince recalled: "When the Dictators were playing at the Savoy, admission was thirty-eight cents for the girls and forty cents for the boys. Can you imagine a live band playing from nine P.M. to one-thirty in the morning, and I mean playing, for a price like that? And these guys were good. On a good night, they got somewhere between a hundred and two hundred people."

It was inevitable that the Sultans and Dictators would someday go head to head. The Sultans' first home also was the Savoy on Springfield Avenue. And they were contemporaries. They had attended the same schools and grown up in the same neighborhoods. Henderson recalled: "This one Sunday afternoon the Sultans were playing the matinee. When they went off on intermission, we went up and played a couple of songs. They had a song called 'Looney.' It was a nickname for Rudy Williams. So, we played it. We actually blew them off the bandstand. We knew we were good.

"We did the same thing with Tiny Bradshaw. They had a fourteen-to-sixteen-piece band, and we only had eight men. They started really listenin' to us and the next week Tiny came back—that was the beginning of World War II—and took Hal, Chippie, Robby, and Scottie, our trombone player, with him.

"Robby stayed with Tiny longer than any of them. Robby let Bradshaw put his name on 'Jersey Bounce,' the theme song he'd written for the Barons of Rhythm when they were playin' out at the Shady Rest Country Club. The song was a hit, and he thought it'd be a credit to the band. Tiny's trombone player made the connections for Robby to get the song published, so he got his name on it, too, and he got the lion's share. Robby didn't make more than two thousand dollars for the song. I think he got around eighteen hundred, and it made millions."

Soon after, Mitchell joined Benny Carter's orchestra. Henderson remained behind in Newark, forming the Picadilly Pipers with his friends Clem Moorman and Ernie Ransome.

Teen Sensations
–The Barons of Rhythm
Chapter 13

The Barons of Rhythm were just a bunch of high school kids making music out of a storefront on Fairview Avenue in Newark in 1938. But they were tight, so tight that after less than a year of rehearsals they began playing regularly at the Shady Rest Country Club in Scotch Plains, New Jersey, watering hole of north Jersey's black social set. They were top-notch young musicians, including two whose talents soon would gain recognition at the national level: Ike Quebec and Bobby Tucker.

Quebec, of course, played torrid tenor, and his innovative style eventually made him one of the world's best on his instrument. In the early 1940s, pianist Tucker accompanied, and perhaps more importantly befriended, Billie Holiday. He was one of her closest friends, buoying her spirits when she went to federal prison on narcotics charges. When she came out, Tucker resumed playing for her when he could. Since 1949 he has been singer Billy Eckstine's accompanist. As Eckstine once joked, Tucker has outlasted his two wives.

The Barons also produced one of music's top arrangers: Walter (Gil) Fuller. Like Quebec, his ideas tended toward the more progressive sound of the emerging behop movement. As a teenager, Fuller wrote for Nina Mae Kinney, Floyd Ray, and Tiny Bradshaw. Subsequently, his genius propelled Eckstine's band and those led by Dizzy Gillespie and James Moody.

Conrad Butler, the Barons' leader, was a student at Newark's South Side High School in 1938 when he decided to form a jazz band. He scouted the city's high schools to find the best young musicians. Butler turned first to his South Side schoolmates, recruiting Connie Williams (who became the editor of the *New Jersey Herald News*), the only girl in the unit, to play piano. The ensemble included South Siders Thomas O. (T. O.) Swangin on alto sax; Leo Salley on trumpet; Bob Washington, trombone; Jimmy (Chops) Jones, a West Side High student, trumpet; and Jimmy Stanford of Arts High, sax. The rhythm section was rounded out by various drummers and bassists.

The Barons of Rhythm, circa 1938: Bobby Tucker, piano; from left, front, Howard (Duke) Anderson, holding saxophone; Thomas (T. O.) Swangin, Bobby Jarrett, and Jimmy Stanford, saxophone; center, Sam Cureton, Leo Salley, and Jimmy (Chops) Jones, trumpet: unidentified and Bob (Wash) Washington, trombone; rear, Clarence Mack, bass; Earl Nelson, drums. Courtesy of Thomas (T. O.) Swangin

At first, the band rehearsed at local schools; then Butler came up with the idea of renting a storefront on Fairview Avenue, between Seventeenth and Eighteenth avenues, where the ensemble played after school and on weekends. The teenagers patterned themselves after their idols, the Savoy Dictators, older Newark musicians who helped them with arrangements and occasionally sat in. "We played for school dances and some local affairs," Jones recounted. "Then we caught on at the Shady Rest in Union County, where Count Basie and big bands headlined. We were like the house band."

Like Quebec, Jones was self-taught, an initial impediment to the group's ability to broaden its musical scope: "Up until I was about twelve, I concentrated just on the drums. I just had a snare drum, no drum set. I'd stay home on Sunday—even when my sister invited me to go along with her to Coney Island—and wait for the Alabams, Leon Eason's group, to come on the radio. I'd play right along with them—on the furniture—anywhere.

"Conrad started me playin' trumpet. I met Conrad one day while I was on my way to a Boy Scout meeting. His mother lived on Lillie Street, but he was staying in Asbury Park at the time. I took his address and he invited me over to practice on his horn. When he went back to Asbury Park, he left his horn with me. I couldn't read [music], but I had learned to blow the bugle in the Boy Scouts.

"Soon after, I got a job with the iceman. It paid two fifty a week. I gave my mother a dol-

Jimmy (Chops) Jones, late 1930s. Courtesy of Jimmy (Chops) Jones

lar fifty and paid a dollar a week to buy a horn from Richards' Pawn Shop on Springfield Avenue. It cost twenty-eight dollars. I taught myself to play by writing the notes on paper. Conrad could read and play better, but I practiced more.

"After we formed the band we practiced at Eighteenth Avenue School, then over at Charlton Street School. I was first trumpet, but I couldn't read a note. We just played stock music—from the store. I'd take it home and my sister, who took piano lessons, would play it until I got my part down. I only knew about ten or fifteen numbers—all by heart. If the guys wanted to play a song from the middle, I'd insist we start at the top.

"Bobby Plater, Clem Moorman, Gates [Luther Willis], and Hal Mitchell was writing for us. We played all the Basie, Lunceford, and Andy Kirk numbers. I'd never rehearse 'cause I couldn't read. I'd always take the music home. My downfall came when Plater had us run through Johnny Russell's 'For Dancers Only.' When I stumbled, I started makin' excuses. First, I said I forgot my glasses. They soon found out I couldn't read. Then Conrad got with me and I started hangin' out with Jabbo [Smith], Little Willie [Nelson], and Little Benny Harris, who was around for a while. That was my education.

"From the time I found a stack of seventy-eights in our cellar, Louis Armstrong was my man. Then one day I went down to Lubinsky's record shop on Plane Street and heard a guy in a booth listening to Roy Eldridge. Little Willie [later a member of Buddy Johnson's band] had copied Little Jazz [Eldridge] note for note. From then on, Roy was my man."

Jones was drafted into the Army in 1939, the first of the regular members to leave the Barons. When other musicians were recruited, the band broke up. "I thought the Army wouldn't take me 'cause I wore glasses, so I went sauntering into the place where we had to report on Avon Avenue hours late," Jones said. "Next thing I knew I was on a bus to Fort Dix. I didn' get out until '43. Hollis Plinton [the Barons' bass player] was a sergeant at Dix and the first dude I met when I got there. He said he'd get me in the band, a five-piece jazz band led by Herbie Fields. They had us playin' all the time. Then I got assigned to Fort Greene in Virginia. Before I left I had three days' leave and played with the Barons at Shady Rest and the Orange Armory.

"After my discharge, I played with Ame Garrison at the Boston Plaza. A fellow named 'Baltimore' played piano and we had a lady bass player named Mary. Then I went with Mandy Ross for a long time."

T. O. Swangin's musical inspiration was Carl Biederman, whose home on South Tenth Street was headquarters for altar boys he recruited from Queen of Angels Church. He melded them into a band that played for parades and other church functions.

"Mr. Biederman, who also happened to be the director of the Newark Police and Firemen's Band, gave one fellow a drum and me a clarinet and started to teach us those instruments," Swangin said. "I caught onto it enough to join the band while I was still in grammar school. I got to play in all the Holy Name parades. We also played for funerals, but mostly we rehearsed all year for the Holy Name affair. We'd play marches and some overtures. Sometimes we'd play for the carnival.

"By the time I got to South Side, Clem [Moorman] was ready to graduate. Rudy Williams [of the Savoy Sultans] was in the band, but he said it was corny and got out. Then, Conrad and Leo [Salley] and I got the idea to start a band—the Barons. We got Connie to play piano and went over to Arts High and got Jimmy Stanford. We started rehearsin' at my house on Eighteenth Avenue, then at Conrad's house on Peshine Avenue.

"About that time, Conrad bought [rented] the storefront on Fairview Avenue, where we played. I think we got three dollars for our first job, but mostly we played a lot of free things— just to get ourselves known. We chipped in and bought a microphone and a stand and after a while we started rehearsin' at the Savoy Ballroom on Springfield Avenue," Swangin recalled.

"Our object was to get to play like the Savoy Dictators. They were our favorites. We got all our arrangements from them—Chippie [Outcalt] and all of them. Up until that time Gil Fuller was doing our arranging, and he'd use a lot of fifths and eighths. When he'd end a song it didn't sound right. Looking back, I guess that's because he was more advanced than most of us. His type of arrangements—bop and all that—was just comin' in. He was full of ideas. Later, he was able to explore them as Dizzy and Eckstine's arranger.

"When the Dictators gave dances, we'd try to sneak in and get on the dance floor. They were all five or six years older than us. All the big bands like Lunceford and Chick Webb were playin' Newark at the time.

"Then we began playing for dances at the YWCA. We'd get together and make up some kind of a contract. Al Terrell was in the band. Connie [Williams] was our first piano player and Bobby Tucker was our last. In between we had several others, including Goose Taylor. We had Johnny Cox on alto—he's dead now— and Jimmy Stanford and William [Buddy] Schenck on tenor when we started out. First, we had Pete Fields [on drums], then a fellow by

The brass section of the Barons of Rhythm, early 1940s: from left, front, Sam Cureton, Leo Salley, and Jimmy (Chops) Jones, trumpet; rear, unidentified and Bob (Wash) Washington, trombone. Courtesy of Jimmy (Chops) Jones

the name of Jabbo [Crowder]. Then we had Earl Nelson and Joe Brakes and sometimes Danny Gibson. Many times, the Dictators, like Danny, [Hal] Mitchell, or Scottie [Howard (Sadiq) Scott], would fill in for a particular job.

"Our trumpet players were Chops, Leo, and Sam Cureton. We had Hollis Plinton on bass, then Clarence Mack. As we became more advanced, we kicked guys out. We began playing together in 1938 and by 1939 had our first jobs. After a while we started playing in taverns like Dodger's Bar and Grill, where Herman Bradley used to have a band. As the war broke out, the band petered out. I was probably one of the last ones to go because I had a family—a wife and a son—and was working in a defense plant. Finally, all my extensions ran out and they sent me to Fort Dix. Almost every one of us wound up in some military band.

"Most of the time I was stationed at Fort Francis in Warren, Wyoming. When I first heard the band playing, I said, That's my piano player, Bobby Tucker. Bobby got permission for me to sit in and play third alto. They needed an alto player, so as soon as I finished basic training I was transferred over to that band and I stayed there until I was discharged. We had a very good swing band. George Duvivier [the bass player] was in it and Sammy Davis was a cadre man. He used to sing with us. We played for USO shows that came in with stars like Mickey Rooney and Tony Martin."

Leo Salley started playing cornet in 1934 as the mascot for the Elks marching band. His father was one of the members: "I really didn't get the knack of it until I joined the South Side High band. I got fired from my first job, subbing for a trumpet player at a tavern. I got paid a dollar fifty, but I could only play about three numbers—'Honeysuckle Rose,' 'Exactly Like You,' and probably 'Hold That Tiger.'

"Conrad organized the Barons of Rhythm and was the leader. 'Jersey Bounce' was our theme song. Bobby Plater wrote it for us. We were the first to play it, though there was no name on it. We just called it 'The 65 Special,' 'cause it was number 65 in the book. Clem [Moorman] really molded the Barons of Rhythm. He made the band what it was. Gil Fuller was our first arranger. Then we had Clem. We had a good jump band. We thought we had the best band around. We thought we were hot stuff. We played steadily at Shady Rest, the country club in Scotch Plains where all the rich black folks used to go, sometimes against eight- or nine-piece bands like Buddy Valentino's.

"I patterned myself after Harry [Sweets] Edison. He was no high note man, but he swung nice. Mostly, I learned the horn by playing one-night gigs at places like the Boston Plaza with Leon Eason—I love that man—and Gus Young. I played second trumpet with the Barons, so I got a lot of solos, like 'Sleep,' and head numbers like 'Baby, Won't You Fall in Love?'

"The war broke us up. We were about to audition for the Savoy Ballroom in New York. We'd patterned ourselves after the Savoy Dictators. We thought they were the best band Newark ever had and we had the same arrangers, so we were called 'The Little Dictators.' Around the time we all got drafted we had a little mixup over money matters. T. O. was the business manager, so he took over the leadership and kept the band going. Then the war came along and I got assigned to an Army band in Tampa, Florida. We played Paris, London, all over, and I had a good time.

"Unfortunately, the Barons never recorded. We made one demonstration record one time, but I lost it. After I got married, I was with Billy Anderson's band for eight or nine years. I just played on the side—weekend jobs. For a while I had my own band, Leo Salley's Orchestra."

Jimmy Stanford was thirteen when he joined the Barons: "I was the baby. My cousin

The reed section of the Barons of Rhythm, early 1940s: from left, Bobby Jarrett, Thomas (T. O.) Swangin, and Jimmy Stanford. Courtesy of Jimmy (Chops) Jones

introduced me to the sax and one of the local fellows, Charlie Shavers, was my first teacher. I took lessons, too, from Count Hastings [of the Dictators], but Walter [Gil] Fuller was really my mentor. He got me into the band while I was still going to McKinley Junior High. We played at Shady Rest, the Masons' Hall in Newark, and Goldman's Hotel in West Orange. We also played a couple of dances in Princeton at the fraternity houses and one for Rutgers."

When the war came along, Stanford served briefly in the Navy, then joined Buddy Johnson's band for four years until 1946: "Gus [Young] got me in by asking me to audition. At that time, Gus, Willie Nelson, Lindsey Nelson, and Frank [Slim] Henderson were with Buddy. So was a kid from Plainfield who played trombone. We called him 'Preacher.' I took [Ulysses] Bubbles Thorpe's place.

"We played all over the country, mostly the southern circuit—Baltimore, Washington, the Carolinas, Georgia, and as far west as California, mostly dances and some theaters like the Royal in Baltimore. In Rocky Mount, North Carolina, we played opposite Billy Eckstine's band when Diz and Parker and all those guys were in it. They were the better band, but we were doin' what the people wanted. It was our territory. Buddy was king down there.

"After the war, I tried to revive the Barons, but it didn't work. Then Pancho [Diggs] got me a job with the Four Chucks. Ame Garrison, the saxophone player, was on vacation. I just stayed. We were together from 1947 to '58 with Joe Watson on bass, Danny Gibson on drums, and Frank [Red] Brown on the piano. First, we played the Howard Bar; then we went downtown to the Stork Club, which later became the Key Club. We also played the T-Bar and Charlie Fusari's place across from City Hall. I got sick in 1964 and haven't played since."

THE CLUBS

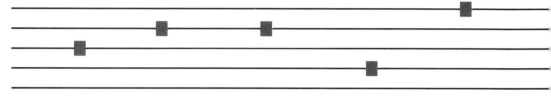

1935-44

The Kinney Club
—Home of the Hustlers
Chapter 14

For a fifteen-year period beginning in the late 1920s, the Kinney Club at Arlington and Augusta streets was the hub of Newark's sporting life. It was at the heart of Newark's Barbary Coast—an area aptly named for its resemblance to the danger-ridden waters traversed by high seas pirates—and because it offered its racially mixed clientele a walk on the wild side.

The Kinney Club attracted a mix of high-class pimps, prostitutes, gamblers, numbers bankers, and hustlers, along with plain folk on hand to see what all the action was about and whites who were "slumming." It had a distinct air of excitement about it, drawing top acts from New York and patrons who often arrived in limousines. Though less extravagant, it was Newark's version of New York's infamous Cotton Club, overflowing with beautiful bejeweled women and men whose bankrolls may have been derived from dubious sources but who were nevertheless fun-loving, big spenders.

At a time when other clubs in Newark closed at 2 A.M., the Kinney stayed open until dawn. Despite an occasional crackdown, there was no need to worry, for the police—especially the top brass—were among the best customers. "If you needed a cop, all you had to do was run up to the Kinney and you'd find one," recounted Wes Clark, who played bass in the band. "The owners were in with the police."

Along with the Palace Lucille on Plane Street and the Radio Inn on Halsey Street, the Kinney Club was one of Newark's first black nightclubs. "The first one [nightclub] I ever heard of, and I was born here in Newark, was over on Tichenor Street," said Uncle Willie Hurt, a Kinney Club patron. "That was in 1909 or '10. Then they moved over to Arlington Street. A man by the name of Louis had a pickup band."

In those days, the place for a young sporting man to be seen was at the rathskeller in the Kinney Club basement, then known as Kinney Hall. "When they first opened up, they had the

A Kinney Club revue, circa 1938: from left, front, chorus girls Ruby Vincent, Peggy Robinson, and Goldie Simpson; center, singer Rita Costello, comedienne Flo Thomas, emcee Charlie Fluker, singer Viola Wells (Miss Rhapsody), singer/comedienne Gladys Webster; rear, Pete Fields, drums; Herb Hensen, saxophone; Gene Ballard, piano; Elmer Chambers, trumpet. From author's collection

rathscalio," said Hurt. "Different bands would come in from New York and different singers. You had to be a big shot to go down in the rathscalio. Like Fox. Fox was a big-time gambler. And Gus Walker. You had two or three of them bigtimers who'd come in and say, 'Give 'em all a drink.'"

In the years when the club was known as Kinney Hall, traveling shows were staged in the basement, a provocative lure for impressionable young people trying to break into show business. Singer Billie Sermond was about twelve when she and her friend Dorothy Bryant went down to Kinney and joined comedian Checkers' revue, which was headed for Pittsburgh. They "got stranded," but fortunately a minister's family harbored them until they earned enough money "singing and dancing around in the costumes we kept from the show" to pay for their carfare back to Newark.

By the late 1920s Kinney Hall had become the Kinney Club, Newark's hottest night spot

Kinney Club waitresses Lucille Dorsey, left, and Estelle Bailey, late 1930s. Courtesy of Lucille (Dorsey) Morton

until many of the musicians went off to war in the 1940s and live entertainment eventually died off.

Trombonist-singer Clyde Bernhardt recalled: "We useta run over [to the Kinney] from the Club Alabam on our break. Richard Cheatham from New York had the band at the Alabam—eight pieces—and Lorraine McClane and Moms Mabley were on the bill as the McClane Sisters. The Club Alabam didn't cater to the average black man—just the ones who had money. Otherwise, it was all white. The Kinney Club was more mixed—black and white. Little Bits Turner [a comedienne] and her partner—he was a hunchback—had it sewn up. People would pack the place and throw money at them. Elmer Chambers, who useta play with Fletcher Henderson, was one

of the oldtimers at the Kinney. He couldn't play jazz, but he was a helluva musician. If you put it down proper, he'd play it."

A decade later the club was going just as strong. Waitress Lucille (Dorsey) Morton was a teenager when she lied about her age to get a waitressing job in 1938: "The men who came to the Kinney Club were much older. Some were dope fiends, old dope fiends, but they were polished. They weren't cutthroats. Newark was on the map, then. It didn't have an actual red-light district, but from William Street to West Kinney, all along Washington, was like a red-light district where all the johns used to go. At that time, people used to hustle. Men would send their girls from Cleveland and two or three other places to the club and the other pimps would protect them. They even

Audrey Armstrong and a muscular partner, circa 1940. From author's collection

had insurance on them. The biggest pimp rode around in a Deusenberg."

When the entertainment was moved upstairs, the floor shows became lavish. To attract a more sophisticated crowd, Benny Gilsider and Herman Pontishoff, the owners, completely overhauled the place, installing banquettes and an elevated bandstand with a railing that separated the entertainers from the customers.

As Morton described it, "You came up a long flight of stairs, turned to your right and walked back toward Arlington Street into a large hall with red and white tables. There was no food.

Beer was fifteen cents a glass. If a customer didn't finish it, we'd bring it back and pour it in another glass. It wasn't a knockdown, drag-out place, but you always had someone who wanted to start something. We had bouncers and a bar downstairs. All you'd [the waitresses] have to do was whistle if someone owed and didn't wanna pay up. No one would start anything 'cause the head waiter was Big Mose—and he was big. We also had [bouncers] Mr. Chips, Gam, and Skee. On New Year's Eve, everyone had a good time all night long. It'd be daylight when you came out. We'd add two or three drinks on the tab. They were drunk, anyway. They were bigtimers and they didn't care."

At the time, the club had three waitresses—Morton, Estelle Bailey, who also sang, and Ann Hensen, a rotund woman whose husband, Herb, was in the house band with Chambers, a jowly trumpet player who had given up a road career with Fletcher Henderson's band because of illness. Gene Ballard played piano with Pete Fields on drums and Wes Clark, bass. At other times, pianist Joe Crump and drummer Gus Young brought their bands in to spell Hensen and company.

For the employees, the Kinney was a gold mine. "The musicians often made more sittin' around drinkin' with the customers than we did playing," Clark recalled. "We got a cut for every drink that was sold. It was like a commission. And you could drink a lot 'cause the liquor wasn't that strong."

Said Morton: "The boss gave us fifteen dollars to start with. It was up to us to make whatever we could before turnin' in our bankroll. I had a bad night if I didn' make a bundle. That meant doing a little bit of everything—singing or dancing if a customer requested, even doing 'ups'—picking up money customers put on a table with your thighs."

During the late 1930s, the club had a number of popular emcees who generally wore tails and could sing or dance. They included Johnny Fussell, Honey Boy Thompson, Little Kenny [Clark], Clarence Ellis, and Charlie Fluker. The shows changed every two weeks or so, although some performers stayed on from show to show. The stalwarts were the three main chorus girls: Peggy Robinson, Goldie Simpson, and Ruby Vincent.

"We had two shows a night, just like the Cotton Club," said Morton. "The revues were built around a theme. The girls would do skits and there would always be a shake dancer. Then Carrie [Marrero] or one of the other singers would do a chorus and walk the floor. If you had a request, she'd come to your table and sing. The show would last about an hour. The emcee would close it by having the chorus come out and do their routine and the band would play a number."

Many of the shows in the late 1930s were produced by Billie Byrd, who often served as emcee. In 1938, one of his "snappy new revues," as it was described in the black press, featured singer Irene Easterly, comedienne Flo Thomas, a Kinney Club regular, and tenor Marshall Haley, a local singer considered to be a big-timer because he had sung on radio on the Major Bowes Amateur Hour. The following year singer/dancer Gladys Webster, Olive Gordon, and Carrie Marrero were featured in Byrd's productions of *Alexander's Ragtime Band* and *Take Me Back to School*.

"I'd say the Kinney Club was the center of entertainment in Newark," said Morton. "All the different ones in show business came here [to Newark] at some time or other to get a gig because we had so many clubs and taverns. Sometimes you could catch an act at Small's Paradise in Harlem, and the next time you saw the performers they'd be in Newark. A lot of people would travel here from New York, even further, because the shows in Newark were a lot less expensive."

One of the "big names" to play the Kinney Club in the early 1930s was blues singer Clara Smith. Although she was a good draw, trumpeter Leon Eason, who was in the band at the time, considered the show less than a success because Smith, at the time, "was on the way down," no longer possessing the powerful blues shouting ability that made her Columbia records solid hits in the black community.

In the late 1930s and early 1940s, Mamie Miller, a big, stout woman from New York, sang the blues at the Kinney Club and coordinated many of the shows. Among the performers and musicians, she was considered "the boss." "She would take the leads," Morton said. "She knew her songs, and could kick high. She'd get a lot of entertainers from New York. If they weren't right, she wouldn't keep them."

"Mamie Miller was a money-maker," said Wes Clark. "She lived in New York all her life and she knew the ropes. She had brains—and money. The women in the shows had to do 'ups' and, I'm telling you, Mamie Miller was a money-picker-upper. She could do it the best.

Bassist Wes Clark, 1929. Courtesy of Wesley (Wes) Clark

She was like a mother, teaching her children. Some of the girls couldn't do it, but Mamie'd break 'em in."

One of Miller's favorite dancing partners was Johnny Fussell, an ace tap dancer who traveled to Europe with Tip, Tap, and Toe and often performed with the Miller Brothers, another top act of the day. At the Kinney, he'd wow the crowd by dancing while sitting on a chair.

Another crowd-pleaser was comedienne Flo Thomas, who played the club for a decade. Born in King Fisher, Oklahoma in 1907, Thomas began her career as a chorus girl in Kansas City in 1925 in a show called *Steppin' High*. At nineteen, she married Dyke Thomas, a black-faced comedian "older than my father," and played theaters with him all over the United States and Canada.

"When he died, I was on my own," said Thomas, whose comical outfits were her signature. "I was living in Brooklyn and came to the Kinney Club at the suggestion of a girlfriend. I never tried out; I just walked in and sang a song and that was it. I liked comedy, so I just kept doing it."

Flo's big number was a risque (for its time) tune called "Old Man Mose." "I don't think I was ever funny offstage, but people were crazy about that number," she said. "You could change it around and get terrific laughs out of it. I was risque. Everything I did was risque and 'Old Man Mose' was the most risque number I did. That's why they liked it so much. And I could pick money off the table, coin by coin. I was the past mistress of that. I used to start with half-dollars, several quarters, nickels, and dimes and take them off one at a time."

"Three-quarters of the customers at the Kinney Club were whites—big spenders who either brought their women or girlfriends with them or came looking for a girl," explained Morton. "Rainy nights always were crowded. There was no gambling, but the girls would sit at the tables with the customers, or, maybe, meet them outside after the show. They'd get a lot of gifts." For many of the young white men who came by trolley from the suburbs seeking an exciting night out at the Kinney Club, the

Dancer Johnny Fussell at the Kinney Club, late 1930s. Courtesy of Lucille (Dorsey) Morton

adventures proved disappointing. My father, the late William (Bill) Kukla, and his younger brother, Fred, were two of them.

"The whole thing was a gyp," said Fred. "I guess Bill was about twenty-one and I was about nineteen when we heard about the Kinney Club through the grapevine. Someone said, 'You should have seen what we saw at the Kinney Club last night.' We decided to go out of curiosity. Newark was a nice place then. There was nothing to be afraid of, so we went. It was right after [the] repeal [of Prohibition]. There was no admission or anything. From what I remember, they were serving beer and light wine then, no hard liquor.

"What stands out most was the waiters who would hover over you if you didn't drink your beer fast enough. There were no waitresses at the time. Beer was served in bottles—a quar-

Exotic dancer Reese LaRue, late 1940s. Courtesy of Gertrude (Turman) Brown

ter a bottle. It was worth it, but they had to make money, so the waiters would stand over you. They didn't say anything [intimidating], but we got the idea fast enough. I think you had to be twenty-one to drink legally, but nobody did much checking in those days. The whole joint was phony. The dancers weren't really dancers. They'd come out and wiggle a little bit. Then they'd get you to put a quarter on the table so they could pick it up. We'd be waiting for something to happen. But it wasn't what we expected. If you looked closely, you'd see them grab it with their hand. The costumes were skimpy, but there were no nudes. A lot of the girls wore flesh-colored panties, and the lights were kept low. They were all very pretty colored girls. Under the dim lights they looked bare, but it was mostly illusion."

All of Newark's top entertainers played the Kinney Club at some time or other, including singer Gladys Heard (mother of author Nathan Heard), comedian Crackshot Hacksley, and the Prysock brothers from Paterson, New Jersey: Arthur, who became one of America's top male vocalists, and Wilburt (Red), who made his own name as a bandleader. For many local entertainers, the Kinney Club was the place to get a start. But some of them also considered it a rough and tumble joint.

"I went to the Kinney Club three times in my life," said singer Celeste Jones. "It was too rough. I just didn't like the crowd. Rhap [Miss Rhapsody] didn't like it either. She'd occasionally play there, but she didn't like it. There was just too much [activity] going on."

"If you had been in the Kinney, you had been somewhere [important]," added singer and dancer Joe Gregory. "But it was risque. All the pimps hung out there. Dodger's [Bar and Grill] was more high-class. The Kinney was more of a solid mixed club. You'd expect to see five or ten white couples."

By the mid 1940s, the club was on a downhill course. Many of the musicians had gone off to war, then returned to "regular" jobs, jukeboxes offered entertainment at a cheaper price, and technological changes, namely television, began attracting nightclub audiences.

When the Kinney Club came under new management in September 1947, there was an attempt to bolster business by establishing a new policy: "Star-studded Hollywood revues." The stars, however, were hardly Hollywood names. One bill, for example, listed blues singer Roebie Kirk, a local performer who had some acting experience but hardly was a box office attraction, comedian Geechie Palmer, shake dance "artist" Watina Allen, and music by "Bob Dawson's Big Little Band."

Subsequently, dancer/choreographer Reese

LaRue attempted to restore the Kinney Club's luster by staging exotic, burlesque-like revues. LaRue, a GI fresh out of military service, was a top dancer and choreographer who had a flair for spicing up his shows with glamorous costumes and a touch of nudity. At the Kinney, he generally teamed with dancer June Fletcher in extravagant shows that were enjoyable, sometimes even controversial. But the age of rhythm and blues was dawning. The Kinney Club had seen better days. Times and tastes mitigated against its continuing success.

In the late 1940s, the club was shuttered, a broken monument to the golden days of Newark nightlife. Ravaged by time and vandalism, the building was bulldozed in 1972. Bob Queen, editor of the *Afro-American*, who was there that day in March, gave a graphic account of what was left: "Windows staring out like eye sockets in a skull.

"It was probably fate that caused this close-up of a building that had stood ravaged and vandalized for nearly twenty years," Queen concluded. "Peeping into the second-floor window in plain view was the skyline blue ceiling, part of the stage, and a piano against the window on the Augusta Street side. The lower section had been boarded for over a year as the former tavern had become a haven for winos and junkies and a giant receptacle for trash, bottles, and beer cans. Passing through Branford Place three days later, the old club had vanished from the face of the earth. Nothing was left but the caterpillar tracks of the bulldozer that had unceremoniously dispatched it to eternity, but not the memories from many who still recall its gaudy days in a rather carefree era."

S on Berry
and the Boston Plaza
Chapter 15

In the late 1930s, the Boston Plaza on Boston Street, three doors in from West Market, was one of Newark's most popular night spots. The owners were the five Berry brothers from Dothan, Alabama—William (Son), Elie (Bert), Ralph, Jimmy, and Rufus. Son Berry, the oldest, arranged the sale from the previous owner, Bill Watson, in 1936. Two years later, Son, Bert (the company president), and Jimmy branched out and bought the Greenbriar in Eatontown near the Jersey shore, a club that catered to an elite black crowd from north and central Jersey.

When the Berrys took over the Boston Plaza, bartender Bill Roberts came with it. Roberts, born in Macon, Georgia in 1904, clearly recalled the changeover: "When Watson opened up the club in 1935 or '6, it was just a plain old bar at 27 Boston Street. Then he bought a restaurant at 4–6–8 Boston Street and sold it to Son. Milton Pittman's was the first band in there. He had four pieces. Frank Cross, who

worked at the post office, was the drummer." Also in the band were two musicians about whom nothing is known, Louis Wright and a fellow known only as Julius.

Congenial and popular, Pittman made the perfect emcee, doubling on piano and as the bandleader. A man with a keen business sense as well, he eventually started an insurance business and opened a club called Pitt's Place on West Market Street. While working at the Plaza, the bespectacled Pittman became the driving force behind a series of jam sessions that rotated from club to club. On Monday afternoons the sponsors were Dodger's Bar and Grill, Fisher's Tavern, and the Villa Maurice. The hosts on Wednesday nights were the Boston Plaza, the Grand Hotel, the Rainbow Inn, and Tyler's Chicken Shack in nearby Avenel.

When Tyler's and the Rainbow Inn withdrew in the spring of 1939, some of the owners objected to a setup that left only two clubs on

The Three Regular Girls

EMMA HAWKINS, LOUISE GORDON and BILLIE SERMOND
Present
A Cabaret Dance and Entertainers Revue

Singers Emma Hawkins, Louise Gordon, and Billie Sermond as the Three Regular Girls, circa 1935. Courtesy of Florence (Hall) McIntyre

Milton Pittman at the time he owned Pitt's Place, circa 1950. Courtesy of Gertrude (Turman) Brown

August, changing the performances to Tuesday nights at the Plaza and Wednesday nights at Steve's Tavern on West Street, owned by the Savarese brothers, John and Butch.

One of the most memorable evenings at the Plaza occurred several weeks earlier when the city's top musicians and entertainers gave a farewell bash for torch singer Louise Gordon. She was returning to Kansas City, her hometown, and all her friends turned out. Soon after, the same crowd threw a birthday party for Pittman, who wowed his friends by singing one of his original compositions, "I'm Still in Love With You,' followed by "Sweet Georgia Brown" and a popular ditty, "Let's Have a Party."

After completing renovations, Son Berry and his brothers opened the Greenbriar in the summer of 1938, dubbing their Monmouth County showcase "The Dream Palace at the Jersey Shore." With summer business waning in Newark, the Greenbriar provided a perfect change of venue for his year-round customers and employment for many Newark entertainers during the slow summer months. As an added touch, he built some cabins in the back and began sponsoring bus rides to the shore area for the weekend. The first two summers Satchel Robinson was the emcee for the floor shows. The thirteen-piece Barons of Rhythm served as the house band.

Back in Newark, Ame Garrison and Her Sirens of Swing were holding sway at a series of Sunday matinees at the Plaza. A multi-talented musician who also played trombone, clarinet, accordion, and organ, she supposedly was the only female maestro of an all-girl group in New Jersey. Garrison, who played mostly "with the guys," subsequently joined the International Sweethearts of Rhythm, an all-girl orchestra that played the country's top clubs and theaters and traveled abroad.

One of Berry's best customers was Pretty Melvin, a big spender who threw exotic parties for stars like Billie Holiday and allegedly ran an opium den in his opulent East Orange digs. "Melvin was a very cultural person," singer Celeste Jones said. "He went around to all the clubs, but he came mostly to the Boston Plaza.

the Wednesday rotation. The rumor around town was that Berry planned to organize his own jam session and buck his former partners by pulling in the Nest Club, the Rin Tin Inn, and, possibly, the Alcazar.

"The jams have been waning in popularity for some months," partly because the owners had alienated their patrons by "sitting at one table and not mixing with the crowd," a *Herald News* entertainment critic wrote. "The power behind the jams has been Milton Pittman, who serves as emcee. It has been his personality, quick wit, and hustle that has kept them alive and booming. Whether he remains is an important factor to the success of the group."

Pittman reorganized the jam sessions that

Except for Dodger's, it had a little better crowd. Son always had music and nice performers. Satchel Robinson was the emcee. He was very popular at the time, a good performer. When Melvin came in, Rhap [Miss Rhapsody] was good for forty or fifty dollars, and I was good for five or ten. 'Prisoner of Love' was his number."

Roberts, who generally was behind the bar, said Melvin "thought nothing of pulling out a thousand dollar bill and buying drinks for everybody in the back. Or, he'd ask for change. One night I flabbergasted him by pulling out a big roll of money and changing it. Was he surprised!"

The bankroll, Roberts revealed, came from Son Berry's other business—illegal booze: "Son was in partnership with Jim Rhett down in Keyport after he bought the Greenbriar. Both of them were three-time losers because of bootleggin' whiskey. If they were caught again, they'd face goin' to jail for life. I was in it with them. For seven years, seven days a week, I drove the sugar and rye down to Keyport and brought back eleven fifty-five-gallon cans of bootleg booze. I knew exactly where to sell it. At the time, a hundred pounds of sugar cost three dollars and fifty-five cents up on Twelfth Avenue. We had vats in the basement where we stored the stuff. Then on Monday I'd put the empty cans in a canvas bag and take 'em down again. I had a souped-up Ford with a special gear. In all those seven years, I never got stopped. When I got back, I'd take out expenses and we'd split it three ways."

When the Berrys decided to enlarge the Boston Plaza in 1941, a controversy arose, prompting a reporter to note: "It is hard to understand the way the minds of some of our leading colored citizens act. . . . Take, for example, the group who went down to the Newark Excise Board the other day to protest the transfer of licensing of the Boston Plaza so that the place could be enlarged to meet the increase in business. Much stress was laid on the proximity of the place to one of our leading colored churches [the old Bethany Baptist building on West Market Street]. Yet the fact remains that these same protesters were con-

Arthur Terry and the Grand Rascal Trio, circa 1945: from top, Clarence Mack, bass; Terry, piano; Eddie Wright, guitar. Courtesy of Jimmy (Chops) Jones

spicuous by their absence when two white taverns—one almost across the street from the said church—received their licenses."

Eventually, the club was enlarged. "They knocked out the wall where there was a restaurant on the other side and made a big nightclub with a stage where they had the piano and the band would play," recalled Earline Berry, Bert's widow. "And they had a little floor for dancing. We used to live on the third floor in the back apartment. I raised my five children there—four daughters and a son. We had the original kitchen and a big back porch. The children would walk down to the second floor, where another lady had an apartment, and go out on the roof to listen to the music. Once in a while, I'd go downstairs," she added. "I remember Sarah Vaughan coming there to sing and dance just before she won the amateur show at the Apollo. Emma Hawkins used to sing there, too."

By 1943, one of the most popular performers appearing regularly was dancer/emcee Allen Drew, whose act "kept the customers in a jovial mood with stories he can tell without stopping for hours. The guy is the best thing that ever did it for my money," a local scribe reported. Another top act was Willie Dukes, a vocalist and female impersonator. "If you didn't know, you'd think he was Billie Holi-day," said one patron. Torch singer Madeline Keith, dubbed "The Girl With 1,000 Songs," was another favorite. From 1942 to 1944 she appeared in most of the revues, doubling for a time as emcee.

In 1945, Berry sold the Boston Plaza to the Fredericks brothers, Otto, Bill, and John, and it became Fredericks' Lounge. Bill, whose nickname was "Porky," had been a bartender at Little Johnny's, a Montgomery Street tavern. The Plaza's profitability enabled them to buy Jim Rhett's Twinlite on Rankin Street in 1946, which they renamed the Three Deuces. Among the headliners booked into their new club were bassist Slam Stewart and Myra Johnson, the former Fats Waller Orchestra vocalist, and blues singer Lil Green.

Mrs. Reeves and the Nest Club
Chapter 16

From the mid 1930s to the early 1950s, the Nest Club on Warren Street—now a vacant urban renewal lot—was one of the few Newark night spots that offered black audiences a "complete floor show." It was also one of the few clubs owned by a woman, the beautiful, businesslike Eurlee Reeves. Unlike the entertainment at the Kinney Club or Dodger's, which often sought big-name acts out of New York, the "stars" were almost always local talent.

Charlie Matthews, who became New Jersey's first black freeholder director (Essex County's chief legislator) in 1961, was the club's first emcee. Other local favorites—like dancers Sadie Matthews, Anna May Hall, Sugar Payne, Abe (Snakehips) Moore, Joe Gregory, and Gertrude Turman, emcee Ernie Ransome, crooner Bob Taylor, blues singer Elsie Paige, and musicians Joe Crump, Hal Mitchell, and Danny Gibson—were among the regular entertainers. Generally, the shows fea-

tured skits, songs, and dance routines based on a unifying theme that incorporated the talents of the entire cast.

" 'Prisoner of Love' was one of our most popular numbers," Gregory said. "I'd come out barechested and barefooted, wearin' just a pair of bathing shorts, while Bob Taylor stood over in the corner singing 'Prisoner of Love.' All the girls would be slithering around my feet. I had this whip, and I kep' fendin' them off, payin' them no mind. Then, Anna May'd reach up and touch my legs, and I'd go wild. At the end, I'd gather her up in my arms and carry her off. The audiences loved it."

Many Newark entertainers got their start at the Nest Club. Lander Coleman of the singing Coleman Brothers was one of them: "Singing at the Nest Club was a big deal. I was just a kid, going to Belmont Avenue School and Oliver Street School. We'd get a dollar fifty, a dollar, sometimes eighty or ninety cents each. We [his singing partners John and James Norris and

A high-stepping chorus line at the Nest Club, late 1930s: from left, Christine Northington, Ernie Ransome, Mary (Sugar) Payne, Abe (Snakehips) Moore, Tat Plowden, Charlie Matthews, Laura Reilly. The band members include Herbie Lee Williamson on trumpet, Teddy Brannon (eyeglasses) on piano, and Hal Mitchell, trumpet. Courtesy of Eurlee Reeves

Robert Tippins] bought four little uniforms—white short jackets and long black pants with a stripe down the side.

"Gracie Smith was on the show. And they had a floor show—the girls dancing on the floor. One of them was called 'Blackie.' There was Sadie [Matthews] and some chorus girls from New York. In later years, [Madame] Pork-chops used to come in. She used to do some of everythin'. Artie Gilmore had the band. Gus

Young had a band. So did Joe Crump. New York bands was coming over, too. Buddy Johnson. Count Basie. Duke Ellington. They was all just getting started. Big acts used to come over to the Nest Club.

"The emcee would come out and announce the different acts they had for that night. They had no admission. You'd just come right in. Mrs. Reeves had food and the bar. Chicken. Hot dogs. Hamburgers. Fish. Chittlins. Name it; they done sold it. It was always jammed—all they could get in there. Just as long as the people could get in a place called a nightclub."

The Nest Club also was a home away from home for many of the performers, a place where they got together to exchange ideas and work for improved working conditions. "Around 1934, everybody was making two dollars and fifty cents a night," said Thad Howard, the Intercity Swing Club's first president. "We wanted to raise the amount, so we started the club. The entertainers were all for it. We wanted to get the musicians, too. We got a lawyer and decided—no gigs under three dollars. It worked. We had about forty performers and about twenty-five or thirty musicians. From time to time, we'd put on all-star vaudeville shows that attracted hundreds of lindy-hoppers—jitterbuggers as they were called then."

When Mrs. Reeves (as she was always known to her employees and customers) bought the Cabin LaBlanche in 1937 and renamed it the Nest Club, her aim was to put the Kinney Club out of business. Actually, the clubs were as different as their patrons and performers. The Kinney Club, with its imported New York acts, was owned by whites. It was the jewel of the infamous Barbary Coast, an area that was home to pimps, prostitutes, and other hustlers, and it was the turf of the big spenders—white men on the prowl and free-spending blacks whose money often came from illicit activities. Ordinary Newarkers patronized it, too, but to a lesser extent.

The Nest Club was considerably simpler in its setting and its style of operation. Yet, in Mrs. Reeves' mind, the Kinney Club was her staunchest competitor, her arch-rival.

Nest Club bill, 1938. Courtesy of Gertrude (Turman) Brown

From the outset, she wanted to "put on better shows," draw away patrons from the Kinney Club, and shut it down. Twenty years later the Kinney Club did close first, but for a variety of other reasons.

Born in Pelham, Georgia in the 1890s, Eurlee Reeves came north as a child to work for the wealthy Landis family of Newport, Rhode Island. She subsequently moved to New York, then settled in Newark, where she raised her children from a second marriage, Jewel, Walter, and Jack Wilkie. A fourth child, Horace

Eurlee Reeves with entertainers, late 1930s: from left, singer Grace Smith; Reeves; singer Elsie Paige; dancer Janie Napier. The others are unidentified. Courtesy of Eurlee Reeves

Wilkie, died while still in his youth. An inventive woman, full of ideas about how to support her children, she decided to start her own business rather than work for someone else.

Her plan was simple—start small and build on the trade. With that thought paramount, she opened a small storefront on Newark Street, selling beer and hotdogs "out of the window."

"At first, that's all I did," she explained. "Then one day some girls came by and told me they wanted to be entertainers, but the Kinney Club had all the shows and 'they don't hire no colored [dark-skinned] girls.'

"I said, Don't you worry your pretty little heads. You just gave me an idea. I'm cuttin' out all of this sellin' hotdogs in the window, and I'm gonna open up a nightclub.

"They said, 'Miz Reeves, you would do that for us?'

"I said, I'm gonna do more than that. I'm gonna hire every one of you, but I'm gonna tell you somethin'. You'll have to make your price reasonable to start with, but as business grows, your salaries will grow.

"They said, 'Do you mean that?'

"I said, Yeah.

"They said, 'Let's shake hands 'cause we ain't gonna tell Miz Reeves no lies.'

"So I said O.K."

Soon afterward she went to Cleveland on a vacation and visited Johnson's nightclub, a backwoods juke joint operated by numbers racketeer John B. Johnson: "That place was jammed with people payin' a dollar a head. That show they put on was superb. When I got back, I told the girls, we're gonna put on the same show.

"They said, 'Really?'

"I said, Now, listen! Y'all don't have clothes.

Teenage tapsters Bobby and
Winnie Johnson at the Nest
Club, circa 1937. Courtesy of
Eurlee Reeves

I'm a little bit ahead of y'all 'cause I lived in
New York. I know all the places where you can
rent costumes. We can keep 'em two weeks,
send 'em back, and get new ones. But I want to
tell you somethin', y'all. You gotta give me
your word of honor. I don't want nobody per-
spirin' or menstruatin' on those costumes,
'cause if you do I won't be able to get any more,
and if you ruin 'em all, I'm gonna have to pay
for them and y'all have no job.

"I said, Before we're in this place three
months, we're gonna put the Kinney Club out
of business; don't you worry. You just do what I
tell you to do, and we'll do it. First thing I'll do
is get Joe Crump for our pianist. He's gonna do
all the playin'. One of you girls is gonna go over
to New York and pick out your costumes for
the first show.

"I said, the second thing you gotta have is an
act, so I went to this place where the fighters
had a club and saw this fellow do a dance. It
was done to the 'Song of India.' I came back
and told the girls: You're gonna learn that
dance. I'm gonna show ya as much as I can.
Anna May Hall—she was my best girl—said
she'd show them, and so we started off, but we
still needed a place.

"I said, We got to have that place that Miz
Henry used to have across the street [the Cabin
LaBlanche]. She couldn't make a go of it, so
she had to give it up. I said, We're gonna have a
man build my own stage. I'm gonna have a

Tropical revue at the Nest Club, circa 1938; from left, Mae Darling, Sadie Matthews, and an unidentified chorus girl. Courtesy of Sadie Matthews

stage so high y'all have to go up steps to get on the stage and come 'round and come down. But ya gotta be careful. I don't want no fallin'.

"So, we went on like that. The first night we put on a big show. I went over [to New York] and got these costumes and I made one girl who was a beautician fix 'em up and do their hair. When we put on that show that night, that did it. I had the show four nights a week—Thursday, Friday, Saturday, and Sunday. The other nights I didn't have no show.

"We had Greenie, the police officer, on the floor, keeping law and order, 'cause we didn't want people actin' like a honky tonk when they came in there. I put this song on, 'Song of India.' I had it on my jukebox, so that's how they rehearsed it when Joe Crump wasn't there. They were really good entertainers. We had Gertrude Turman and Anna May Hall, Joe

Crump on piano, and Gus Young played the drums. Just the piano and drums. That's all we had. Sometimes we had another fellow that played the trumpet—once in a while.

"Stepin Fetchit [the Hollywood actor] married one of my girls, Winnie Johnson. She was beautiful. She and her brother, Bobby, danced together, but they were too young to go out dancin', so their mother and father used to bring 'em. I did everything within the law, so I never had any complaints. I never had any trouble at all.

"When I went on vacation, I'd go to Cleveland, Ohio, where all those big shots had nightclubs and they'd take me a thousand miles into the country and I'd go to these nightclubs and see their shows. I'd find a show that I liked and I'd come back and show the girls. Anna May would take it from there. When I'd get through tellin' her, she'd know just what I wanted, and she'd perform it just like that."

Little Sadie Matthews became one of the club's chorus girls. She was from Philadelphia and had worked in Baltimore and Atlantic City previously, singing and dancing with Banjo Bernie's band: "After my baby was born, I decided to follow my sister, Mandy, to Newark. So we came to Newark. That's when I opened at the Nest Club. It wasn't the Nest Club. Had another name.

"I worked at the Nest Club seven years, two shows a night. 'Round ten, the show would come on and the band would be playin'. We'd do bits—everything. One bit was 'bout Dr. Fojo Bones. Georgie Rollins was dancin' in the show and so was Jackie [Mandeville] and Fats [Jennings] and Anna May Hall and Bill Chapman. He and Anna May used to dance together. He used to wear a derby and she was a good tap dancer.

"Sometimes I'd do a bit with Anna May. One time I tripped her. We were doin' the dolly dance. Anna May got embarrassed and wouldn't come back [on stage], but the people loved it. They thought it was in the show. All of us had to be in the chorus. Frances Herbert was the shake dancer. That was her specialty. She used to crawl on the floor and shake. We used to do a lot of Indian dances; then the show would change after two or three weeks."

"We put on such fine shows that the Kinney Club went down—sooooo low," Mrs. Reeves said. "I told the girls I heard there was nobody in the Kinney Club last night. My girls had been worryin' and worryin' and worryin' 'cause the Kinney Club was gonna beat 'em. Well, the Kinney Club didn't beat 'em. And we put the Kinney Club out of business. [Actually it was economics and changing trends in entertainment.] We sure did! I told the girls, Now how do you feel? 'Cause we put on a show that was out of this world. And they were all colored girls. I loved them all. I just loved my girls. Nobody taught me how to do this. I just laid down at night and thought about what I wanted to do. I wanted to be big. I wanted to come out big, and I did it—all by my damn self!"

Pop Durham's Alcazar
Chapter 17

The Alcazar tavern at 72 Waverly Avenue was as ordinary as any other corner saloon in Newark in the 1930s, but under the proprietorship of Iva (Pop) Durham it became a favorite gathering place of musicians and one of the city's most popular bars run by blacks. Durham, who came from Texas and looked "just like a Texas ranger," according to trumpeter Leon Eason, had been a hod carrier before he bought the corner saloon. He had worked hard, and still did, but he also enjoyed fraternizing with friends and neighbors while running his business.

"Pop turned what had been a dinky saloon into a place where he made plenty of money," said pianist Clem Moorman. "When I was a young man, the Alcazar was it. More than anything, it was an orderly place; there were no fights." "Mr. Durham wasn't urbane by any stretch of the imagination, but he was all business," said Connie (Williams) Woodruff, who grew up in the neighborhood. "He was a big man, and he always drove big cars—great big cars. He enjoyed the place as much as his customers."

Durham also had the distinction of being the first tavern owner to sell Heineken beer. "But it cost a buck, and we couldn't afford it," recalled guitarist Willie Johnson. "We drank what we could afford—Krueger's and the other slop that sold for twenty or twenty-five cents."

The Alcazar was not fancy—just a huge room with a double horseshoe bar and a bandstand and a few tables in the back where the musicians played and other entertainers dropped by to do a number or see their friends. Like many taverns, it had a side door for the ladies, who came straight out of church for Sunday shows wearing wide-brimmed hats. Sitting at the bar not only was unladylike, it was off limits—at least until the war years. By that time, female factory workers came attired in overalls.

The Alcazar, late 1930s. Courtesy of William (Willie) Johnson

"The most exciting day was the Monday after Easter," recalled Florence (Williams) Henderson, wife of Al Henderson, the bassist. "Each Easter Monday we'd all wear our Easter outfits and go to the Alcazar." In retrospect, she explained, "it was just a big old family bar with a dingy little room in the back, a typical dive. But when I was a teenager I was dying to get in because I was in love with Bob Taylor, the singer. I had to wait until I was nineteen because Pop Durham knew my people and would have told my mother. When I heard Bob Taylor sing, I thought, This man should be on Broadway. I can still hear him. He used to sing the tune Leon Eason wrote, 'Beverly.' He was a very romantic singer. And he was nice looking—tall and big, like [the actor] Danny Glover. But he was very dark. If you're real black, people don't always see you as good looking."

At the time, Taylor was about ten years older than his teenage admirer, "a big difference if you're nineteen," said Henderson. To make matters worse, he "was in love with a tall, very striking girl named Thelma, so what kind of chance did I have? Eventually, I got over him."

The two performers most closely associated with the Alcazar were Eason, whose band played there for years, and emcee Matty Alston, whose specialty was jump tunes like the catchy "Upstairs" when he wasn't talking "a whole lot of stuff." While Eason, dapper as ever, remained a local favorite for many years, Alston disappeared off the scene long ago.

Short and squat, Alston had none of the good looks or charm of a Satchel Robinson or Babs Gonzales, who provided the female draw at other Newark clubs. Yet the sheer force of his personality made the Alcazar a rendezvous

Singer/emcee Matty Alston and guitarist Willie Johnson, mid 1930s. Courtesy of William (Willie) Johnson

Eason was a package of unadulterated talent, a gifted trumpeter and inventive vocalist like his idol, Louis Armstrong. To Newarkers, he was and remains their Armstrong. As a teenager, he and his friend Herbert Harper formed a dance team and appeared in vaudeville shows. "Then, when I was about twenty, my mother bought my brother a trumpet. He didn't play it much, so I started fooling around with it, and the first thing ya knew I got a tune out of it. They had a band over at the Y where they had basketball games, so I'd go over there and sit in."

After debuting in a six-piece band led by Hubert Ravenue in 1930, Eason joined a traveling show with the Alabams at Newark's Orpheum Theater and stayed on the road for five years. As the band's featured trumpet player, he gained enough experience to form his own band after returning home. For the next year or two he led small combos at three white clubs in Newark—the Blue Goose on Frelinghuysen Avenue, the Park Rest at Virginia and Frelinghuysen, and the Club Miami on Clinton Avenue, where Jackie Gleason was the emcee.

"Blacks had to do what they had to do," Eason said. "It was a rough thing, tryin' to stick with show business. Work ain't out there most of the time. Years ago everyone was looking for work. All a lotta the guys wanted was a Cadillac and a woman."

In 1937, Eason moved his band into the Alcazar to begin his first lengthy stay at a black club: "Rain or snow, we played seven days a week with two matinees on Sunday—nine shows a week for three and a half years. We went in with Gene Holder on piano, Butch Robinson on tenor, Albert Best on bass, and Charlie [Brother] Kelly, drums." Their theme song was "I Can't Get Started With You," a tune that Bunny Berigan's trumpet solo subsequently made a national hit.

"Kelly was a woman's man," Eason noted. "When he was mad at a woman, he was mad with the world. I got tired of that. A guy from Rahway called me for a gig at the Lion's Share in Elizabeth. Joe Gregory was the drummer, but at intermission this kid named Joe Brakes would play and everybody would gather

for entertainers and musicians. Some celebrity always was dropping in to see Alston, seated on a chair on the bandstand, small talking and keeping the crowd in stitches while introducing the acts.

In retrospect, Alston was more of a stylist than an entertainer. In Moorman's opinion, he was "a jive emcee," clicking his fingers to the beat of "Savoy" or swinging through "That's What I Like About the South." After working at the Alcazar, Alston traveled with Count Basie's band, then dropped out of sight. His friends believe he "moved down South somewhere."

Leon Eason's band, circa 1940: from left, Duckey Massey, piano; Carl McIntyre, saxophone; Clarence Mack, bass; Kenny Richards, drums; Eason, trumpet. Courtesy of Carl and Florence (Hall) McIntyre

'round him. When Kelly quit the band, I hired him. After that, we had Kenny Richards on the drums.

"Everybody used to hang out at the Alcazar," said Eason. "Thad Howard [singer/ emcee] and Joe Timmons [another popular singer] were two of the regulars. I put everybody on if they could do somethin'. We'd make up an impromptu show. That's how I had most of my fights. A lot of people would come in and want to sing, but they can't. Wouldn't let 'em."

The atmosphere at the Alcazar was marked more by fun than fights, thanks to Eason's good-natured ability to handle most situations. No matter how he tried, his straight-to-the-point mannerisms failed to hide a kindly disposition evident in his ever-ready smile.

With Alston and Eason as a team, Pop Durham hit paydirt. His club was teaming with performers or would-be performers clamoring to get onto the bandstand. By then, Eason had developed an easy-going, humorous singing style, patterned after Satchmo, handkerchief and all: "I used to sing with the Alabams. Then, when I came back home I used to sing on the radio—WHBI on Shipman Street—on Sunday afternoons at three o'clock. It was a half-hour show and we had twelve guys in the band, some of the same guys, like Bobby Williams, who were on the road with us."

Eason was not only a top-notch trumpeter, he was a first-rate singer and composer. Like Armstrong, his singing style packed a witty wallop, and at times a tinge of the romantic. In his inimitable version of "Honeysuckle Rose," for example, he sings: "Charlie is a jerk, never goes to work," playing wickedly with the words while rolling his eyes impishly at his audience. His only recordings, made in the late 1940s for Blue Note, include "Just a Gigolo" and "On the Scene," one of his compositions. The most popular tune he wrote was "Beverly," named for a former girlfriend. "I didn't sing it too much because I had no copyright on it," he explained. "I knew they [white promoters] would steal it."

Virtually all who heard him agreed that Eason's talent was profound, that he should have "gone places." He did have many offers to travel and become better known. But the problem was always the same: no money. "I could have made it," Eason revealed. "I had an invitation to go to California and have an act in a club built around me. And there were plenty of other offers. But there was no money in it. There still isn't. All the other guys [managers, promoters, record company officials, et cetera] make the money while the musicians keep runnin' and scufflin'. I didn't want to be like that. I've been to Louie's [Louis Armstrong's] house [in New York], and it was just an ordinary house, just like the ones in this block where I live [in East Orange, New Jersey]. All the other people got the money he made—big money—not Louie."

At the Alcazar, Eason was able to eke out a living. But his best-paying job was at the Park Rest at Virginia and Frelinghuysen avenues in the industrial section of the city near the airport, a white nightclub where he worked in 1935 and 1936. "It was the midst of the Depression," he recalled. "As part of my act, I wore a porter's hat, carried a dust pan and broom, and sang 'Pennies from Heaven.' It was a good job. Sal Mandell, who ran the place, was my best boss. He paid top money and gave me a chance to make something. Pop [Durham] was O.K., too. But the pay at the Alcazar wasn't all that good. Nobody was makin' much of anything at that time."

By the time Willie Johnson joined Eason's combo at the Alcazar in late 1937, the pay was seventeen dollars a week. "I guess Leon was making twenty or twenty-five dollars because

he was the leader and had all the headaches," said Johnson, who replaced vibraphonist Pete Diggs. "At that point, we had Duckey Massey on piano, Kenny Richards on drums, Al Best, who was my classmate in school, on bass, Carl McIntyre on sax, Leon, and me. We worked hard, seven days a week, with matinees on Sundays and Thursdays, but it was enjoyable.

"Leon had me do 'Gone With the Wind,' emulating Charlie Christian [the famous Benny Goodman guitarist who died at age twenty-one], and I was given a lot of spots. Sometime I'd take the part of a third horn, like a trombone. Mostly, we'd play head stuff, whatever came into our heads. We played most of it so much we didn't have to practice. Carl and Leon did the arranging. We didn't have any money for orchestrations. They'd buy sheet music and take it from there.

"All the guys in the big bands that played Newark came to the Zoo. That's what everyone called it—not the Alcazar. Tricky Sam Nanton, the trombonist, used to hang around. He was a friend of Cecil Jenkins, who was in the Alabams with Leon. Sy Oliver from Jimmie Lunceford's band would show up from time to time. They came because they all knew Leon. He had a mystical drawing power. He was charming. Everybody liked him and loved to hear him play."

Because of Eason's affability, a young girl destined to become an international star unofficially launched her career at the Alcazar. Sarah Vaughan was a teenager when "she'd sneak in the side door, and Leon would let her sing," Johnson recalled. "Pop Durham would let her do a tune or two, then he'd say, 'Daughter, you're nice, but you gotta go.'"

Because Durham was such a sport, the Zoo was a central gathering spot for Newarkers and their friends who liked a good time and good music. "All the brothers and sisters would come in straight from church on Sundays for the matinee," Johnson said. "Pop had booths, so the men could sit with their ladies. They'd all say, 'Meet you at the Zoo at one o'clock.' At two o'clock, Pop would come down and give everybody a drink. He and his wife, an Indian woman all the customers and musi-

Cladys (Jabbo) Smith with a Newark band led by Larry Ringold, early 1940s: from left, Smith, trumpet; Alexander (Buster) Stothoff, piano; Gus Young, drums; Mack Walker, bass; Ringold, saxophone. Courtesy of Lucille (Dorsey) Morton

cians called 'Mom,' lived upstairs. She was the one who really ruled the roost."

With the advent of the 1940s, Eason was in and out of the Alcazar for long stretches. One of the groups that filled in and eventually stayed was led by the legendary Jabbo Smith, perhaps the most underrated trumpeter ever to play the instrument. Despite his stature among his peers, Smith preferred Newark to New York, so much so that he stayed on, perhaps because of "some woman," perhaps because he was a small-town southerner who tended to retreat from city life. Whatever the reason, Smith shunned the limelight, opting to play at small, unknown clubs like the Alcazar.

"I lived in Newark five years," said the reticent Smith. "When I came to Newark I played first in a group with Arthur Terry, Herman Bradley, and Ike Quebec. I'm not sure where. But I played the Alcazar and the Kinney."

Smith was at the Alcazar in 1939 with a group led by Carl McIntyre. Then he formed Jabbo Smith and His Ambassadors of Swing, a combo that played for parties and other functions around town. At the Zoo, he often teamed with Alston and accompanied blues singer Albennie Jones.

"Jabbo could play the sweetest figures behind someone singin' a ballad," bassist Al Henderson recalled. "What a waste! He came here with a band that was playin' out in the Meadows during the 1939 World's Fair. The way I heard it, he got in a tussle with the union and the union socked it to him. They wanted local musicians, so they got somethin' on him, fined him, and put him out."

"Jabbo was just a nice guy," said emcee Joe Gregory. "He was always smilin' and would listen to your ideas. You could learn a lot from him. No matter where he went, he always had his trumpet. Always."

Later, the band at the Alcazar—with Johnson still a member—was led by Larry Ringold, a talented musician who played many instruments and was a fine arranger.

Pop Durham continued to do business at the corner of Waverly Avenue and Barclay Street into the 1950s and 1960s. Eventually, business slackened and Pop sold the property to the City of Newark. In 1980, Johnson, who idolized his former boss, bought a bar on Sixteenth Avenue in Irvington, near the Newark line, and named it the New Alcazar. At the opening, Durham, then in his nineties, was the guest of honor. He died later that year. Today, the voices of children playing outside the Louise A. Spencer Elementary School ring out at the spot where Eason, Smith, and Johnson once made some of Newark's best music.

The Pipers —Clickin' at the Pic

Chapter 18

I've got you under my spell;
How long I can't tell.
When you love and touch me,
Sure does upset me;
Don't stop now!
(Words and music by William Campbell)

Those were the opening lines of the song that topped Newark's black hit parade in 1942, a popular tune that became a hit on jukeboxes up and down the East Coast. "Don't Stop Now" was so appealing it prompted Herman Lubinsky of Savoy Records to stop by the Picadilly at Waverly and Peshine avenues in Newark to see what all the hubub was about.

Lubinsky not only liked what he heard, but realized he had a potential blockbuster on his hands—at least, locally. Barely missing a beat, he invited the Picadilly Pipers—Clem Moorman, Al Henderson, and Ernie Ransome, along with their pert little vocalist Melba (Bonnie) Smith—to a recording studio to wax the song

and several others. The way Henderson figured it, seventy thousand or more records were sold, virtually all the profits going to Lubinsky and Savoy and just a pittance to the Pipers.

The Pipers, whose original vocalist was Jewel Collins, were the first hit act at the Picadilly at Waverly and Peshine avenues in Newsicians and performers worked from inside the bar. "I don't think there were more than twenty, maybe thirty barstools," said writer Connie (Williams) Woodruff. "The audience either sat at the bar or stood. It was a very, very small place."

Until 1941, when the club changed hands and became the Picadilly, it was called the Kit Kat Club, a favorite watering hole where drummer Gus Young entertained seven nights a week. When it became the Pic, it was run by Georgie Haber and Roddy Rodberg, alleged associates of city crime bosses who had a stranglehold on virtually every illegal activ-

Bonnie (Davis) Smith, left, and the original Picadilly Pipers, early 1940s: from left, Jewel Collins, vocals; Al Henderson, bass; Clem Moorman (holding guitar), piano; Ernie Ransome, guitar. Courtesy of Clem Moorman and Al Henderson

ity in the Third Ward, especially those run by blacks.

"The white club owners always took care of the people in the neighborhoods," said Woodruff. "Most of them were Jews. Many of the people in the colored neighborhoods were domestics and chauffeurs who worked in their homes. Some were their customers. They could always run a tab at places like the Pic, if they wanted. The boys [mobsters] always made sure they had food or anything else they needed. Sometimes, they bought surplus food and distributed it."

For Neal Patterson, whose family lived upstairs over the Pic in a five-room railroad flat, life was an unending series of thrills. "When we were real little the entertainers thought we were cute kids, and used to toss us nickels and

dimes," said Patterson, who became a Newark police lieutenant. "When I got older, we'd all line up on the firescape on the side of the building, pretending to play the piano as we looked inside."

At thirteen, Patterson came face to face with jazz great Charlie Parker. "Hank Mobley [the terrific tenor saxophonist who went on to play with Dizzy Gillespie] was in charge of Monday jazz sessions. A lot of the New York stars would come. That's how I met Bird," he recalled. "I was just a kid, but he took the time to talk to me. He was a real nice guy.

"We never thought of the music as noise or an annoyance," said Patterson, whose mother worked at Unique Art, a toy factory directly across the street from the Pic, and whose stepfather was employed at the nearby Reynolds factory, which manufactured foil food wrappers. "We listened to it at night, and it was beautiful."

Like most of Newark's other neighborhood nightclubs, the Pic was nondescript, a simple clapboard building at the corner of Waverly and Peshine avenues in the old Third Ward, topped by four second-floor flats. Its *pièce de résistance* was its blue and white awning, stretching from the front door to the sidewalk, beckoning patrons from the Peshine Avenue side.

The Pic's interior was dominated by an oval bar with a piano in the middle. Risers holding a few tables were situated on either side, while a rear hallway led down a couple of steps to a cubbyhole on the Peshine Avenue side of the building decorated like a grass shack and called the Tahitian Room. That was where Bill Goode held sway on piano and organ and the musicians played for tips during their breaks.

As tiny as it was and inconsequential as it seemed, the Pic attracted a string of top hometown acts, first the Pipers, then the Velvetones and Madhatters. When the local entertainment wasn't varied enough, the owners looked to New York, booking some of the biggest names in show business as the main attractions, including Parker, Erroll Garner, and singer Ruth Brown. Even Billie Holiday played the Pic.

Three shows a night were staged on weekends, while Goode and other keyboard artists kept things lively in the Tahitian Room. "If You Click at the Pic, You'll Click With the World." That was the club's motto. The Pipers, with Moorman on piano and Solovox, Henderson on bass, Ransome on guitar and tipple, and Smith handling the vocals, was the group most closely associated with it.

Smith, who recorded on Savoy as Bonnie Davis, was a co-ed from Bessemer, Alabama when she "got the singing bug and headed for New York," according to Moorman, whom she eventually married. "Until then, she wanted to be a teacher. For three years, she was a student at Alabama State on a scholarship from U.S. Steel."

After landing a job in New York with Teddy Hill's band in the late 1930s, Smith was booked into the Picadilly in 1942. With a boom in business created by defense plant workers out to spend some of the money they were making by working double shifts, the Pic and other local clubs increasingly turned to importing entertainers from Harlem, depending less on local talent. "Eddie Mosby, the manager, would contact Do Pop—he was a singer and songwriter—and he'd send singers over to the Picadilly," Moorman noted. "Bonnie became the favorite singer."

As the Pic's house band, the Pipers adopted a breezy style on the order of the Nat King Cole Trio. Moorman wrote much of their material, sharing the vocals with his wife-to-be on a number of catchy little tunes like "Upstairs."

"Union musicians were on strike at the time," said Henderson, "so when Lubinsky came looking for us at the Picadilly to record, we had to use another name. Or else, we'da lost our cards." The pseudonym chosen— probably by Lubinsky—was the Bonnie Davis Trio. On some records, it became the Bunny Banks Trio.

From the perspective of female fans, Ransome, nicknamed "Skeets," was the definite draw. "Ernie was very handsome, and everyone liked him," Henderson said. "He wasn't a great musician—he played the tipple like an overgrown ukelele—but he could pick out tunes and do alright. And he sang ballads that all the women liked. We played the Pic easy three or four years. We were there when Pearl Harbor was bombed. It was a Sunday afternoon. We were playin' a matinee, and we heard about it over the radio."

When Moorman and Ransome left Newark in 1943 to play a string of engagements in Philadelphia and Atlantic City, Henderson took over the trio at the Pic, hiring Pete Diggs on vibes and Johnnie Bell, a pianist, as the vocalist: "Johnnie was a good left-handed piano player and he sang good," Henderson said. "He and his wife both turned preachers. They had a temple up at Springfield and Belmont."

Two of the most popular male singers to play the Pic were Merle Turner, the Erskine Hawkins vocalist, and Tony Jenkins, who sang

Smooth singer Tony Jenkins at Dodger's, mid 1940s. The band members are unidentified. Courtesy of Jackson (Flap) McQueen

for a while with Andy Kirk's band. Turner doubled as a bartender at the Pic in the early 1940s. After serving in the military, he was booked into two other Newark clubs, the Twin-lite (Three Deuces) and Fredericks' Lounge (the old Boston Plaza). Jenkins, whose arsenal when he arrived at the Pic in 1946 included an array of romantic numbers like "Begin the Beguine," was described by one reviewer as "being able to sing anything, anytime, anywhere."

The Velvetones, who made several well-received recordings, took over at the Pic in the summer of 1945. With the exception of Enoch Martin, the piano player and arranger and a graduate of Barringer High School, the quar-

tet's members were alumni of Newark's South Side High School. Sam Rucker, who played guitar and sang first baritone, lived nearby on Spruce Street, while Madison Flanagan lived on Somerset Street. Walter Dawkins, who later sang with the Ray-O-Vacs and ran the Key Club, was the fourth member.

During 1945, the Velvetones made six recordings on Coronet, including "One Day," "Easy, Baby," and "Sweet Lorraine," then signed with Sonora. On Sonora, Pops Little replaced Dawkins.

Eddie Mosby, who began his nightclub career as manager at Skateland, also was responsible for bringing another popular singing group, the Madhatters, to the Pic in 1945. For the next two years, the group was in and out of the Pic, doing four shows nightly, featuring Linwood Proctor. Don Banks was on guitar and a fellow named Gary played bass.

By the end of World War II, almost every big name in show business had played Newark at one time or other. During one three-week stretch in 1947, for example, Una Mae Carlisle was holding forth at the Pic at the same time singers Savannah Churchill, Dinah Washington, and Madeline Green, comedian Mantan Moreland, and balladeer Warren Evans were appearing at other black clubs in the city. Lil Green, whose big hit, "Romance in the Dark," was on top of the charts, was on her way into town. By 1950, the Pic had turned to a "stars only" format, booking acts like pianist Billy Taylor and his quartet and Erroll Garner. Shut down in the 1950s, the Pic became an old tire shop. It was demolished in 1968. Today, the Harold Wilson School occupies the property where Newarkers once thrilled to the music of some of the world's greatest jazz artists.

Dodger's Bar and Grill –The Suburban Draw
Chapter 19

While the Kinney Club was catering to high livers and the city's sporting life and the Nest Club was drawing neighborhood folks, Dodger's Bar and Grill, 8 Bedford Street, was the social hub of the black middle class. A good part of its trade was built on the following of suburbanites from nearby towns like Montclair, Summit, and Morristown, along with Newark's in crowd.

"Dodger's was one of the most popular places in Newark at the time," said Celeste Jones, who often sang there. "The people from Montclair and places like that used to come on Sundays. I used to sit in a corner and watch them. They used to laugh and get drunk and do the same things everybody else used to do, even though they were supposed to be dicty [high class]."

Before it began offering entertainment in the mid 1930s, the club was a nondescript bar owned by "Old Man" Campisi, whose family lived upstairs. Then it was called the Club Par-adise. Ma and Pa (Josh) Frazier operated it for two years or so afterward, but turned it back to the Campisis' son, Gus, a small-time gangster, in the late 1930s.

The Fraziers, who were black, and their partner, Wes Saunders, also ran the popular Omega Bar and Grill in Roselle. At Dodger's they began staging "All-Star Revues" featuring top local talent. Among an ever-changing array of emcees were Johnny B. Gardner, Charlie Matthews, Thad (Chuck) Howard, Abe (Snakehips) Moore, Bob Taylor, Ernie Ransome, and Jimmy Anderson.

Among the first entertainers to play Dodger's were Milton Pittman, whose band played from a little gallery near the ceiling, and a blues singer named Hattie Dukes, who went to work in a defense plant after World War II. Two of the most popular emcees were Satchel Robinson and Charlie Matthews, suave and sophisticated performers who set female patrons' hearts aflutter.

Patrons at a Newark nightclub, mid 1940s. The woman in black, center, is Annabelle Sellers. Courtesy of Lucille (Dorsey) Morton

Matthews was a teenager when he took over as emcee. Born in Daleville, Alabama in 1917, he moved to Newark from Philadelphia while he was in grammar school: "I came from Philly doin' the five-tap Charleston. After a while I started going down to the rehearsal hall where Bill Chapman and Arthur [Prince] Hall used to dance. They were my classmates. Bill and Arthur started teaching me new steps, 'specially the time step."

Around 1935 Matthews joined the Works Progress Administration (WPA) Federal Theater Project, where he met Charles Walker: "They called him 'Cornbread.' He taught me a lot of new things Bill and Arthur didn't know. There were certain basic routines everybody could do, certain steps that were interchangeable."

Tall, handsome, and driven by a desire to

make money and a name for himself, Matthews began "going around on gigs" with Chapman and Ike Quebec, then a hoofer and piano player: "One night Bill invited me up on stage at the Colony Club and from then on I started getting paid jobs. The first ones were at white spots, Glockie's and Pat and Don's in Harrison."

When the Fraziers hired Matthews to emcee their shows at Dodger's he stayed three years, teaming with the best entertainers in Newark. They included Emma Hawkins, the "Queen of the Blues," singers Louise Gordon and Billie Sermond, bandleaders Sonny Murray and Hubert Ravenue, and pianist June Cole, whose brother, Cozy, was the famous drummer. "I'd open the show by saying, Good evening, ladies and gentlemen. Here we are meeting you once again from the mecca of New Jersey's gay

Satchel Robinson in a publicity shot, circa 1940. From author's collection

night life, Dodger's Grill, 8 Bedford Street. This is show time, and show time is your time. Then I'd break into a little song and dance, usually 'Whatcha Gonna Do When There Ain't No Swing,' or 'Sing Me a Swing Song and Let Me Dance.' Sometimes I'd do 'I've Got Rhythm' as the band joined in and the drummer picked up the beat."

At Dodger's, Matthews also found romance:

"Emma Hawkins, who was about thirty-five, took a liking to me and did everything she could to help me. When she demanded a raise, she demanded one for me, too. Wasn't long before I was makin' five dollars more a week. My specialty was swing tunes. I also was one of the few male performers to do 'ups.' In between shows, you had to do an 'up.' That's how I started singin'. You couldn't dance on an up."

As a song and dance man, Matthews teamed with Ernie Ransome or Abe (Snakehips) Moore for WPA shows at the Adams and Empire theaters: "Ernie and I had a little number we did together. He would be like a straight man for me. We'd pick up stuff. We'd go to shows and steal material. At the time, they were paying laborers fifteen dollars a week, so we were making big money—forty-seven dollars every two weeks. At the same time I was working at Dodger's and later at the Nest Club."

Thursday nights at Dodger's in the late 1930s were devoted to amateur nights given by Guy Gordon, mini-versions of those taking place at New York's Apollo Theater. The two winners got to appear at the grill on Saturday and Sunday nights. The black press described the contestants as "ambitious . . . swarming the place while seeking their first break."

One of the most popular bandleaders at Dodger's was Herman Bradley, a drummer who led the Rhythm Dons, forerunner of the Savoy Sultans. From the time Bradley organized the band in 1933 it had tremendous popular appeal, first at the Old Pasadena Club on Orange Street near the East Orange city boundary, then at Dodger's.

On Bedford Street, the Dons reigned over Sunday night jam sessions, lively events that brought swingsters spilling out of the suburbs. Early signs of the band's abilities became evident at band battles staged at the Essex Theater at the foot of Springfield Avenue where the Dons warred with Pancho Diggs's band in a nightclub band versus dance band format.

In bassist Wes Clark's opinion, the Dons were the best band in town, especially when they went head to head with other groups in the band battles: "Me, Little Willie [Nelson]—he could hit those high notes and hold them—

Slim Henderson, and Teddy Brannon. We took it all. There was always a contest at Dodger's."

In the spring of 1939, Dodger's began sponsoring jam sessions on Monday afternoons in an unsuccessful attempt to revive its sagging business. Fortunately, a letdown in live entertainment did not last long. With the start of World War II, jobs became plentiful—even in the black community. Workers, with newfound cash to spend, were out in droves looking for fun. "It was a war economy and the factories were booming," said pianist Duke Anderson. "People often had to work two shifts—sixteen straight hours—if they wanted to keep their jobs. When they were off, they wanted a good time. That meant plenty of business for the clubs and for us musicians."

To attract new patrons, club owners began pumping profits into renovations. In early 1943, Dodger's announced a gala "grand opening" to show off its spiffy new decor. The focal point of "the new, bigger and better Dodger's Cocktail Lounge" was a huge oval bar, surrounded by red-topped, softly upholstered chromium stools, shiny new metal bar tables, and red leather chairs. The old entrance was sealed and what formerly was the bar became a four-step balcony, reaching from the new entrance about midway into the room. All of this was set off by knotty pine wainscoting, inlaid linoleum, and colorful Venetian blinds.

On opening night, Gertrude Turman, Fannie Akridge, and Skippy Williams, a fair-skinned beauty who was Gus Campisi's girlfriend, provided the entertainment. Soon, the emphasis turned to importing bigger names, spurred in part by the loss of local musicians to the war effort. Boots Marshall, formerly the emcee at Harlem on Hudson on the Jersey Palisades, was brought in to head the revues. Williams, a vocalist/comedienne who sometimes entertained at the Kinney Club, had the run of the place—coordinating shows, singing, and serving as mistress of ceremonies when necessary. She subsequently became the vocalist with Mandy Ross's Orchestra.

"Everyone knew she was Gus's girlfriend. Gus was like the Godfather," said Anderson. "Skippy could go anywhere she wanted in

Piano player Humphrey (Teddy) Brannon and trumpeter Herb Scott, mid 1930s. Courtesy of Wesley (Wes) Clark

Newark and do anything she wanted. The cops didn't bother her, and they didn't bother Gus. The cops never came near Dodger's."

"For me, Dodger's was like my kitchen sink," explained Miss Rhapsody. "Gus was a great person to work for. He was real nice and almost as quiet as Jay [June] Cole." A favorite at Dodger's, Rhap dispensed tunes like "Hey

Lawdy Mama" and "Bye, Bye Baby" from inside the bar where the band played. When she took off again for Washington in 1944, "they put Bea Morton in my place. She had big busts and she'd slap 'em in your face or on your head. I don't know why. She had a voice, but she insisted on doin' all this other stuff."

Another popular singer at Dodger's was Lillian Highe, who appeared in Lew Leslie's *Blackbirds* in 1925. She was a versatile stylist with a repertoire ranging from a distinctive version of "Wagon Wheels" to a compelling interpretation of "On the Sentimental Side."

Herb Scott was also a top draw, rolling the crowds in the aisles by playing his trumpet upside down on "Mrs. Skeffington" and delivering "I Can't Give You Anything but Love, Baby" in rapid-fire pantomime. "Scotty would take his trumpet and turn it upside down. Instead of pressing these fingers [demonstration], he had his hands backwards," Wes Clark said. "He'd play solos that way. I've never seen another trumpet player do it."

In 1949, Bill Cook, a radio personality who managed singer Roy Hamilton, took the helm at Dodger's. Under Cook's management, the establishment became the Caravan Club. "Caravan" was Cook's theme song and "Musical Caravan" was the title of his radio show. On opening night, the bill read like a mini "Who's Who" of show business. The guest artists, according to the ads, included Buddy Johnson, Sarah Vaughan, Illinois Jacquet, Ella Johnson, Arthur Prysock, George Shearing, and Al Hibbler.

One of the most popular entertainers to play the Caravan was Little Jimmy Scott, a wisp of a man with a falsetto voice who catapulted to international fame with his Roost recording of "The Masquerade Is Over." By the time Scott arrived in Newark, he was a veteran of the Lionel Hampton Orchestra and had recorded more than a half-dozen songs on Decca with Hamp, including "Everybody's Somebody's Fool" and "I Wish I Didn't Love You So."

"Tiny Prince deserves a lot of credit for helping a lot of us," said Scott. "He said, 'C'mon, man, work with me.' Tiny was doin' a little jive promoting at that time, and he was running *After Hours* [a magazine about Newark nightlife]. Anybody who was anybody mingled here in Newark," added Scott, a Cleveland native who made Newark his "real home." "They played Newark, then they'd jump off to New York. They'd leave here and go on to their successes."

Despite Cook's efforts, the Caravan never attained the magnetism of Dodger's. In the early 1950s, bandleader Jerry Bogar and his wife, Nancy, made another valiant effort at getting it going, but were forced to sell it again little more than a year later when business foundered. Like the other nightclubs of its genre, it eventually gave way to the wrecking ball. In the 1970s, low-income housing was built on the site by the New Community Corporation of Newark.

TWO INSTITUTIONS

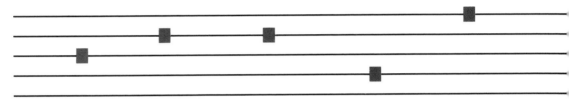

1939–49

The Coleman Hotel —"For Negroes Only"
Chapter 20

When black entertainers played Newark they generally had a choice of staying at a rooming house or with a friend. As in the rest of the nation, the city's public accommodations were strictly segregated. Until the Coleman Brothers seized on the idea in the 1940s, there was no major hotel that catered to blacks. Because of the brothers' ingenuity, the Coleman Hotel on Court Street near Washington became a hub of black entertainment and social life, and they were counted among Newark's most successful black businessmen.

Centrally located in the heart of the city's tenderloin district, the hotel was just two blocks from Broad Street and barely a block from the old Orpheum Theater, which had been renamed the Newark Opera House in 1937 and was struggling to stay afloat by staging popular revues. Every inch of the hotel had a purpose. From the ground-floor lounge, radio programs were broadcast to the black community. The basement housed a restaurant, a bar-

ber shop, and a recording studio, where the Coleman label was launched.

The Colemans' success was built on their knowledge of the entertainment industry. The brothers were prominent entertainers, pioneers on the order of Sister Rosetta Tharpe, who popularized church music by performing in night clubs. Their initial investment in the hotel came from the money they made entertaining on nationwide radio and in theaters and clubs. Six nights a week, fifteen minutes a night, they had their own WCBS radio program. When President Roosevelt died in 1945, they performed three nights straight in tribute to the fallen leader, singing "almost every hymn or spiritual ever written."

Russell Coleman, barely seventeen when he joined the group in the mid 1930s, still contends that Lander, one of his older brothers, was the only one in the clan who really could sing: "The rest of us just hid behind him," he demurred. But the Colemans' harmony was so

The Coleman Hotel, mid 1940s. Courtesy of Lander Coleman and the Rev. Russell Coleman

at his nitery of the same name in Greenwich Village.

When the Colemans sang, their most faithful fan sat front and center each night—their mother. "Our father never did approve of our singing in nightclubs," said Russell, retired pastor of Newark's Zion Baptist Church. "To me, music was music—pop, jazz, or whatever—but he never took to the idea. He was a preacher, a Baptist minister just like our grandfather—in Virginia where we came from."

"My father's mind was on his church and his pastoring," said Lander Coleman, the group's lead singer. "He didn't know the name of a club, even if you called it. He was strict, so strict I shudder now just to think of him." Their mother, on the other hand, was their staunchest ally. "Except for when we were on the road, she attended every one of our performances for twenty-five, maybe thirty years," Russell noted. In all, the Reverend William Coleman and his wife, Lillie, had twelve children—ten sons, seven of whom were musical, and two daughters.

As far back as Lander or Russell can remember there was a Coleman Brothers singing group. "The first was my uncles on my father's side," explained Lander, the sixth born. "My father's younger brothers [Levi, Lewis, Matthew, and David] started the quartet. That was around 1918. My father couldn't sing a note. When they came to Newark—to New Jersey— they were singin'. That was the [family's] first quartet, the first Coleman Brothers. They sang standard hymns and spirituals. I can remember them singing 'Ezekiel Saw the Wheel.' Another one was 'When the Roll Is Called Up Yonder' and 'Walking in the Light.' Another they used to sing was 'My Lord Said If You Go, I Go With You.' They'd just get a tune and rearrange it to suit their harmonizing. No music. No nothing. Just four voices. It was the same way when we first started off. We had no music, no accompaniment at all.

"My older brothers was the second Coleman Brothers—Everette, Wallace, and Jack—with two friends, Robert Tippins and Howard Har-

special, so gloriously uplifting, that Barney Josephson, a prominent New York nightclub owner, believed their sacred music could attract patrons in a secular setting. In 1947, Josephson, who had integrated jazz by hiring Billie Holiday, booked the Coleman Brothers into Cafe Society uptown. At the same time, singer/guitarist Josh White was the headliner

The singing Coleman Brothers, mid 1940s: Everette on guitar; center, Lander, Melvin, and Russell; rear, Wallace and Danny Owens. Courtesy of Lander Coleman and the Reverend Russell Coleman

ris. Then, around 1927, when we were living in Glassboro, New Jersey, my brothers Octavius [then sixteen], Melvin [fourteen], and I formed the Jubilee Four with Robert Bright, who was just twelve, Sidney Russell, and Leroy Thomas.

"We joined in with our older brothers in 1932. The third Coleman Brothers singing group was composed of Wallace, Everette, me, Russell, and Melvin. Danny Owens, who later sang with the Four Tunes, was the sixth. That was the group that made the records and sang on the radio.

"In the beginning, our uncle used to take us out to Reading, Pennsylvania or Nyack, New York. He was a minister, too. He started us off in his church. Whatever was in the offering, we split fifty-fifty. Sometimes we got fifteen cents each, sometimes a little more. That was big money then: thirty-five or forty cents in one night. We used to sing at Adam Clayton Powell's Church in Harlem—Abyssinian Baptist—and at the Golden Gate Auditorium. Promoters would hire us to sing at all the big auditoriums.

"We gave our first anniversary [concert] at the Robert Treat School in Newark. We were the ones who started the idea of having all the other groups join in. That was in 1933. The second anniversary was in Orange at the armory. That place was just filled to capacity. We had a guard there that night. There was no black police officers on the force then. He was a special. Slim O'Neill. He was watching at the door, when we was collecting the money. He was tall, like a giant. I think it was thirty cents to get in, children fifteen. We had a six or seven hundred dollar house and that was money back in those days.

"Over the years I worked with several other groups while my brothers continued to sing together [in various configurations]. In 1934, I toured sixty Warner Brothers theaters on the East Coast with the Chain Gang Quartet, mostly up in New York State. We started out at the Steel Pier in Atlantic City. Robert E. Burns, who escaped from a Georgia chain gang and settled in New Jersey, told his story on stage and we sang, mostly spirituals. His story was made into the movie *I Am a Fugitive from a Chain Gang*, starring Paul Muni. Years later I sang at his funeral. At that time, we were making twenty-two dollars per man, working on the Steel Pier [in Atlantic City]. That was big money."

From 1935 to 1942, with Lander as soloist, the Coleman Brothers made a series of tours through the South and West and were heard regularly on two New Jersey radio stations, WHBI in Newark and WPAT out of Paterson. The biggest break in their career—a move that propelled them to national attention—came in 1943, when Milton Lesnik became their manager. Under Lesnik's tutelage, the brothers signed with Decca records and WABC radio and were booked into Cafe Society. Soon after they became the "staff vocal group" at WCBS radio. Then, in 1948 and part of 1949, they were on staff at WRL in Cincinnati. A number of their records on Decca were long-selling hits, among them "Low Down the Chariot," "Milky White Way," and "My Prayer"—the spiritual version.

"The first time we sang in a nightclub was at Cafe Society, but that was years later," said Lander. "As a teenager, I used to work in the Nest Club [in Newark], but not as the Coleman Brothers. I had a side group called the Four Shadows. We did Mills Brothers type singing. Around 1931–32. James and John Norris and Robert Tippins, who was with the second Coleman Brothers, were in it. The Norrises grew up right here [in Newark] on West Kinney Street. John played a little tenor guitar—four strings. Tippins liked my voice and he contacted me to become the fourth member of the group. We sang whatever part the song called for. If one couldn't make it, we'd just switch that part."

Many entertainers squandered away earnings that seemed like a small fortune at the time, but not the Colemans. Together, they pumped their profits into a chain of businesses in Newark, where their family settled after coming north in 1925. In 1944, they pooled twenty thousand dollars and bought the seventy-two-room hotel on Court Street where the parking lot of *The Star-Ledger* presently is situated. "We sold every one of our cars except one

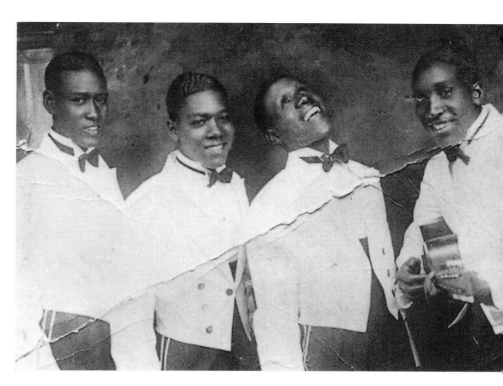

The Four Shadows, 1933: from left, Robert Tippins, Lander Coleman, James Norris, and John Norris. Courtesy of Lander Coleman

and put together every dollar we had to get it," said Russell. "At that time, twenty thousand dollars was a fortune."

Black ownership of the hotel filled a void in Newark and proved to be a smart venture. As many musicians attest, they often "went home with some woman" just for a decent place to stay. The Colemans knew the scene. "When we were traveling, we'd stay in the Y or some little honky tonky rooming house," Lander explained. "I'll never forget a little place in Toledo, Ohio. They called it the Ritz Plaza. Or the York Hotel in Baltimore. When we walks in the place that night, the guy's showin' us the rooms. Everything was just clean and white, but when he pulled on the light a row of roaches walked across the bedspread, just like they were following one another. We turned around and went right out. Was no way to sleep.

"We had the first real black hotel in Newark. They had a couple of little joints. The Grand Hotel. Little honky-tonk places. In our hotel, Sonny Oliver had a barbershop in the basement. And we had a recording studio operat-

ing down there. Then we had the cocktail lounge. Brooks Alexander used to sing and Emerson Yearwood used to sing and play piano. Millard Thomas played the organ. He was the guy who wrote 'My Prayer.' He played for the Coleman Brothers when we were on staff at WRL. We just had piano or organ music. No groups. Sometimes Henry Polite would sing, too." According to Russell Coleman, Polite was "Mr. Everything" at the hotel—"our manager, the bartender, and the cook, too," as well as the employee who catered to its famous guests.

Dinah Washington stayed at the hotel," said Lander. "So did Big Maybelle. Ruth Brown. Billie Holiday. Little Jimmy Scott. When they was playing anywhere in the area, they'd stay. Sometimes they'd be singing in Newark, maybe at the Hi Spot or the Hi Hat, sometimes in New York."

When the Colemans started their record company "down in the basement," they turned first for talent to local artists like June Cole and Google Eyes, whose big number was "I'm a Young Boy." Probably the most important record issued on the Coleman label was "I'll Al-

The Ray-O-Vacs, mid 1940s: from left, Lester Harris, vocals/cocktail drums; Jackson (Flap) McQueen, bass; Joe Crump, piano; Leoparte (Chink) Kinney, saxophone. Courtesy of Lucille (Dorsey) Morton

ways Be in Love With You," a tune made popular by the Ray-O-Vacs, a local singing group. While the tune remained popular enough to warrant reissuing by Decca, it never made any real money for the foursome or for the Colemans.

"We were cheated," asserted Lander. "Herman Lubinsky of Savoy Records took it and made a master. No permission. No nothin'. Then he sold it all over the South. He had all the money, so we couldn't do nothin' about it." In the long run, though, he acknowledged, "Lubinsky gave a lot of artists a lift. He gave them a start. Otherwise, their talent might never have been recorded."

Aside from their run-in with Lubinsky, the Coleman Hotel and the record business con-

tinued to thrive. In 1950, three of the brothers bought a place called Ernie's Fishing Club at 81 West Street, "put up a little motel in back," and called it the Dreamboat.

"Wilbert Harrison, who sang 'Kansas City,' started off there," said Lander. "Sam Cooke used to work in there. So did Wynonie Harris, the Ray-O-Vacs, Carrie Smith, and Larry Darnell. In the 1960s I put up two brand new buildings down along the [Passaic] river and ran that myself. That was the Dreamboat, too. That was during the time the hotel was closing."

Eventually, the hotel was razed, but the Dreamboat still stands along the river. In early 1991, it was a nightclub known as After Hours.

Herman Lubinsky and Savoy Records

Chapter 21

One of the key figures on Newark's music scene in the 1930s and 1940s—a man despised by black musicians—was a colorful character named Herman Lubinsky. Lubinsky owned the Radio Record Shop, 58 Market Street, now a parking lot for Macy's (formerly Bamberger's department store). More importantly, he founded the Savoy Record Company, one of the industry's most successful independent labels.

Lubinsky was a short, stubby cigar smoker, endowed with a shrewd business sense. His initial formula for success appropriated the idea Columbia records used to corner new trade two decades earlier—race records. In the mid 1940s, he expanded his business by recording key innovators in the transition from swing to bop, capturing the youthful tones of artists like Charlie Parker, Miles Davis, and Dexter Gordon. Next, the company branched out, though less successfully, to rhythm and blues, recording artists like Varetta Dillard, Big Maybelle, and Nappy Brown. In the 1960s

and 1970s, Savoy's emphasis shifted once again, this time to gospel music, a highly successful venture that made church singers like the Reverend James Cleveland and Dorothy Norwood household names in black neighborhoods nationwide.

Officially, Savoy was launched in late 1942 with the release of four tunes by the Savoy Dictators Lubinsky had recorded in a hall above Harris's tavern in 1939. The company remained in business in Newark until Lubinsky's death in 1974, when his heirs sold everything but the gospel rights to Arista.

Initially, Lubinsky sought out the top talent at local clubs. In the late 1930s, Newark had joints jumping on every corner of the Barbary Coast. With jukeboxes gaining popularity, Lubinsky realized he was onto something big. His real love was electronics, but he also sold used records out of his radio parts store. It was this endeavor that paved his entry into the recording business.

Stories about Lubinsky's avarice are leg-

Herman Lubinsky and Viola Wells (Miss Rhapsody) at a Savoy recording session, 1944: the musicians, from left, Freddy Webster, trumpet; Eddie (Lockjaw) Davis, saxophone; Cozy Cole, drums; Harold Underhill, guitar; Billy Taylor, bass; June Cole, piano. Courtesy of Sheldon Harris

endary. Clearly, he was obsessed by money and went to extraordinary lengths to get and save it. On balance, he was a complex, often contradictory, man. One of his friends recalled how he would circle and recircle the block of his New York apartment in search of a parking spot. Yet his wife and children didn't drive so he often sent them home by taxi.

"He was paranoid about money," his eldest daughter, Lois Grossberg, revealed. "It consumed him like a burning fire. He had a reputation as an ogre in the business. You had no

idea of the cheapness. He paid his bills, but he was always arguing with the repairmen. He always thought he was getting gypped. Other than a Fleetwood Cadillac and a boat at the Shore, he didn't have any simple pleasures. He never enjoyed his money."

In 1924, Lubinsky launched New Jersey's first radio station, WNJ, from the attic of his house at 89 Lehigh Avenue in Newark. "We had a tower in the backyard," Lois recalled. "My father called himself Alex Smith. That was his radio name. I guess he chose it not to sound

Jewish. He was gearing himself to black people."

Fifteen years later, Lubinsky entered the recording business. By today's standards it was no big deal. He simply took a crude recording machine to a warehouse over Fatty Harris's tavern at William and Halsey streets and invited the Dictators to perform. Although the records were not immediately released, they gave birth to Savoy Records.

"It spoils my whole day to mention Herman Lubinsky," said Al Henderson, the Dictators' leader. "There ain't nobody who has ever had a kind word to say about him. The S.O.B. was the worst thief in the world. He made millions on us [black musicians] and he wouldn't pay you nothin'."

To Henderson, each detail of the events that day at Harris's remained painfully clear. "We had Clem Moorman on piano, Danny Gibson on drums, Bobby Plater on alto. Count Hastings was on tenor, Hal Mitchell and Chippie Outcalt on trumpets, Howard Scott, trombone, and Willie Johnson, guitar. We made four or five sides with this little portable recording machine and a little crystal mike under the worst conditions. There were no acoustics, no studio, and the piano was outa tune. The recordings were poor, but the band was tight, so together it sounded good. We were cookin'."

Lubinsky conveniently failed to inform the band of his plans to wax records and capitalize on the musicians' popularity to sell them. To a man, they thought they were auditioning for a show. The real reason for the session became evident only after Lubinsky formed Savoy and began selling their records. "We learned later that Lubinsky had pressed a hundred records from the masters and they went like hotcakes," Henderson said. "Eventually, we got a few dollars; that was it."

Lubinsky generally had the musicians he recorded in some kind of bind. Times were hard. When they needed money, he was right there with a few bucks to fill the need. Rarely was the money commensurate with their talents.

As Henderson found: "We didn't know the potential of the recording business, but Lubinsky realized there was a lot of money in it and our band was the only band he knew in Newark. Jukeboxes were catching on and distributors were clamoring for new material."

Harold Mitchell: "We made a record, but we had no idea we were makin' one. Lubinsky had this radio tubes and parts store on the corner of Plane and Market Street at the time. All he had in it were thousands of radio tubes. Somehow, Babs [Gonzales] was involved when we made that first record. Babs was busy promotin' whatever he could promote at the time. Somehow, he hooked up with Lubinsky, who said to bring us down to this deserted warehouse up over Harris's saloon. We didn't get paid. It was supposed to be an audition.

"All he [Lubinsky] had was this broken-down upright piano that had all of sixty-six keys and this recorder that was like a standard shift car. We set up and Clem was there bangin' away, tellin' us, 'There ain't nothing [much of a piano] to play.' If you listen closely [to the records], you can hear some real odd stuff. I'd say we made about five songs, 'Heyfus Geyfus,' 'Rhythm 'n Bugs,' 'I Know Words Cannot Express,' and a couple others. [Three years later] I was out in California with Benny Carter and Babs sent me a postcard that said, 'Hey, Mitch. That motherfucker just released your record,' knowin' that I would know just who that motherfucker was. There was nothin' I could do about it at the time. When I came back, I had one great battle with Lubinsky and he finally consented to give us a penny on each record. Each of us got one-eighth of a cent. I think we collected about thirty dollars apiece."

Despite the raw deal, Henderson and Moorman got burned again in 1941, when their trio, the Picadilly Pipers, recorded "Don't Stop, Now" on Savoy. At the time, Local 16 of the musicians' union was in the midst of a strike that prohibited members from making recordings. The penalty for evading the sanction was the ultimate: loss of the member's union card.

Henderson remembered: "We were hot and Lubinsky seized on it. He came to the club and promised us two cents a record to record the

Richard (Dick) Harvest, on bass, with Robert Roebuck, drums, and Alexander (Buster) Stothoff, piano, mid 1940s. Courtesy of Meredith Gordon

number Bonnie was knockin' the customers dead with. We couldn't go under the Picadilly Pipers 'cause we'd lose our cards. So we made the recording under another name. Lubinsky had us by the balls. 'Don't Stop Now' [a hit on city jukeboxes] sold eighty thousand records. That meant Lubinsky owed us eight thousand dollars. He gave us seventy-five bucks to divide between the three of us [musicians]. There was nothin' we could do about it, and he knew it. The union would have jumped on us, 'cause the union didn't even want us [blacks] to have cards."

From the artists' perspective, Lubinsky was a wily, unethical shark out for bucks, a man who could locate a vulnerable point, then go for the jugular. The sum and substance of Lubinsky, they thought, was his desire to steal their songs and talents for a pittance of their worth. But times were hard, opportunities limited, and money tight, so they tended to set aside their fears and suspicions, succumbing to what often amounted to their only chance to record their music.

In retrospect, Lubinsky used many tactics to lure musicians to his label and sell records. His grandson, Bruce Grossberg, for example, told how he circulated a rumor that he had impregnated Varetta Dillard, one of Savoy's stars of the early 1950s, "to heighten interest in her records." Dillard was a top talent. In *Honkers and Shouters*, author Arnold Shaw described her as "singing in a style that invited comparison to Dinah Washington," purveying "R & B best-sellers from 1952 to '54." One of her biggest hits was "Johnny Has Gone," recorded in 1954 under the tutelage of Savoy's Lee Magid.

Some musicians contend Lubinsky got them drunk, then had them sign a contract for a few bucks. Some say he dealt outright, offering what he wanted and leaving it up to the performer to take it or leave it. From all indications, these business deals were a two-way street. In some instances, Lubinsky sought out the performers who recorded on Savoy. At other times, especially as his business grew, the performers came looking for him.

Fred Mendelsohn, now retired and living in Lake Worth, Florida, was one of Lubinsky's closest associates over the years. After Lubinsky's death in 1974, he ran Savoy for a decade until it was sold to Arista. Mendelsohn disputed the musicians' contentions of being cheated and used: "Herman was a very tough, hard individual, difficult to work for and often an intolerable man. But he was honest. None of the musicians really were robbed. They all signed contracts and got five percent royalties. The fact was the money for the session had to be recouped before they got royalties, not just at Savoy, at every company.

"As far as publishing was concerned, the publisher had a staunch rule. The publisher got fifty percent of the earnings and the writer got the other half. Any musician who sold his songs and retained his name as a writer should continue to receive royalties when his song is played on the air. Otherwise, he should sue. Mr. Lubinsky paid all their royalties if they were due, when they were due."

The musicians, of course, had no access to the company's books and had to rely on Lubinsky or his designees to say how many records had been sold. Many were poor and ill educated; others, simply powerless and caught in his grip. In their view, the results were generally the same: Lubinsky made whatever money there was to make while they got a few bucks and a shot at glory.

Savoy continued to flourish. By the mid 1940s, the company had recorded practically every major artist to come out of Newark, among them the Dictators, the Pipers, and Miss Rhapsody. Often, these local artists gave Lubinsky access to bigger names in the music. For Miss Rhapsody's 1944 Savoy sessions, for example, she gathered a group of some of the top musicians of the time, including drummer Cozy Cole, trumpeter Frankie Newton, and saxophonists Eddie (Lockjaw) Davis and Walter (Foots) Thomas.

The Ray-O-Vacs, a popular 1940s quartet based at Lloyd's Manor on Beacon Street in Newark, also got stung. "Lubinsky cut our money in half by bringing in the X-Rays to record our number 'I'll Always Be in Love With

Eddie Wright, guitarist, with Herb Scott's Scotty and His Frani-Kats, circa 1945: from left, front, Bill Goode, drums/vocals; Wright; Frank (Red) Brown, piano; rear, Scott, trumpet; Al Best, bass. Courtesy of Wesley (Wes) Clark

You,' said leader Jackson (Flap) McQueen. "He bought the masters from the Coleman Brothers [who made the original] and got all the royalties. We coulda killed 'im."

Eddie Wright, who played guitar with Four Bars and a Melody, told this tale: "I used to see Lubinsky a lot at Penn Station and he'd always say, 'You're the only guy who ever made money off me.' I was a businessman, so when he wanted us to record I got a fabulous

Trombonist Clyde Bernhardt in a publicity shot, circa 1982. Courtesy of Clyde Bernhardt

sum. I got a thousand dollars just to do 'Near You'—just that one tune. And it was a hit.

More often than not, the artists' dealings with Lubinsky resulted in a love-hate relationship. To this day, many of those who didn't record when he came calling consider it a badge of honor.

Leon Eason is one of those proud men who refused Savoy's offers to record. "Lubinsky was a thief," Eason asserted, accenting the final word. "He used people. But he never got me."

"I was afraid of him," admitted Clyde Bernhardt, who also turned down all invitations to record on Savoy.

"Lubinsky got me out of the business," stated singer Nate Brown. "He wanted me to sing the blues, but said I didn't sound negroid enough. With that, I got out of the cab we were in on the way to a studio and caught a cab back home."

For all his avarice, Lubinsky was a key contributor to Newark's music history. If local musicians didn't record for Savoy, they probably didn't record at all. Their only legacies are their live performances, etched in the memories of those who heard them in their prime, recollections faded and lost over time.

Said Tiny Prince, who covered the nightclub scene for the *Herald News* in the 1940s: "There's no doubt everybody hated Herman Lubinsky. If he messed with you, you were messed. At the same time, some of those people—many of Newark's top singers and musicians—would never have been exposed to records if he didn't do what he did. Except for Lubinsky, all the hot little numbers, like Buddy Johnson's 'Cherry,' would have been lost. The man may have been hated, but he saved a lot of our history—for us and for future generations."

A NEW GROOVE

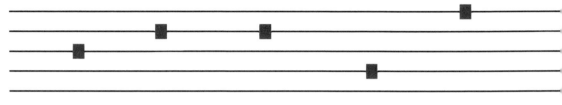

1942-50

Ike Quebec
–Torrid Tenor
Chapter 22

Ike Quebec, who was born in Newark, was one of the world's greatest saxophonists in the 1940s, an innovator whose ideas and associations made him an early proponent of a new style of music—bebop. In the course of his short life, little more than four decades, he propelled his way to musical stardom among his peers and jazz aficionados. Critic Leonard Feather described Quebec, who was equally at ease with slow blues or soaring swing, as "a superior tenor man of the [Coleman] Hawkins school with a big tone and firm, vigorous style." Jazz historian Bob Porter called him "one of the best tenor players who ever lived." Writer Michael Cuscuna concluded: "Ike was the man who knew all the modern innovators and urged them to consider this music [bebop]." Quebec's enthusiasm, Cuscuna believes, was "pivotal" in moving the Blue Note label beyond traditional jazz and boogie woogie to more progressive musical forms as the 1950s arrived.

Ike was a teenager living on Avon Place in Newark's old Third Ward when he broke into show business in the early 1930s. He was playing piano—just beginning to noodle around on sax—when Little Sadie Matthews, a veteran performer, got him a job at Dave and Maney's on Parrow Street in Orange, where she was singing the blues. To her, Ike was "just a young kid" accompanist. Little did she—or anyone else for that matter—surmise that Ike would become a world premiere tenor player—and so quickly. By the time Quebec was in his mid twenties he had been in and out of Cab Calloway's orchestra and was emerging as one of the jazz idiom's most original instrumentalists.

Matthews recalled: "I laugh when I think back on Ike. He lived right across the street from me. Every night he'd drive me to work 'cause I didn't have no car. Just when I'd be out on the floor, goin' table to table, he'd drag out this ol' saxophone and start playin' behind me, and I'd say, get out of here with that old thing. Let me do my number."

Ike Quebec on saxophone, early 1940s. Courtesy of Jimmy (Chops) Jones

How Ike came to be known as "Quebec," a name adopted also by his nephew, tenor player Danny Quebec, remains a mystery to his friends. Born Isaac Abrams in Newark on August 17, 1918, he used the name "Quebec" as far back as anyone remembers. To his friends, he was "Que." Wes Clark, whose father was a nephew of Quebec's father, believes Quebec's wife, Kathleen (Brown), gave him "his musician's name." "Don't know where it come from," Clark admitted. "Maybe the street. He never would stay in. He was streetwise. Raised hisself."

"Ike was a helluva pool player," recalled Jimmy (Chops) Jones. "We'd all hang out at Ratty's Poolroom on West Kinney Street, near Monmouth, waiting for gigs. Whether you had a gig or not, you'd go there, hang around, and play pool. Ike would hustle you while he was talking to everyone. I'd be taking my best shots, and he'd be knocking in ball after ball and never stop talkin'. That was because he was streetwise. He was only a year or two older than us, but to him we were kids."

Quebec, who came from a family of three boys and a girl, started in show business as a tap dancer. At sixteen, he won an amateur contest at Miner's Theater downtown on Washington Street. He began playing piano while broadening his horizons in a traveling show called *Harlem on Parade*. He also played at the Waverly Tavern with drummer Herman Bradley's band. "He was gifted," Clark asserted. "He just picked it [piano] up, and he was a good player, somethin' like [the legendary stride giant] Donald Lambert." Said pianist Floyd Lang: "Ike used to sit up under me all night at house rent parties. Wasn't long before he could really play [piano]."

One of the clubs where Quebec played was at West Market Street and Rankin Street, Clark recalled. "That was where all the colored policemen used to hang out. There was three pieces—Ike on piano, a saxophone player named Horace—he had his leg shot off overseas—and Brooks, the drummer."

"Ike played in a group that I had that played everywhere around Newark, no special place," said Leon Eason. "He played by ear, but he was good. He knew all the tunes. He was a good entertainer. He could sing and dance and play. When I was at the Alcazar I used to run jam sessions on Mondays. One Monday he came up at intermission with a horn and asked if he could sit in. I said, Yeah; anyone could sit in. Whatcha wanna play? Ike said, 'Body and Soul,' and he played it just like Hawk—Coleman Hawkins. That kind of surprised everyone, 'cause they [only] knew he played piano. But he was original—that came from playin' the piano—and he had a big tone."

About the same time, Hal Mitchell recalled Quebec walking around the streets of Newark "as if he were playin' the saxophone. He was

Bandleader Conrad Butler and Ike Quebec, front right, with the Barons of Rhythm at the Shady Rest Country Club, circa 1940. Quebec is joined on the front line by Jimmy Stanford, Bobby Jarrett, and T. O. Swangin. Courtesy of Thomas O. (T. O.) Swangin

still playin' the piano, so the fingerin' came automatically. His idol was [pianist] Earl Hines."

Quebec supposedly taught himself to play soprano saxophone first, then tenor. According to Eason, he learned sax by locking himself in a room for weeks and not coming out " 'til he could play that saxophone better than anybody. The guys in the band taught Ike to play [better], but he cut right through it," Eason added. "Pretty soon he could play better than anybody. That made a lot of the guys jealous."

"No matter where Quebec went, he always had his horn with him," said Connie (Williams) Woodruff. "Always. And he was always practicing. When I was about fifteen or so, I used to play piano with the Barons of Rhythm. Ike and Kathleen lived right across the street from the storefront where we practiced on Fairview Avenue. He was always stopping by

and sitting in. He wasn't a regular member of the Barons. To me, he was more like a star, an older guy who everyone looked up to because he was such a good musician."

Quebec's wife, said Woodruff, was "a good-looking light-skinned girl" whose father, Harold T. Brown, was one of Newark's most prominent black undertakers. "The Browns were friends of my mother and father, and Kathleen was my babysitter when I was about ten. When I got older I used to go to Ike and Kathleen's a lot. Most of the time he was away, out playing somewhere with a band."

"Kathleen never came to the clubs," said Eason. "I don't think her people wanted her to marry Ike. They didn't think he was good enough for her. They were opposed to people in show business."

"Ike was a very nice person, quiet, but not

shy," Woodruff added. "What I remember most about him was that he had big, thick lips, the biggest I'd ever seen. They were gigantic."

Quebec had another peculiarity—unusual fingers. "They had the oddest shape, very slender but with big ends and curved fingernails that set over the keys 'til you couldn't see them," said Chops Jones. "They looked like leopard pads." Said Eason: "I used to call them horsefingers."

From the time Quebec began playing tenor, it was clear that he possessed a raw, natural talent, one that eventually made him a standout on his instrument. His "total mastery" of the saxophone, according to Cuscuna, was apparent to "all who chose to hear." By 1942, he was darting in and out of Harlem, playing in a bunch of New York bands including those led by Frankie Newton, Roy Eldridge, and Benny Carter. Just as importantly, he had found his modernist soul mates in a circle of new friends who included Thelonius Monk, Tadd Dameron, Bud Powell, and Kenny Clarke, with whom he wrote the bop anthem "Mop Mop." Eventually, he moved to New York, although he still played lots of Newark gigs.

As jazz legend goes, bebop was born at Minton's Playhouse, the Harlem hotspot where Ike, Clarke, Dizzy Gillespie, and others on the cutting edge of musical change jammed through the night, trading licks and building on each other's themes. Soon, he and Gillespie began gigging around together. "Ike used to work with me a lot," Wes Clark said. "Whenever he wasn't workin', I could get him. Ike and Butch Robinson used to play in the middle of the bar at the Horseshoe Bar. They worked there for about two years. Then Ike formed his own group. They made quite a few records."

Ironically, it was Robinson who was being scouted by Cab Calloway for a spot in his band when Quebec decided to audition. Quebec played his head off and was hired on the spot, according to Eason. "Butch was devastated," said Eason. "Cab wanted a tenor player, and Butch thought he had the job. When Ike went with Cab, Butch went crazy. It broke him. He took off for New York. We heard about him, but we never saw him again."

In 1944, around the same time he joined Calloway, Quebec made his debut on Blue Note as a leader, the start of what became his most prolific period musically. In time, he became the artist and repertoire (A & R) man for the label, giving Eason a chance at one point to record six sides. From 1944 through 1951 he moved in and out of Calloway's orchestra, but he never strayed far. For a while he played with Newton, then with Hot Lips Page. Then he began forming his own groups. Along the way, he won several *Esquire* magazine top sax ratings.

By then, he was a stone drug addict, a habit that eventually affected his playing and claimed his health. "After he and Kathleen split, I used to go over to his house on St. Nicholas Avenue and 149th Street," said Eason. "One time when I went Ike and this little trumpet player were at the table cuttin' coke, choppin' it up. They asked me if I wanted some, but I said no. I didn't go for it. My mother was a minister."

"I heard about it [Quebec being on drugs], but I thought he was on marijuana, not hard drugs," said Woodruff. "A lot of people in show business—show girls and musicians—smoked [marijuana]. In the community at large, drugs were forbidden. Our parents made us scared stiff of them. Drugs would make you do weird things, even attack your mother, we were told."

Ironically, Kathleen Quebec was a registered nurse who tried desperately but unsuccessfully to get her husband off drugs. Eventually she left him. Eventually, too, his illness forced him to stop playing. He worked for a while as a chauffeur in the late 1950s. In 1963, he died of lung cancer at age forty-four. About the same time, Kathleen moved to Washington. Jones thinks she married a doctor. Eason is certain she never remarried.

"When I think back, I guess Ike must have spent a lot of money on drugs," Woodruff said. "They were poor. They never had much of anything. They lived on the third floor of that apartment on Fairview Avenue all their married life, a cold-water flat with no indoor plumbing. The bathroom was out on the back porch. That was typical in those days, especially in the old Third Ward."

Eason believes Quebec, like many other black musicians, was a victim of his own talent. "No matter how you cut it, we made nothing," he asserted. "If the clubowners didn't get you, the agents and the managers would. That's the way it's always been for us. No money."

Sarah's Gonna Sing
—The Early Years
Chapter 23

Sarah Vaughan was a high school teenager, a product of Newark's old Mt. Zion Baptist Church on Thomas Street, when her rendition of "Body and Soul" mesmerized the audience at the world-famous Apollo Theater in 1942, winning her a week's engagement at the famous Harlem hall. That night the career of one of the world's most soulful singers was launched.

As if fate somehow had touched her doubly, Billy Eckstine happened to be in the audience. Captivated by Vaughan's stirring way with a song, Eckstine raced backstage to talk to the fledgling singer, then went looking for bandleader Earl (Fatha) Hines to inform him of his "find." In early 1943, Hines signed her to sing with his band and, when the occasion arose, back him up on piano. Sarah was on her way.

Strangely enough, Vaughan's many friends back home in Newark didn't know she could sing. To them, she was simply the talented piano player who accompanied the church choir and school orchestra, the girl whose house on Brunswick Street was the focal point for their "Friday night socials." Like their parents, Sarah's mother and father, Ada and Asbury Vaughan, were members of Mt. Zion and pillars of the black religious community.

"We all grew up in the same church," said Phyllis Brooks, whose grandfather, the Reverend John Richard Brown, was the pastor, "so we all knew each other for years and years and years. When we were in high school, the kids would gather at Sarah's house and dance and play records. Sarah would do a lot of the piano playing for us. She sang in the choir and she played for the junior and senior choirs and took lessons from Miss King—Josephine King. Sarah was our alto in the choir, but she did very little solo singing. Her voice was very tiny. She couldn't project much beyond six benches."

Evelyn Greene, a retired Rutgers University music professor who lived on Pennington

Street at the time and was in the church choir, recalled: "Sarah just sang insignificant alto. There was no sign of any kind of voice."

After she entered secondary school, Vaughan also was the organist for the boys' glee club at East Side High, where she played for the dance orchestra.

"In our choir at Mt. Zion we had a lot of talent, Sarah included," said Brooks. "Besides Evelyn, we had some local talent that didn't quite make it to the top. One was Ralph Sanders. He used to do a lot of church-type singing around. We had a lot of good voices. Sarah and I used to alternate playing for the junior choir. Miss King used to allow to play for the church service on Sunday morning. Sarah would play sometimes, and sometimes I would play. We were the star pupils."

Like others their age, the young people of the church were even more attracted to the popular music of the day. With the encouragement of Sarah's parents, they began flocking to the Vaughan home at 72 Brunswick Street on Friday nights.

"I have no idea how her house became the center of our social life," Brooks said. "Sarah was a shy girl, very shy, so I guess it just was because the kids were welcome. Her parents were very open and supportive of her and they didn't mind the kids gathering there or being dispossessed every weekend. I can still see the house. It was a small, two-family house. They lived upstairs. When you walked in the kitchen you'd have to walk up the stairs to get in. They had a very tiny living room and her little piano was over on the side. Every Friday night we'd go over to Sarah's house and drive her parents out of the living room. Out in the kitchen they would stay for the rest of the night. Ten o'clock was our curfew. They had their house back at ten o'clock."

Brooks was among the regulars with her cousin, Jeanne Brown, her girlfriend Marion Wilson, Sanders, and Ralph Jacob, as well as "loads of kids" who lived in the immediate area: "We were doing all the latest jitterbug dancing. When we grew up, you couldn't dance in my house. You couldn't do any of those things. If you went to the movies, you'd have to

Sarah Vaughan, early 1950s. Photo by Al Henderson; courtesy of Florence (Williams) Henderson

go when my grandfather didn't know about it."

About the same time, Vaughan began developing a jazz piano repertoire. "She'd race home from school at lunchtime. She had some favorite jazz musician she liked to listen to on the radio," Brooks said. "He played piano and was a national name—Howard something or other [possibly Herman Chittison]. Every day he'd be on about fifteen minutes. She wouldn't miss this program. She was very enthused about him. That was the first time I heard her play what was pop music. She'd demonstrate these chords to me and my cousin, Alma Brown. She also loved Ella [Fitzgerald], so she'd play 'A Tisket, a Tasket,' which also was getting a lot of air play."

None of her peers, however, seemed aware of Vaughan's growing interest in singing, a talent left largely undeveloped until she transferred from East Side to Arts High as a sophomore. With the change in schools, the emphasis of her social life changed, too. Intrigued by the city's nightlife and the abundance of talent among the musicians and singers, she began hanging out at local clubs, begging to sing when she had the chance.

"Because Sarah did so little solo singing while we were growing up, we all were shocked when she went over to the Apollo," Brooks recalled. "She didn't spread the news around that she was going to do it, so we were all surprised. While she was at the Apollo, I went over with her mother one night. She had a week's engagement. That was her prize. I remember going backstage afterward and being very disappointed because I thought it was horrible back there. I guess I expected more glamour. After Sarah signed with Earl Hines, our getting together drifted apart. I used to see her when she'd come back home. By that time her family had moved to [tree-lined] Avon Avenue. I dropped in once or twice. Then we got further apart."

Although her friends at Mt. Zion had little knowledge of Sarah's involvement in the city's nightlife, the word somehow got out that she planned to sing at the Apollo. "We heard that Sarah was gonna sing at the Apollo," said Greene. "It was all over the church. So we all tuned in. The show was broadcast every Wednesday night and was the only entertainment of that kind we had. Most of the time we didn't know who the contestants were. When I heard Sarah, I said, Wow! Sarah's singing! I didn't even recognize her [voice]."

Sarah's winning the Apollo amateur con-test, however, came as no surprise to many of Newark's musicians or the patrons of the clubs she frequented to gain the confidence she needed to go on stage and make her amateur night debut. "I can recall her coming into the Alcazar when she was just a kid," said Carl McIntyre, who led a quintet there in the early 1940s. "That's where she got her start. I'd say, Sing, girl! She'd say, 'I'm scared.' All the girls wanted to sound like Billie Holiday. She was big time. But Sarah had a style all her own."

Thad Howard, then a popular emcee, also remembered Vaughan appearing at the Alcazar: "The first time I ever saw her was at the Alcazar on Mother's Day. She was the last one up. I introduced her, and she sang 'I Cried for You.' I stood there dumbfounded. I couldn't believe it. She was just a kid. Seven or eight months later she won the contest at the Apollo and went with Billy Eckstine. Golly, she had a voice."

Miss Rhapsody, one of Newark's most popular singers at the time, recalled the night Vaughan signed with Hines: "It was at the Hydeaway on Halsey Street," she maintained. "I was right there. I knew Earl because he used to come into my place while I was working in Kansas City."

With Hines, Vaughan began life on the road, tracing and retracing her steps over the next fifty years. In the 1960s, she bought a sumptuous home in Englewood Cliffs, about twenty-five miles from Newark. But she remained a Newark girl, never too big to sing at a local club or stop by and "hang out" with friends. In 1946, the year *Esquire* voted her "The New Queen of Song," she appeared with saxophonist Don Byas at the Club Supreme, a part of Graham Hall on Belmont Avenue. The following year she shared the bill with her friend and fellow Newarker Ike Quebec at an "Old Home Night" show at Graham's. At Christmastime in 1949 she was the "guest artist" at the Caravan, the old Dodger's Bar and Grill on Bedford Street, where she sang as an amateur.

In the early 1950s, a columnist wrote: "Sarah was back home, hanging out with friends at Lloyd's Manor, complete with slacks, while looking relaxed and as happy as one could

Sarah Vaughan, mid 1950s. Courtesy of Newark Public Library

imagine. Our Sarah is one of the most gracious and unaffected persons you could meet."

Further into her career, Vaughan frequented the old Key Club on Halsey Street, one of the few spots that still offered live music into the 1970s. Or she might stop at the Bridge Club on Washington Street, which serves terrific soul food. Once the word got out, especially at the Key, lines suddenly formed outside, creating a crush to get in.

In February 1957, the City of Newark proclaimed "Sarah Vaughan Day" and gave one of its most famous daughters a royal homecoming. With her parents proudly looking on, Vaughan received a scroll from Mayor Leo Carlin during ceremonies at City Hall, then was honored at a Mt. Zion Church dinner at which her "ethereal tones" and "God-given voice and talent" were extolled. The proceeds were part of a $35,000 campaign to build a church youth center.

As the scroll she received that night indicated, Sarah had done the impossible: she had bridged the gap between sacred and secular music. It read in part: "In highest praise for the creativity you have manifested in translating music and song into a universal language of love, hope and understanding."

Not only was Sarah one of the world's most celebrated singers; she was one of its best, blessed with a magnificently luxuriant voice that she could stretch, bend, and otherwise mess with from the bottom of the basement to a skyward falsetto. And she was versatile, at first a band singer, then a virtuoso who could handle pop tunes and jazz with equal aplomb. One night she might sing at a small club like New York's Blue Note, the next in a tremendous hall, surrounded by a symphony orchestra.

Like her friend Eckstine, she was basically a hipster, full of fun and ready to explore new worlds. On stage, in her high-pitched speaking voice, she was shy and childlike, teasing her fans by inviting them to choose a tune, then launching into her own choice, invariably "Send in the Clowns." Offstage, she loved to party, preferably in the company of a small circle of close friends that included Ella Moncur, Clyde Golden, Tom Guy, and Roberta and George Alford, rather than luxuriate in the more public trappings that her fame offered.

With time, other singers vanished from the scene, but Sarah's voice amazingly grew richer in tone and timbre, never failing her. For five decades, she continued to record and perform all over the world, seemingly invincible. But she was not, destined to die before her time. One of her last appearances was with Quincy Jones and the scores of musicians who recorded "We Are the World" to benefit hungry children worldwide. She was ill, but she made the date.

Sarah Vaughan died of lung cancer April 3, 1990 in her home in Hidden Hills, California, one week after her sixty-sixth birthday. Following services in Mt. Zion Church on Broadway (an offshoot of the church in which she grew up) in Newark, arranged by her eighty-seven-year-old mother, her body was taken by horse-drawn carriage to Glendale Cemetery in nearby Bloomfield, New Jersey. She was buried in the family plot next to her father.

Bopping at the Manor
–A New Brand of Music
Chapter 24

The importance of Lloyd's Manor as a focal point of Newark nightlife in the late 1940s rivaled the prominence of the Kinney Club and other popular neighborhood clubs a decade before.

Clubs like the Three Deuces and Fredericks' Lounge on Boston Street and the Silver Saddle over on Clinton Avenue, once a whites-only venue, had sizable followings, too, but Lloyd's at 42–48 Beacon Street was the home of bebop, a hangout for hep cats and promising new musicians. Prohibition, the Depression, the Swing Era, and the war years had given way to a new period of prosperity. Times were changing and so were tastes in popular music and entertainment.

"Lloyd's was the beginning of music for our generation," said singer Nate Brown, who studied music on the GI bill. "Newark was a different world then. The emphasis was on families and neighborhoods and Lloyd's had everything—a dance hall, a bar, food, and big-name entertainers like Nat King Cole and Billie Holiday. We all got our start there. Moody. Babs. Hank Mobley. Charli(e) Persip. Danny Quebec. Jimmy Ponder. Even George Benson. From 1946 or so 'til 1958, it was one of the key spots in town."

Bill Lloyd supposedly won the spacious club atop a bowling alley in a card game and lost it the same way a decade later. Whatever happened, he ran a successful business until it changed hands and became the Penguin Club in 1956. Once the home of Dreamland Academy, where bands like Pancho Diggs's and the Barons of Rhythm held sway over throngs of frenetic jitterbuggers, Lloyd's was the center of all that was hep, the headquarters for the city's beboppers and early proponents of rhythm and blues.

When Lloyd took over, the upstairs was still a ballroom where dancers paid a dollar and a quarter or so to hear big-name bands led by Lionel Hampton, Luis Russell, Willie Bryant,

Wynonie Harris, and Oran (Hot Lips) Page. But the real action was in the lounge off the main entrance, presided over by local innovators of bop.

One of the first events was "The Carnival of Swing," prompted by the inequities created by double standards for black and white musicians. According to the black press, the show was staged because "Local 16 has never gone to bat properly for our colored musicians who are always paid below scale. Our boys have had to watch New York musicians walk into town and take over juicy spots, particularly downtown, where several attempts to hire local colored bandsmen were refused. Some of the nightclub owners who wanted them badly had to admit that union pressure forced them to hire white bands. Yet when our Newark boys go to New York they hardly get a chance to toot two bars before an 802 delegate is asking for credentials."

Newark's black musicians were told the only jobs open required them to play continuously for five or six hours, mostly accompanying entertainers. With the high cost of arrangements and instruments, they came away with little to call a salary.

In self-defense, 125 musicians joined forces in 1946, forming the Musicians' Staff Club, Newark's version of a union. The line-up for the first fund-raiser at Lloyd's read like a "Who's Who" of talent in the colored community: Chink Williams' band, Brady Hodge, Ernie Phipps, Bobby Jarrett, Sonny Marshall, Harold Ford, and Allen Gibbs.

The following spring the members took over the former Servicemen's Center at 15 Belmont Avenue as their headquarters. Pancho Diggs was named president; Duke Anderson, vice president; Al Henderson, secretary; Gene Kee, recording secretary; and Harold Underhill, sergeant-at-arms.

Part of Lloyd's popularity can be attributed to the Ray-O-Vacs, who had Newarkers flocking to Beacon Street to hear their jukebox hit "I'll Always Be in Love With You." Led by Jackson (Flap) McQueen, the group featured Lester Harris from Paterson, who began singing at

Lloyd's with Arthur Terry and His Grand Rascals. The customers immediately proclaimed him "Mr. Blues."

Three key figures were in the forefront of the progressive jazz movement spawned at Lloyd's: Danford (Larue) Jordan, Babs Gonzales, and James Moody. Together, they fed off each other's genius and shaped their musical ideas.

"Larue was considered a genius," said Bill Roberts, the bartender. "One night he started playin' 'Smoke Rings,' slow-like for [singer] Billie Sermond, and just kept goin' on and on. Lloyd got disgusted, so we went down to a place on Washington Street to hear Gus Young. We heard Gus play about three numbers and when we got back up there Larue was still playing the same number—two hours later. I said, What is it? Larue said: 'Progressive jazz.'"

Saxophonist Connie Lester, barely out of his teens when he got his first gig at Lloyd's, remembered Jordan as an innovator: "A lot of my phrasing comes from Larue. He did some strange things."

Jordan had begun singing and playing piano professionally a decade earlier with a group called the Four Shades. Even then, he was into bop, long before Dizzy Gillespie, Kenny Clarke, and other innovators popularized it at Minton's Playhouse in Harlem.

Joe Gregory, one of the Shades, noted: "We worked one time at the Kit Kat Club before it became the Picadilly, but we never got off the ground. We went downtown to the five and ten and recorded a tune called 'Baby, Won't You Fall in Love With Me?' That's as far as we got.

"Babs [Gonzales] was always hangin' around at the rehearsals of the Four Shades," Gregory said. "He used to hang out with us. That was his gang—Larue and Bill Goode. That was when all the boppin' stuff started. We used to talk about it. A horn would make a sound like 'bip' and Larue would say 'bop-ba-doo, bebop-baba-do-lee.' You'd get the sound of the instrument. Babs or Dizzy, I don't know who, introduced the idea. We all used to talk about it. I wasn't too much of an outstanding

Larue Jordan plays progressive jazz with drummer Danny Gibson, bass player Curley Bell, and saxophonist Rudy (Bones) Williams at Lloyd's Manor, circa 1945. Courtesy of Al Henderson

figure, but I was doin' it. Diz and Babs got it together. In the early part of his career, Dizzy spent a lot of time in Newark."

Several years later, Gonzales formed his Three Bips and a Bop with the creative Tadd Dameron on piano. Together, they matched innovative sounds to their music, producing a seemingly nonsensical but fluid vocalese that caught on so quickly the group was invited to headline a show at Carnegie Hall.

Gonzales's recordings of "Bebop Santa Claus" and "Oop-Pop-a-Da," either with his own group or backed by Moody's band, are bop standards. The latter tune was so ear-catching it prompted Gillespie to record a more popular version.

"I formed the Bips," Gonzales told writer Ira Gitler, "because I felt bebop needed a vocal

bridge to the people. The fire was there. Bird was cooking, and Oscar Pettiford and Dizzy and them with their little group. But it wasn't reaching the people."

Babs' music was much like his personality, fluid and fun-loving. He was a genuine "hep cat," eccentric from a mainstream viewpoint. At times, as Gitler noted, he wore a turban and called himself Ram Singh. Or, at a moment's notice, he was Ricardo Gonzales. As the stories go, his antics included an endless enchantment with wild stunts, like posing as a homosexual to avoid the draft during World War II.

Gonzales, whose real name was Lee Brown, was called "Little Babs" because his brother was "Big Babs." Even as a youngster it was clear he possessed an unusual talent for promoting practically anyone or anything, partic-

Babs Gonzales, circa 1945. Courtesy of Lucille (Dorsey) Morton

Advertisement for a bebop session at Lloyd's Manor, early 1950s. Courtesy of Gertrude (Turman) Brown

ularly himself. His was a lifetime of wheeling and dealing, cut short at sixty-two by hard, fast living.

Over the years, Babs dabbled in everything from playing piano and singing to writing books and publishing his songs. He was in constant motion, moving from project to project and place to place, "flopping" wherever he could find a free "pad." For a while in the forties, he lived in California and reportedly was actor Errol Flynn's chauffeur. Later, in Paris, his was the opening act for Josephine Baker.

Primarily he was what author Roy Carr and his co-authors called "a bebop babbler," with Eddie Jefferson, Slim Gaillard, Leo Watson, and a few others, one of the "precursors of today's rap raconteurs."

"Babs was the forerunner of whatever was happening," recalled pianist Duke Anderson. "He was a singer; he played a little piano, but not that much, but he had the originality that nobody else had. Babs really was a genius, but no one knew he was a genius 'cause he was always a conman. Whatever Babs said was the law. He would say things in the conversation that would make you stop and think. He knew

all about life when he was nine or ten years old. He could sit right here and have all your money in a minute. That's how persuasive he was.

"And he could get away with a lot of things because he was so little and nobody would hit him. I don't think Babs weighed more than a hundred and ten pounds. Geronimo [real name Herbert Johnson] was another cat like that. He was a hustler, too. He wasn't as good as Babs, but he was suave. Sharp. He was street-smart. Babs loved him. All the tricks that Geronimo had, Babs taught him."

Although he was younger than his fellow beboppers, James Moody also got his start at Lloyd's. "Moody came out of the bop experience," said Anderson. "He was a child prodigy on the piano, classically trained. I saw him first when he was about seven years old. He played a program I was involved in at a church down in the Neck [the Ironbound section of Newark] and it was very remarkable. That was around the late 1930s. Then he switched off to tenor."

Moody recounted: "The reason my mother moved to Newark was because they had me in

Lloyd's regulars, late 1940s: from left, Clarence Mack, bass; unidentified; George Gordon, piano; Togge Smythe, saxophone. Courtesy of Meredith Gordon

a school for retarded children where we lived in Reading, Pennsylvania. The reason they did that was because I was hard of hearing, but they didn't know it. They thought I was out of it. I was raised at Pennington Court [one of the Newark's first public housing projects]. From there, I went to Arts High School, then to East Side High. Then I got drafted.

"I started playing when I was about sixteen. I liked saxophone from listening to records, mostly Jimmy Dorsey, Lester Young, and Charlie Barnet. Duke [Anderson] is very kind, but actually I could only play a couple chords on piano. When I was coming up, the musicians I heard about in Newark were guys like Pancho Diggs, Gene Phipps, and Ike Quebec.

Actually, I didn't play in Newark in the beginning, not until I came back from the Air Force—the black Air Force.

"As a kid I used to go in the Kinney Club, Dodger's Grill—all of them. Grace Smith used to be my buddy. She used to be swinging, and I just dug her. And I can still remember Gus Young doin' 'When a Woman Needs a Man.' They used to call him 'Mr. World.' In those days, everything was segregated. That was in 1946.

"My first paid job I played up at Lloyd's Manor. That was before I went with Dizzy—in the latter part of '46 or early '47. I got seven dollars a night. That was good money. The piano player was Larue. But who was the bass player or drummer, I can't recall. We played in the bar. Sometimes, we'd go in the back for dances. We played bebop—always bebop—but Babs was way ahead of me.

"I guess I was about twenty-one when Babs told Dizzy about me. I had seen Dizzy down in Greensboro when I was playing down there in the Air Force. Dave Burns, a friend of mine from Perth Amboy, got me in the band. Thelonius Monk was the piano player. Ray Brown was the bass player; Milt Jackson, the vibraharpist; Connie Cockrell, the drummer; and Walter [Gil] Fuller was the musical director."

Another young musician who got his "start" at Lloyd's was Ken Gibson, a teenager at the time. Years later, after becoming Newark's first black mayor in 1970, Gibson recalled sharing the bandstand with some of the biggest names in the business. As mayor, Gibson did not forget his friends or his musical roots, encouraging the city's Parks and Recreation Department throughout his sixteen years as Newark's chief executive to hire groups of older musicians to play outdoor concerts in the summer and headline special events. From the perspective of younger musicians, Moody and the other innovators who ruled the lounge at Lloyd's were musical giants, mentors whose teachings were incorporated into their feeble attempts at replication. "If you didn't know your horn," said saxophonist Connie Lester, "you couldn't come to Newark."

James Moody, 1950s. Courtesy of Meredith Gordon

The Dawning of Rhythm and Blues
Chapter 25

By the late 1940s, nightlife in Newark that centered around its swing musicians was dying off for a variety of reasons, in part because of a growing interest among more avant-garde fans and musicians in the impressionistic sounds of bebop and a fascination with two new inventions: the jukebox and television.

In a sense, the musicians who were talented or fortunate enough to record their music were simultaneously major contributors to the demise of the nightclub scene and their livelihoods. As they soon found, it was substantially cheaper for club owners to buy a jukebox and have the patrons pump in nickels to hear their favorite tunes than hire live entertainment. The issue of recorded music was a thorny one, met head on in the early 1940s by James Petrillo, president of New York's Local 802 of the American Federation of Musicians.

Confronted by the immense popularity of radio programs that depended on recorded shows to attract millions of listeners and the

burgeoning success of the record industry, Petrillo demanded from the companies royalties and other benefits for his musicians. In 1941, he imposed a ban on union members' making studio recordings after the companies adamantly refused to meet his demands to pay up. Even President Franklin Roosevelt's intervention failed to stem the controversy. For three years it raged on, until finally, in November 1944, the union came to terms with Columbia and RCA Victor records.

According to Robert D. Leiter, Petrillo's biographer, "about six hundred companies established a fund controlled by the union" into which they paid varying fees for each record, generally "a quarter of a cent for thirty-five-cent disks to five cents for two dollar disks."

The end of World War II saw the return home of many musicians who had been assigned to play at military camps or USO shows. Scores of them headed straight for the recording studios, eager to find fame and earn

Harold (Hal) Mitchell and writer Connie (Williams) Woodruff, 1988. From author's collection

royalties. As Leiter noted, an "acute shortage of shellac," an ingredient that "kept surface noise down," was over, and the market was being flooded with recordings by hundreds of new and exciting artists.

New jukebox machines, "mechanical wonders," as writer Bob Queen called them in 1947, were popping up at clubs everywhere—eyecatching with their chromium-plated designs, earcatching because of the popular tunes emanating at the mere drop of a coin and flick of a button. By the mid 1940s, the shiny new machines at venues like the Dug Out Bar and the auditorium at Graham's Hall in Newark and Ruth's Dining Room in Orange began rivaling live shows.

Installing a jukebox at a local club or tavern meant big money for the gangsters who owned and controlled them. It was their new gig. "Mobsters either owned the taverns or the owners were so in debt to them they had to take the jukeboxes whether they wanted to or not," said Connie (Williams) Woodruff, then city editor of the *Herald News.* Woodruff knew the scene firsthand because she also worked in a record store on Orange Street operated by

Bill Osgood and B. F. (Mac) Macfarlane, Newark's first black jukebox owners.

"Jukeboxes paid big, big money," said Woodruff. "It was a big, big take. The owner of the jukebox would take a certain amount of money off the top, maybe two dollars or five dollars. The rest would be divided between the jukebox owner and the tavern owner. The money charged by the owner of the jukeboxes was supposed to cover general maintenance of the machines, his expenses, and time spent running around supplying and changing the records.

"As a fledgling employee at the store, I rolled many nickels, dimes, and quarters. If a tavern owner got in trouble financially and needed five hundred or a thousand dollars, all he needed to do was call the guy who owned the jukebox. If he had a real, jumpin' joint, it was nothing for them to take a hundred dollars a week out of a machine; fifty or sixty was standard in those days. He could get a loan and pay it back from the money he got on the machine. It was a painless way to get a loan and repay it."

Even more popular was the strange new

Bob Queen, circa 1982. Courtesy of Bob Queen

new home appliances and to acquire telephones and automobiles. As a result, live entertainment was replaced by home entertainment. In the black community, new heroes, like Robinson and Nat King Cole, a consummate performer whose easygoing style was a natural for television, were emerging.

As Bob Queen wrote in the *Afro*, the musicians soon found themselves "stumbling over each other, lugging their horns just to keep from getting lonesome." Things were so bad, at least two clubs were "paying below scale."

"Is swing dead?" Queen asked in an October 1947 edition of the paper. "It is my opinion," he wrote, "that if it is dead or anywhere near that state, it certainly has a way of popping up, full of life, in the most unexpected places." Yet he lamented that, "while jazz fans are ringing the tills merrily at Town Hall on the Fred Robinson bass sessions and Carnegie Hall romps with Illinois Jacquet's exciting saxology," night spots in Trenton (Newark, too) suddenly were turning to bebop.

For the moment at least, the more focused sounds of swing had been replaced by a new musical energy, the frenetic hard licks of bop with its crop of younger musicians and their followers. An explosion of new music had arrived: "cool jazz," rhythm and blues, and rock and roll, followed eventually by rap. Swing was not dead, but in the face of all these newer musical styles, its popularity was on a back burner, taking with it the livelihoods of Newark's "oldtime" musicians and entertainers. As in the waning days of vaudeville, the era of live nightclub shows and revues was approaching its end.

With bop as a transitional force, a more explosive era of rhythm and blues, rooted in gospel influences, had arrived, driving its fans into record stores to make small fortunes for independent labels like Newark-based Savoy and Regal, whose owners were financially keen enough to catch the trend.

Ever rich in talent, Newark rose to the challenge, producing a host of top musical practitioners in the 1950s and 1960s. Among the biggest names were Moody, Mobley, Persip, Wayne Shorter, Woody Shaw, Houston Person, Rah-

medium of television. For four or five hundred dollars, club managers like Eddie Mosby of the Picadilly found themselves in the avant garde, luring new business to watch TV while saving money on live entertainment. In the black nightclubs like the Pic, television's powerful new draw was the dynamic young baseball player who broke the sport's color barrier. Instead of billing musicians, the advertisements invited patrons to see "Jackie Robinson versus the Giants," quite a feat for just one man, even one as great as Robinson.

With the postwar boom came an age of rampant acquisition and materialism as Americans, hungry for new gadgets and appliances, strove to keep up with the Joneses. Consumerism reached an all-time high, prompting a rush to buy television sets, phonographs, and

Cissy and Whitney Houston at a concert at Essex County College in Newark, 1983. Courtesy of New Jersey Newsphotos

saan Roland Kirk, and Vinnie Burke. Over the years, the city has also served as the launching pad for the careers of some of the nation's top singers. In the early 1950s, Ruth Brown, queen of Atlantic records, practically called Newark home. At the same time, Faye Adams, whose popular recording hit was "Shake a Hand," and Florence Wright, who hit the charts with "Deal Me a Hand" and "The Game of Broken Hearts," were Newark girls. Carrie Smith, one of the stars of the long-running Broadway hit musical *Black and Blue*, is a product of Newark's Greater Harvest Baptist Church. Savion Glover, the talented teenager who appeared in the same show and was featured in the movie *Tap* with Sammy Davis Jr. and Gregory Hines, is the grandson of two of Newark's finest entertainers, Anna May Lundy Lewis and Billy Lewis.

One of the most versatile entertainers to call Newark home is Melba Moore. A terrific singer—like her mother, Bonnie (Smith) Davis—she is also a talented actress and comedienne.

In recent years, Newark's brightest lights—Dionne Warwick and her cousin, Whitney Houston—graciously have followed sister Sarah Vaughan's lead by crediting their hometown with their successes worldwide. Like Vaughan and Smith, their music is rooted in the church, Dionne's at St. Luke's African Methodist Episcopal Church in Newark, where she and her sisters began singing as children, and Whitney's at Newark's New Hope Baptist Church, where her mother, Cissy Houston, is minister of music. These entertainers have inherited a rich legacy. Collectively, they are the musical children of Miss Rhapsody and Newark's other pioneering performers.

APPENDIXES

Who's Who of Newark Nightlife, 1925–50

Ackis, Dewey Photographer and writer. Came to Newark in 1929 after studying law at Howard University; Works Progress Administration (WPA) police photographer during Depression; covered Newark nightlife for *New Jersey Herald News*.

Adams, Carrie Blues singer, dancer, and comedienne. Born in South before 1900; wife of Clarence Adams; appeared with Ma Rainey in Winston-Salem, N.C. (1919); played carnivals, sideshows, theaters, and clubs; considered Newark's grand old lady of local entertainment; played the Eagle Bar (1951); died while "dancing somewhere on Staten Island" in 1960s.

Adams, Clarence Clarinetist and saxophonist. Played in Orpheum Theater pit band; taught many younger musicians rudiments of music; husband of Carrie Adams.

Akridge, Fannie Singer. Born in Lawrenceville, Virginia; sang at Dodger's (1943); died c1945.

Alexander, (Little) Joe Singer. Sang at Lloyd's Manor (late 1940s); also with Billy Anderson's band; style akin to Billy Eckstine's.

Alexo, Tony Tenor saxophonist. Appeared with Two Notes and a Tempo (May 1945) at Jim Rhett's Twinlite, with Danny Gibson on drums and Danford (Larue) Jordan on piano.

Allen, Grace Bawdy blues singer. Often appeared at Dodger's and Kinney Club; featured in Dodger's revue (1942) with Reese LaRue, Jazzlips Richardson, Lillian Bryant, and Crackshot Hacksley.

Allen, Tony Pianist. Appeared (mid 1940s) with Del Mar Boys, with Danny Gibson on drums and Emzey Waters on saxophone.

Alston, Canty. Popular bandleader (late 1940s). From Jersey City.

Alston, Matty Emcee. Mainstay at Alcazar (1939–43); appeared at Hydeaway (1944) and Twinlite (1945); kept things lively, making Alcazar a rendezvous for other performers.

Clem Moorman: "Matty was the first guy I heard do the words to 'Savoy.'"

Anderson, Howard (Duke) Pianist, arranger, and bandleader. Born Aug. 28, 1917 in East Orange, N.J.; ran away from home at 12; joined Ida Cox's road show in Baltimore; teenage house rent party sensation in Orange (early 1930s); learned arranging from Don Redman and Edgar Sampson; pianist and arranger for Buddy Johnson, Tiny Bradshaw, and Dizzy Gillespie (early–mid 1940s); bold style described as "heating the ivories like thunder in a storm"; toured with Bradshaw (1943–45), Gillespie (1945–46), and Ike Quebec (1946); subsequently formed own band; recorded "Salt Lake City Bounce" with Bradshaw; accompanist for June Richmond, Lil Green, and T-Bone Walker; arranged for Louis Armstrong, Eddie Vinson, Flash and Dash, Conway and Parks, Tip, Tap, and Toe, and Patterson and Jackson; vice president, Newark Musicians' Staff Club (1946); formed orchestra with brother James (Billy) Anderson (late 1950s); filled in for Count Basie (late 1970s–early 1980s) when Count's health began to fail; leads small groups locally and teaches his "tetrachord system" at colleges and universities.

Anderson, James (Billy) Acoustic bassist and bandleader. Born Aug. 13, 1919 in East Orange, N.J.; influenced by mother and older brother, Howard (Duke), who both played piano; patterned his style after Ray Brown, bassist for Duke Ellington; first gig a house rent party for which he got $5; before forming the Billy Anderson Orchestra (late 1950s), played with Ernie Phipps Trio and Dicky Thompson Trio; recorded six sides on Savoy with blues singer John Lee Hooker.

Anderson, James (Jimmy) Emcee, singer, and dancer (late 1930s–early 1940s); not to be confused with saxophonist having same name.

Herald News (July 30, 1938): "His show at Dodger's sets so terrific a pace one of the patrons fell out in a dead faint. It surpasses anything Ma and Pa Frazier [the owners] have done."

Leon Eason: "We called him 'The Demon.' One time he bought a horn and thought if he practiced enough he could sound just like Ike Quebec."

Anderson, Louie (Lucky Louie) Emcee, singer, and dancer. Trademark white tie and tails.

Bob Queen: (*Afro-American*): "His act lit up the Colony Club on Broome Street like a beacon."

Anderson, Mildred Blues singer. Performed at Kinney Club (1947); sang "I Ain't Mad at You" at a New Year's Eve bash at Masonic Temple (1947).

Anderson, Nate Popular pianist (late 1940s).

Annetta Dancer. Performed with Whitey's Lindy Hoppers (late 1930s); wife of emcee Thad (Chuck) Howard; deceased.

Armstrong, Al Fine arranger and trombonist (late 1940s).

Armstrong, Audrey Exotic dancer. From New York; toured with Alabams in *Harlem on Parade* (early 1930s); featured in *Parade of Stars* revue at Dave and Maney's in Orange, N.J. (1939).

Arnita Sweet singer. Played Caravan Club, formerly Dodger's (late 1940s).

Avant, Billy All-around entertainer; emcee, singer, tap dancer, and guitarist. Came to Newark's Boston Plaza (early 1941) "direct from the Club Harlem"; emcee at Twinlite, Kinney Club, and Son Berry's Greenbriar in Eatontown, N.J.; husband of Kitty Avant.

Avant, Kitty Dancer and singer; given name Marsha Nell Moses. Sang with Ray Green (early 1940s); played Dodger's, Nest Club, Boston Plaza, and Nitecap as single or duo with her husband, Billy.

Afro-American (June 22, 1946): "Crowds always want her rendition of 'Ol' Man River.'"

Willie Johnson: "She was from Newark. We lived on the same street."

Bailey, Estelle Singer. Singing waitress at Villa Maurice, Reservoir Club, and Kinney Club (late 1930s); appeared in show at Rainbow Inn in Rahway, N.J. arranged by Milton Pittman (1939); noted for rendition of "I Think of You With Every Breath I Take" and "Brown Gal."

Charlie Matthews: "She was brown-skinned, very pretty and dainty—a lady."

Herald News (1939): "She had the joint jumpin' at the Club Del Rio on Washington Street."

Ballard, Freddie Tenor banjo player. Performed with Dick Matthews' band at Dave and Maney's in Orange, N.J. (late 1930s).

Ballard, Gene Pianist. Performed with Dick Matthews' band at Davey and Maney's in Orange, N.J. (late 1930s).

Banks, Helen Singer. Cute little singer. Played in *Gay Paree* revue at Kinney Club; local girl with good voice who sang on amateur night programs.

Banks, Robert Pianist, organist, composer, arranger, and teacher. Born in Newark, Feb. 3, 1930; calls his musical talent "a gift from God which has taken complete control of my body and soul"; early training from his uncle, Eugene Faust, a "musical genius who played thirty-five instruments and received a scholarship to the Boston Conservatory"; first paid gig at Coleman Hotel on Court Street; soon afterward "discovered" by guitarist Horace Sims, who took him on road with El Tempos, Sims's group; repertoire ranges from "Bach to rock to gospel"; recorded on Savoy (late 1950s), including "Shangri-La," "On the Street Where You Live," and "Trees."

Baxter, Ann Singer. Finished third among female singers in 1949 *After Hours* magazine poll.

Beans Pianist; given name unknown. From Montclair, N.J.; lived in Newark; performed as single and pit man in Orpheum Theater orchestra; played many local spots, including cabaret on Branford Place (late 1930s) with Mixie Moorman's Red Hots.

Floyd Lang: "He was Donald Lambert's only competition. They had a style almost alike, but Donald was the master."

Bell, Johnnie Pianist. Considered "good, legitimate player" by peers; often worked at Picadilly (early 1940s) with Al Henderson Trio; became preacher.

Bennett, Bernice Singer. Sang sweet songs at Kinney Club (late 1930s).

Bernhardt, Clyde Trombonist, blues singer, and band leader; recorded also as Ed Barron. Born July 11, 1905 in Goldhill, N.C.; began playing trombone in 1922 in Harrisburg, Pa., where his family moved; got $3 for first job in band led by his cousin, William Eady; on road with Grear's Midnite Ramblers (1927); in band led by Herbert Cowans (Sept. 1928); played at Club Alabam, "one of the leading and biggest night clubs in Newark," with Richard Cheatham Orchestra, an 8-piece band (Nov. 1928); played with King Oliver (1931), Marion Hardy's Alabams (1932–33), Vernon Andrade's Orchestra (1934–37), Edgar Hayes (1937–42), and Horace Henderson (1941); toured with Fats Waller and Jay McShann (1942), Cecil Scott (1943), and McShann (1944); played Club Zanzibar in New York with Claude Hopkins (1945) and Dud Bascomb's band (late 1940s); freelanced and led own groups (1950s–60s); co-leader of Harlem Blues and Jazz Band with June Cole (early 1970s); toured Europe with Barry Martyn's Legends of Jazz (late 1970s); author of *I Remember: Eighty Years of Black Entertainment, Big Bands and the Blues*, his autobiography, as told to Sheldon Harris (1986); died May 20, 1986.

Best, Albert (Al) Bassist. Known for work on bass with Heat Waves and with Leon Eason's aggregation at Alcazar (1939–40); played with Three Blue Notes at Roselle's Omega Bar and Grill (1943), Arthur Terry Trio at Hydeaway (1944), Billy Moore Four at Dodger's (1946), and Ted McRae's band at Harlem's Club Sudan (Jan. 1946); deceased.

Bey, Andy (Wideman) Popular singer and pianist. A 6-year-old prodigy "banging out boogie-woogie" on piano (1946) while an honors student at Newton Street School.

Biddle, Vernon Pianist. Played at many local and New York clubs, including Downbeat; on keyboard at Newark's Hi Spot with Slim Henderson on saxophone and Wesley Clark on bass (early 1940s); went to Hollywood to arrange music for movies.

Blackmon, Lou *Herald News* writer known as the Nightlifer (late 1930s–early 1940s).

Blackwell, Eddie Guitarist. Remains active locally.

Blango, Florence Pianist; married name Smith. Played in all-girl band (1930s); sister of bassist Richard (Dick) Harvest.

Bogar, Jerry Bassist and bandleader. Born in Dothan, Ala., Jan. 17, 1906; played trumpet in youth; led Jerry Bogar's Royal Club Orchestra (1940s–50s); played at Three Towers in Somerville, N.J. (late 1940s); featured at Carnegie Hall in Vauxhall, N.J. (c1950); bought Caravan Club (1953) and operated it for next year or so; died Feb. 19, 1985.

Bonner, Bill Drummer. Played with Dick Matthews' band at Dave and Maney's in Orange, N.J. (late 1930s).

Bradley, Doryce Exotic dancing star. Born Oct. 18, 1914 in Albany, Ga.; came to Newark with parents at age 5; toured (1930s) in *Harlem on Parade* and RKO circuit with Bill Robinson and Buck and Bubbles; headlined at Atlantic City's Club Harlem (1938); played clubs in 1940s including Dan Montgomery's in Buffalo, Club De Lisa in Chicago, and Plantation Club in St. Louis; played Star Dust Inn in Washington, D.C. (1945), Club Bali in Washington, D.C. (1946), Crystal Caverns in Washington, D.C. (1946), Small's Paradise in New York (1946), and Town Club in Virginia Beach, Va. (1946); toured with USO (1945); appeared in Mantan Moreland movie *Mantan Messes Up* (late 1940s).

Bradley, Herman Drummer. Born June 2, 1908 in Charleston, S.C.; moved to Newark in childhood; made $2 at first job at Paterson, N.J. Junior Order Masonic Hall (with Johnny Williams on piano); influenced by Buster Tyler; worked with Joe Crump's band in Bayonne, N.J. (1929); played at Small's Paradise in New York (1929–30); organized Rhythm Dons, who played locally at Dodger's and New York's 101 Ranch (1930s); won many band battles in 1930s; joined Benny Carter's band (1942); played with Freddie Mitchell and Buddy Lucas, making many recordings, including "Easter Boogie" with Mitchell; teamed with pianist

Reno Brooks at Gulliver's, West Paterson, N.J. (1970s); led duo at small clubs in Connecticut (1980s); incapacitated by stroke (1987).

Bradley, James (Jack) Bandleader. Toured with Drake and Walker minstrels as head of their band (1920s); brother of drummer Herman Bradley.

Bragg, Maude Emcee. One of few female emcees of early 1940s; followed Charlie Matthews into Nest Club to announce shows.

Brakes, Joe Drummer. Teenage sensation from Elizabeth, N.J. whose furious solos caught on when he sat in with Barons of Rhythm at Shady Rest County Club (c1940); played with Pancho Diggs Orchestra (early 1940s); replaced Charlie (Brother) Kelly at the Alcazar (early 1940s); with Jerry Bogar's Royal Club Orchestra (1940s–50s); deceased.

Branch, Count Saxophonist and bandleader. Stalwart in Jerry Bogar's Royal Club Orchestra (1940s–50s).

Brannon, Humphrey (Teddy) Pianist and arranger; nicknamed for Teddy Wilson. Born Sept. 27, 1917 in Moultrie, Ga; moved to Newark at age 4; took lessons at home at mother's insistence; influenced by musicians in shows at Elizabeth's Ritz Theater, including Earl Hines and Claude Hopkins; first paid jobs with Gus Young (1937) and Heat Waves at Nest Club (late 1930s); played with Hal Mitchell Trio at Hi Spot until he and Mitchell joined Benny Carter's band (c1942); traveled with Carter for 2 years, playing one-nighters at local halls and making sound tracks for 2 movies, *Thousands Cheer* and classic *Stormy Weather*; drafted into Army and played in several military bands; played with Roy Eldridge's band at Chic in Canada; played and arranged for Paul Gayten and Ravens; performed with Jonah Jones on supper club circuit; traveled with George Foster "as far as Australia and Monaco"; backed artists including Don Byas and Lester Young on recordings on Savoy, Prestige, and Atlantic (1940s–50s); preferred playing in small groups "so I can build my own backgrounds"; lived in Newark until his death, Feb. 24, 1989.

Brinson, Carl Talent scout and promoter; better known as Tiny Prince because of his diminutive frame. Born in Newark, May 12, 1918; one of Newark's best lindyhoppers (1940s); wrote column in "jive" language for *New Jersey Herald News* (1940s); founded *After Hours*, black entertainment magazine (1949); discovered singer Roy Hamilton; served as affirmative action officer of City of Newark (1970–86)

Brinson: "Harry Webber, Al Madison, and I decided to start *After Hours* after we got laid off from the *Herald News*. We met on the unemployment line. It was a recession. All the black newspapers were suffering for advertising. They were depending on whiskey and cigarette ads. We came out with *After Hours* in 1949, a year before John Johnson started *Jet*."

Brock, Roy Bandleader (late 1940s).

Brooks, Kitty Singer. Born in Ozark, Ala., March 26, 1929; church singer since childhood; sang with Pancho Diggs Orchestra (1948) and bands led by Charlie (Brother) Kelly and Jerry Bogar; also sang with Snookum Russell's and Happy Rose's big bands; sang "a little of everything," from sentimental love songs and jazz to blues tunes like 'King Size Papa.'"

Broome Street Slim Pianist; real name unknown. Popular house rent party piano player (early 1930s).

Wesley Clark: "I used to hang out with him at the pool room at Broome and Spruce. All the musicians went there to get gigs."

Brown, Bobbie Bandleader. Worked in Canada (1920) and fronted quartet (1921) with Bingie Madison on piano; led Bobbie Brown's Society Orchestra and Bobbie Brown's Syncopators (1921–26), which included tenor saxophonist Happy Caldwell.

Brown, Frank (Red) Pianist and organist. From Jersey City, N.J.; played with Bennie (Red) Robinson at Hi Spot (1947), Howard Bar (1951), and T-Bar, replacing Grachan

(Brother) Moncur's group (1952); switched to organ; regular at Pitt's Place on West Market Street (1960s); deceased.

Brown, James (Brownie) Trumpeter "from the old school." Mother played piano; raised in orphanage near Buffalo, N.Y., where he learned music; played for a while in Works Progress Administration (WPA) Negro band (1930s); performed in several Newark groups (early 1930s) with Bobby Plater, including Heat Waves, at club in Bayonne, N.J. and at Spadaro's, a Catskills resort in Ellenville, N.Y.; wrote and read music; moved to California (1940s); deceased.

Brown, Laura Pianist. Listed in D. Antoinette Handy's *Black Women in American Bands and Orchestras* as playing ragtime piano with Peerless Orchestra in Newark "in the second decade of the century."

Brown, Lee Pianist, drummer, singer, and songwriter, and Newark's most notable hepcat; known internationally as Babs Gonzales, also Ricardo Gonzales. Born Oct. 27, 1919 in Newark; posed as homosexual to avoid draft during World War II; toured as vocalist with Charlie Barnet and Lionel Hampton (1944–45); played at Minton's Playhouse (1946–47); took his Three Bips and a Bop into Carnegie Hall in New York (1947); appeared on Arthur Godfrey Show (1947); James Moody's manager (1952); recorded hits including "Be Bop Santa Claus" and "Oop-Pop-a-Da" with Moody (late 1940s); traveled to Europe with Manhattan Singers (c1950); jailed for drug use (1968); lived in Sweden for several years, opening for Josephine Baker in Paris at one point; appeared on Johnny Carson Show (1972); wrote and published two autobiographical books, *I Paid My Dues* and *Movin' on Down the Line;* died Jan. 23, 1980 in College Hospital, Newark, at age 62.

Brown, Nate Singer. Born in Durham, N.C., c1923; used GI bill benefits to study singing at school "on the corner near Lloyd's Manor," where he began performing with James Moody, Babs Gonzales, Hank Mobley, Danny Quebec, George Benson, and Jimmy

Ponder; played with Arthur Terry and His Grand Rascals at Lloyd's (1946), Pancho Diggs's band at Skateland (n.d.), and Terrace Ballroom (1947); recorded Diggs's popular number "Swanee River" on Coleman label; considered himself more of "a hustler than singer"; blackjack dealer at Caesar's casino in Atlantic City until his death Feb. 6, 1989.

Bill Roberts: "Nate had funny ways. He was ornery—a loner. Once he had an audition with CBS and he never went. He never had a [regular] job. He was independent."

Brown, Oliver (Butts) Editor and publisher. Born in Flemington, N.J.; roommate of poet Langston Hughes at Lincoln University; one of owners of *New Jersey Herald News*, defunct black weekly newspaper based in Newark (late 1930s–50s); deceased.

Brown, Vick Popular crooner. Sang with Ame Garrison's Sirens of Swing (1938); appeared at Boston Plaza (late 1930s–early 1940s); stationed at Camp Pickett, Va. (1943).

Bill Roberts: "One time we went to see Erskine Hawkins. I told Hawkins I had a friend from Newark I wanted him to hear sing 'Until the Real Thing Comes Along.' Vick blew the house down."

Brown, Winnie (Wini) *See* Johnson, Winnie (Wini).

Brownie *See* Brown, James.

Bryant, Jimmy Singer. Performed with Barons of Rhythm (1940).

Bryant, Lillian Sweet singer. Regular in revues at Dodger's (1942–43).

Buchanan, Cliff Emcee. Appeared at Kinney Club (1930s); had act with Bernice Scott.

Burford, Alphonso Musician. Played tipple, banjo, and guitar at house rent parties (1930s); later wrote church music for Seventh-Day Adventists; died 1976.

Burwell, Al Singer. Appeared at Hydeaway (1943) with William (Bass Byrd) Lindbergh, Anna May Lundy Lewis, Billy Lewis, and Ann Brown.

Butler, Billy Drummer; not to be confused with guitar player from New York. From Montclair, N.J.; played with local groups; brother-in-law of Leon Eason.

Butler, Conrad Founder and bandleader of Barons of Rhythm, talented junior version of Savoy Dictators who performed at Shady Rest Country Club in Scotch Plains, N.J. (late 1930s); played baritone and sang; stepped down as group's leader (1941); became musical director at MGM; deceased.

Butterfield, Erskine Pianist and singer. Born in Syracuse, N.Y., Feb. 9, 1913; moved to Newark at age 5; took standard piano and harmony lessons while attending grammar school in Newark; started playing popular music demonstrating tunes for New York publisher Clarence Williams; played for 3 years during Depression with Newark's Russell Mann and His Royal Ambassadors; worked with Noble Sissle; joined NBC studio staff (1938); recorded on Decca and other labels alone and with small white groups (early 1940s); featured twice weekly as "The Singing Vagabond of the Keys" on the Mutual Broadcasting System on WOR in New York (1941); after stint in Army, moved to Minneapolis, where he led trio; subsequently returned to studio music; died in New York City, July 1961.

Clyde Bernhardt: "He got further than [Donald] Lambert, but he wasn't as good. He was plain, down to earth. He didn't boast like Lambert, though Lambert could back it up."

Byrd, Bass *See* Lindbergh, William.

Byrd, Billie Producer and performer. Wrote, produced, sang, and danced in spate of shows for Kinney Club (1938–39); with partner, Thelma, did "a springy, tapping number" in which they supposedly "made a new dance out of the Susie Q" (1938); brought "all-star cast shows from Harlem" into Kinney every 2 weeks.

Cabell, Conrad (Connie) Guitarist and ukelele player. Played at house rent parties (early 1930s); also played bass; died in Sept. 1986 after long residency at Old Soldiers Home in Cranford, N.J.

Campbell, William Writer and producer. Produced and wrote *The Big Plantation* revue and other shows for Boston Plaza

(1942); brought all-star revue featuring Pearl Swan (The Atomic Bomb of Rhythm), Billy Avant, sweet singer Lynn Pinckney, and blues singer Eudora Blake to Twinlite (Dec. 1946).

Carey, George Tenor saxophonist. Played in band led by Russell Mann (1930s).

Carmen, Herb Early 1940s bandleader. Became New Brunswick cop.

Caros, Betty Dancer. Clever little Spanish dancer at Dave and Maney's (1938); appeared in Asbury Park, N.J. clubs.

Carruthers, Leon Drummer. Played in early (c1918) Newark nightclubs like Palace Lucille and Perkins; father was minister.

Carruthers, Swifty Pianist; first name unknown. Played Palace Lucille and Perkins (c1918) with brother Leon.

Caston, Bobbie Female singer. Got rave reviews with Sonny Woods' group at Three Deuces (1947); gained popularity as vocalist with Louis Armstrong's Orchestra; Newark favorite.

Cateye See Roberts, Leon.

Cato (also Kato), Billy Trombonist and bandleader. Played in Bingie Madison's (1926) band, which, according to writer Albert McCarthy, "disbanded in Newark, New Jersey"; bandleader (1927–32) out of Vauxhall part of Union Township, N.J.; his group played at Rose Danceland in New York with Jellyroll Morton; recorded with Morton (1928) and Coleman Hawkins (1940); also worked at Savoy Ballroom in New York with 12-piece band.

Leon Eason: "Bobby Williams got arrangements from Cato's band by sitting in in New York and copying them."

Clyde Bernhardt: "He was one of the best trombone players in New York."

Cawthorn, Carrie Sweet singer. Appeared in shows at Picadilly (1943).

Chambers, Elmer (Frog) Trumpeter; also nicknamed "Muffin Jaws" because of his jowly appearance. Born c1897; met Sam Wooding in Army during World War I; played with Wooding's Society Syncopators in Atlantic City (after war), Fletcher Henderson's Orchestra (1924–26), and Billy Fowler's Strand Roof Orchestra (1926–27); toured with traveling revues (1930s); brought his Blue Streaks into Kinney Club (1938); his arrangement of "Honeysuckle Rose" a house hit; died 1952.

Lucille (Dorsey) Morton: "He was a big, fat man who played potty tot [old-fashioned, syncopated rhythms]. I used to call him 'Apple Jaws.' "

Al Henderson: "He was a crackshot musician, but I was into swing. He would play what we called potty tot, which made me realize what I would sound like if I was playin' the same stuff years later."

Chambers, Frankie Drummer.

Chapman, Bill (Robinson) Dancer. Teamed with Anna May Hall (1930s–40s) in Newark's most popular twosome; deceased.

Chapman, Jack Guitarist, banjo player, and arranger. His arrangements considered pivotal to success of Savoy Sultans; arranged for Alabams and other groups.

Clem Moorman: "He taught me the real meaning of syncopation. All his arrangements were punctuated with it."

Bill Roberts: "At intermission, all the rest of the boys would be drinking and he'd be back there [at the Boston Plaza] arranging music."

Chinn, Cornelius Saxophonist. Played with Joe Crump's Band of 1,000 Themes when it got off ground at Colony Club (1936–37); deceased.

Clark, Larry Pianist. Played with Russell Mann and His Royal Ambassadors (c1931).

Clark, Wesley (Wes) Bassist (originally banjo player). Raised in Newark; played banjo in first job, with June Cole on piano, saxophonist Bill Schenck, and Trombone Red from Hackensack, N.J. at prizefighters' camp in Greenwood Lake, N.Y.; played with Gus Young (1936–44), including New York's Savoy Ballroom; in and out of Newark's Hi Spot for 5 years (1940s), first with Hal Mitchell and Teddy Brannon (1942), then as leader of trio featuring Vernon Biddle and Slim Henderson; played with Picadilly Madcaps (1943).

Clark, Willie (Bub) Ace guitarist and banjo

player. Made what Willie Johnson calls "flukie" guitars out of wood; one of most sought-after house rent party musicians; couldn't read a note; prized possession, a gold-plated Gibson; deceased.

Coates, Clarence Drummer. Played in 1930s groups with Leon Eason; member of Melmore Stompers; played in band led by Carl McIntyre at 42nd Club in Orange, N.J. (1947–52); died Aug. 16, 1990.

Cole, Blanche Singer. Married pianist Teddy Cole (1930s); sang at Colony Club and other Newark clubs and at Crystal Caverns, Washington, D.C. (1941).

Charlie Matthews: "She could sing, and she was equally temperamental."

Cole, Donald Reuben (June or Jay) Pianist. Born April 27, 1919 in East Orange, N.J.; brother of jazz great Cozy Cole, pianist Teddy Cole, and drummer Herbert Cole; graduate of Paul Hill School of Music, New York; called by writer Bob Queen "The Quiet Man of the Jazz World" who "spoke loudest with his piano"; influenced by Art Tatum's "distinctive style and musical clarity" and by Dodo Marmarosa and Bud Powell; played East Coast theaters and clubs with Miss Rhapsody and Her Three Sportsmen of Rhythm (mid 1940s); recorded 12 sides on Savoy with Miss Rhapsody (1944–45); recorded with Deek Watson and Brown Dots on Manor, and on Savoy and other labels with brother Cozy ("Cozy's Caravan" and "Concerto for Cozy"); co-leader with Clyde Bernhardt of Harlem Blues and Jazz Band (1973–75); died Feb. 4, 1975 at Presbyterian Hospital, Newark.

Cole, Teddy Pianist. Brother of Cozy, June, and Herbert; played with Newark's Matinee Idols (early 1930s), group heard each Sunday on WHBI radio; played with trumpeter Roy Eldridge at Chicago's Three Deuces; recorded with Lil Armstrong and Her Swing Band on Vocalion (1937); died in Portsmith, Va. (c1982).

Coleman, Lander See Coleman Brothers.

Coleman, Roy Electric bassist. Played with Al Henderson Trio at Dodger's (1943).

Coleman, Russell See Coleman Brothers.

Coleman, Smokie Emcee and tap dancer; first name unknown. Appeared in Crackshot Hacksley's 1942 revue at Dodger's; played local circuit.

Coleman Brothers Radio recording personalities and concert artists: singers Everette (who also played guitar), Lander, Melvin, Russell, and Wallace, and Danny Owens. Of 10 brothers, 7 were musical, 3 became ministers; had 15-minute daily radio broadcast on WCBS (1945); played uptown at Barney Josephson's Cafe Society and other top New York night spots (late 1940s); several, owners of Coleman record label and Coleman Hotel on Court Street (1940s); radio broadcasts emanated from hotel's Musical Lounge.

Collins, Lester (Shad) Trumpeter. Born in Elizabeth, N.J., June 27, 1910; played with Eddie White's Orchestra (late 1920s–early 1930s); fronted for vocalist Cora LaRedd as member of Charlie Dixon's Band (c1930s); played with Chick Webb (1931), Benny Carter (1933), Tiny Bradshaw (1934), Teddy Hill (1936–37), (including trip to Paris), Count Basie (1938–40), Freddie Moore and Lester Young sextet (1941), then Buddy Johnson; replaced Dizzy Gillespie in Cab Calloway's band, playing on and off with Calloway (1941–46); made 4 sides with Johnson on Decca (c1940); husband of Billie Peterman, who was with Teddy Hill's Orchestra and ran rooming house at 320 Norfolk Street, Newark, which catered to musicians (early 1940s); died in Jersey City, N.J., June 1980.

Cook, Bill Broadcaster and manager. Turned to broadcasting and musical management after operation changed his tenor singing voice, but gave his speaking voice a sonorous quality that made him a natural before the microphone; one of few black disc jockeys of his era; managed singers Roy Hamilton, Florence Wright, and Platters (late 1940s–early 1950s); began broadcasting his "Musical Caravan" from Graham Auditorium and on WAAT from Coleman Hotel, playing current pop tunes (1940s); remembered for his opening theme, "Caravan," and closing recitation of "Ave

Maria"; manager of Caravan Club (late 1940s); died c1984.

Cook, George Trombonist. Played in Frank Gibbs Orchestra (1934).

Cooper, Al Saxophonist, clarinetist, bandleader, and arranger. Born 1911 in Miami, Fla.; half-brother of Grachan (Brother) Moncur; led Savoy Sultans; died Oct. 1981.

Albert McCarthy (*Big Band Jazz*): "As a soloist, [Cooper] did not feature himself a great deal; clarinet passages on 'Looney' and 'Norfolk Ferry' are pleasant, 'Looney' having a mellowness that one associates with New Orleans clarinetists."

Cooper, George Drummer. From Florida; came to Newark from Miami and got job upstairs at White House, club on Halsey Street (1930); played with Eddie Wells' band (early 1930s); best known as member of Matinee Idols, who broadcast regularly on WHBI (early 1930s); also played in Kinney Club rathskeller with Joe Crump (1930s).

Cooper, Ralph Emcee and producer. Emceed shows at Orpheum Theater (1938) before going into movies; produced and emceed shows at Harlem's Apollo Theater (late 1930s–early 1940s); present the night Sarah Vaughan won Apollo amateur contest (1942); judged Newark band battles; managed revived Apollo amateur night shows, *Showtime at the Apollo* (late 1980s into 1990s).

Copeland, Johnny Pianist. From Montclair, N.J.; led local bands at Bungalow on Route 23 in Passaic County, N.J. and Fountain in Belleville, N.J.

Corley, Mary Singer; better known as Skippy Williams. Shared vocals with Horace Sims for Mandy Ross and His Walkin' Rhythm, local band that toured South (1944); coordinated acts, sang, and emceed at Dodger's (early 1940s).

Costello, Marguerite (Rita) Feisty and vivacious singer and dancer. From Ohio; played Kinney Club for 6-month period and headlined at white club on Broad Street (1938–39); brought new interpretation of "Copper Colored Girl" to Kinney; billed as "Queen of

the Shake Dancers" at Club Bali in Washington, D.C. (1943); performed at Offbeat Club in Washington (1943); stopped singing professionally to raise family.

Cousins, Johnny Guitarist. Played Picadilly (1947) with Togge Smythe, saxophone, and June Cole, piano.

Cox, Johnny Saxophonist. Original member of Barons of Rhythm (mid 1930s).

Cross, Frank Drummer. Played with Joe Crump's Band of 1,000 Themes at Colony Club (1936–37); forte was brushes; used drums that supposedly had only one skin; became milkman; deceased.

Hal Mitchell: "He could read better than any one of us. I've never seen anything like it since. He would play the lines we had on the horns."

Crowder, Jabbo Dancer and drummer. Performed at spots including Del Mar Bar (1940s).

Joe Gregory: "He was my main buddy. He was a couple of years younger than me, but he liked to hang out with me 'cause I could dance and he was learning to dance. Finally, we got a couple of little jobs together."

Crump, Joe Bandleader and everybody's piano player. Born c1900; lost several fingers in factory accident; led Joe Crump and His Band of 1,000 Themes (c1936) at Colony Club and Nest Club; led postwar jam sessions at Dodger's on Monday nights (1945–46); went into Lloyd's Manor (1946), where he joined Ray-O-Vacs; toured with them for next 14 years, recording on Decca and Coleman labels; deceased.

Thad Howard: "There was nothing he couldn't play."

Tiny Prince: "He and Gus Young were like 'Mr. World' to everybody. Every musician looked up to him."

Cuba Trumpeter; full name unknown. From Vauxhall section of Union Township, N.J.; played a lot with pianist Donald Lambert; deceased.

Cureton, Sam Trumpeter. Played with Frank Gibbs Orchestra (1934) and original Barons of Rhythm (mid 1930s–early 1940s); died May 1981.

Darling, Mae Sweet singer. Also danced in chorus line at Nest Club; described as having pleasing personality and voice; girlfriend of Coco Darling, popular entertainer and bass player who danced around stage with his bass fiddle.

Sadie Matthews: "She was a prima donna. She didn't want to, but Mrs. [Eurlee] Reeves [who owned the Nest Club] made everyone wear costumes and be in the chorus."

Davis, Earl Saxophonist. Played with Omega Bar and Grill Trio with Ala Mae Miller, piano, and William (Bass Byrd) Lindbergh, bass (late 1930s).

Davis, Melba (Bonnie) *See* Smith, Melba.

Day, Eddie Trombonist. Played in theater pit bands; used to "pass the hat" at local bars to get by during Depression.

Willie Johnson: "He didn't get that many gigs, so he started playing around for the hat; I did it a lot, too."

DeGaston, Zidora Singer. Sang at Dodger's (1930s).

Derricks, Lavinia Singer. Rendered "Lonesome Road" and "Trees" at Milton Pittman's birthday party at Boston Plaza (July 1939).

DeShield, Kitty Shake dancer. Performed at Kinney Club (1948).

Dickenson, Vic One of jazz world's premier trombonists. Born in Xenia, Ohio, Aug. 6, 1906; called "the best in Newark" when he played with Frank Gibbs' band (1938); played with Blanche Calloway (1933–36), Claude Hopkins (1936–39), Benny Carter (1939 and 1941), and Count Basie (1940); died in Nov. 1984.

Dickson, (Little) Willie Emcee. Worked at Nest Club (on and off, 1939–45).

Herald News (July 29, 1939): "Little Willie had the joint jumpin', singing 'Well, All Right' before the introduction of each number."

Diggs, Alton (Pancho) Handsome bandleader and saxophonist. Led orchestra at Skateland, the Montgomery Street dance hall catering to young swingsters twice a week (late 1930s); served as bandmaster with Army's 770th Regiment (1942–45); re-

organized band fronted by singer/comedienne Nina Mae McKinney (c1945); president of Newark Musicians' Staff Club (1946); played at Lloyd's Manor (1947); remained active musically into 1970s as secretary, later business agent (1977) of Local 16, Musicians' Guild of Essex County; considered by black musicians as their man at union; died Dec. 1982.

Douglas, William (Dee) Drummer. Led first band in which saxophonist Bobby Plater played.

Drew, Allen Emcee and dancer. Performed at Boston Plaza (1943); teamed with comedian Johnny B. Gardner at Grand Hotel (1943).

Afro-American (Nov. 20, 1943): "[Drew] had customers in a jovial mood with stories he can tell without stopping for hours; for my money, the guy is the best who ever did it."

Dukes, Hattie Blues singer. From Philadelphia; stopped show at Milton Pittman's 1939 birthday party at the Boston Plaza with her rendition of "St. Louis Blues"; regular in Boston Plaza floor shows; performed at Baltimore's Club Harlem (1942); became defense factory worker (1943).

Bill Roberts: "I recall her working the Palace Lucille on Plane Street between Market and Bank. She sang like Anna [Mom] Pease."

Durham, Joe Bassist. From San Marcos, Texas; oldest brother of trombonist/guitarist Eddie Durham, arranger for Count Basie, Glenn Miller, and other big bandleaders, pianist Roosevelt Durham, and clarinetist and saxophone player Earl Durham; with Roosevelt, made Newark his home after blues singer Mamie Smith's *7-11* traveling show shut down at Miner's Theater (c1926); joined Blanche Calloway's band, which wound up in Kansas City (1931); played with band led by Jasper (Jap) Allen (1932); played at Omega Bar and Grill, Roselle, N.J. with Three Blue Notes (early 1940s); deceased.

Eddie Durham: "Joe also played trumpet and violin. He played all instruments. In fact, he taught me from the beginning."

Durham, Roosevelt Pianist. From San Marcos, Texas; brother of Eddie, Joe, and Earl; rival of stride piano king Donald Lambert; often engaged in cutting contests; had band at Fisher's Tavern with Leatha McCraw handling vocals (1938); also played violin; deceased.

Dyla, Roscoe Emcee. Worked at Kinney Club and Dodger's (1948–49); teamed with Crackshot Hacksley and Wynonie (Mr. Blues) Harris for southern tour (late 1940s); subsequently played Newark club dates.

Eason, Leon Trumpeter and singer. Born Nov. 12, 1910 in Rich Square, N.C.; began playing violin and clarinet as teenager; formed vaudeville dance team with Herbert Harper, debuting at Newark's Branford Theater; began playing trumpet (1930) in Hubert Ravenue's band; toured with Alabams in *Harlem on Parade* (1931–35), accompanying Buck and Bubbles and other top acts; formed own band (1936), playing Newark's Park Rest, Club Miami, and other white spots; led band at Pop Durham's Alcazar (1937–40); served in Army (1943–44); toured with Gene Phipps' band (1944); played with Tommy Gill (1945), Grachan Moncur and His Strollers (1947), and Red Lincoln (1948–51); soloist with Jack Albertson's band (from 1952); led trio at Pitt's Place, Newark (1956–68); recorded 12 sides, including "Lazy River," "I'm in the Mood for Love," and "Just a Gigolo" for Blue Note (1959); witty grace and style like that of Louis Armstrong, his idol.

Billy Anderson: "Leon was one of Newark's most refreshing personalities."

Miss Rhapsody: "Leon plays as much horn as Louis Armstrong ever played. Louis just admired him and loved him 'cause he was [just like] Louis Armstrong."

Easterly, Irene Singer. Had unusually expansive range; sang "Can't Face the Music" in Kinney Club revue starring Flo Thomas (1938).

Elliott, Lucy (Lu) Singer. Featured with Eddie Heywood's Orchestra (1947); sang with Duke Ellington (1950) and Erskine Hawkins (1951); began singing in Atlantic City casinos, mostly at Golden Nugget (late 1970s–mid 1980s); wife of guitarist Horace Sims; died of cancer March 4, 1987.

Ellis, Clarence Kinney Club emcee (1942).

Erwin, Dave Guitarist. Played with Three Blue Notes at Roselle's Omega Bar and Grill and with Picadilly Madcaps at Newark's Picadilly (1943).

Ethridge, Erma Singer; married name Winslow. Born Oct. 1, 1923; sang "Pennies from Heaven" on Newark radio station at age 6; as little girl "saw Sammy Davis Jr. and the Will Mastin Trio at the Orpheum Theater" and was "enchanted with all the beautiful girls who came on stage to sing and dance"; South Side High School graduate; began singing professionally in 1943; appeared with Madhatters at Newark's Three Deuces (1948); toured Canada and Midwest with Johnny B. Gardner; traveled with Redd Foxx; played top New York clubs and theaters (early 1950s), including Apollo, Baby Grand, Elks Rendezvous, and Cotton Club.

Evans, George Trumpeter. Performed in area clubs with Smilin' Bill Stewart, bandleader from Philadelphia; died in Jan. 1987.

Evans, Warren Singer. Sang with Buddy Johnson's band; big hit, "Baby, Don't You Cry"; recorded "Don't Be Late" and "I Still Love You"; performed at Cafe Superior (1947) and Dodger's (1948).

Ferguson, Arthur (Fergie) Trombonist. Played for walkathons with Al Henderson's Orchestra (c1936–37); performed with Ted McRae's Orchestra at Harlem's Club Sudan (1946).

Fields, Pete Drummer. Played with Elmer Chambers' Blue Streaks at Kinney Club (late 1930s) and with Bennie (Red) Robinson at Hi Spot (1947).

Fletcher, June Contortionist. Described in *Afro* as "twisting in corkscrew fashion" in 1946 show at Kinney Club; featured at Kinney (1947) in Reese LaRue's *Tropical Revue*.

Fluker, Charlie Producer and emcee. Came to Kinney Club (1939) after playing New York's Apollo Theater; emcee (summer 1938) at Savoy Ballroom at Springfield and Belmont avenues.

Lucille (Dorsey) Morton: "Another boy who put on good shows."

Ford, Harold Pianist. Born Aug. 19, 1919 in Okolona, Miss.; came to Newark in 1931 to live with aunt and uncle; first job (1940) at Riviera Hotel, 169 Clinton Avenue, Newark ("I wore a tux and got five dollars"); made demo at Hertz Studio and was hired by owner to work there playing piano; played with Gene Phipps Orchestra (1942–45); recorded "a sweet number and the blues" on Manor with Phipps; led quartet at Picadilly (1946) and piano orchestra at Lloyd's Manor, Club Theresa, and other local spots (late 1940s); became postal worker "after music styles changed" because he did not "choose to change my format"; continued playing part time with Warren Gordon and His Orchestra.

Ford, William (Billy) Trumpeter and singer; nicknamed "Weasel." Joined Pancho Diggs Orchestra out of Bloomfield (N.J.) High School (1936); with his frantic trumpeting, caught attention of Tiny Bradshaw (c1944), who signed him as featured artist and vocalist; performed with Cootie Williams until he formed own band; wrote "I'll Live True to You," made popular by vocalist Trevor Bacon (1942) as GI's lament for girl he left behind; headlined Bradshaw's *King of Jitterbugs* show with Lowell (Count) Hastings at Howard Theater, Washington, D.C. (1945); with his group, won *Herald News* Band Popularity Contest twice; fixture at Broad Street's Nitecap (1951–52); teamed with Lillie Bryant as Billie and Lillie, recording million seller "La Dee Dah" (1957); later led U.S. State Department tour of Billy Ford and His Thunderbirds; proponent of soft swing; died 1984.

Hal Mitchell: "He was a well-taught musician—in the classical vein. 'Flight of the Bumblebee' was his specialty. To play swing, we had to teach him to 'bend' a note. He was like the Wynton Marsalis of fifty years ago."

Fulford, Clarence (Mouse) Trumpeter. Mainstay of Matinee Idols; also played saxophone and clarinet; brother of pianist who played with bands in New York, possibly Chick Webb's.

Fuller, Walter (Gil) Pianist and arranger. Born in Los Angeles, 1920; first arranger for Barons of Rhythm; arranged for Savoy Dictators and subsequently for Tiny Bradshaw (c1942), Dizzy Gillespie, and Billy Eckstine (early 1940s).

Stanley Dance (*Jazz Era: The Forties*): "He was the first arranger to adapt innovations of the new jazz to large ensembles effectively. In their brilliance and force, his scores continued the tradition of the virtuoso arrangements."

Fussell, Johnny Ace dancer. From Newark; traveled widely on national circuits; toured Europe with Tip, Tap, and Toe; performed with famous Miller Brothers dance team out of New York (1930s); white tails his trademark; mainstay at Kinney Club (early 1940s); deceased.

Leon Eason: "He'd come out, sit down on a chair, and dance."

Gardner, Johnny B. All-round emcee, comedian, dancer, and talent scout. Star of summer shows at Rockhead's Paradise in Montreal; packaged Newark nightclub and theater shows (1930s), creating jobs for many local entertainers; known for his spicy yarns and clever chatter; billed as "All-American Half-Wit" in *Darktown Follies* at Republican Gardens in Washington, D.C. (Sept. 1941); deceased.

Bob Queen: "Johnny used to lay 'em out in the thirties at the Cotton Club, Villa Maurice, Kit Kat, and Kinney Club."

Charlie Matthews: "The man talked a lot of crap."

Garland, Mose Bandleader. Led Mose Garland and His Syncopators (late 1940s–early 1950s), dance band that appeared regularly at Terrace Ballroom.

Garrison, Amelia (Ame) Acclaimed saxophonist. Born in Charleston, S.C.; doesn't tell her age, but is "no chicken"; graduate of Central High School in Newark, where she "played fiddle"; organized Newark Elks Band in which she played trombone; also plays clarinet, organ, and accordion; played with famous International Sweethearts of Rhythm, all-girl orchestra that traveled world; with Sweethearts, appeared 5 times at New York's Apollo Theater; brought her all-girl Sirens of Swing into Boston Plaza for Sunday matinees (1938); performed with Three Chucks and Chick (1949).

Gates *See* Willis, Luther.

Geech *See* Smalls, Julius.

Gersh *See* Sutton, Frank.

Gibbs, Allen Saxophonist. Brother of band-leader Frank Gibbs; described by Lou Blackmon in *Herald News* as "the best alto in town" (1939); played with Pancho Diggs Orchestra (early 1940s); played with a band while in Navy.

Gibbs, Frank Trumpeter and bandleader. Brother of Allen Gibbs; led band (1931) including Willie Johnson, Collins Murphy, Connie Cabell, Allen Gibbs, and Earl Nelson; subsequent members were Al Henderson, Clem Moorman, and Lowell (Count) Hastings in a group that competed for top spot in local band battles; in 1938 interview, said he felt snubbed by selection of Pancho Diggs's and Herman Bradley's bands as Newark's top groups; attributed subsequent breakup of band to "jealousy"; died in Jamaica, N.Y.

Frank Gibbs (1938 interview): "Who selects the bands, anyway? My boys are the rightful holders of the swing championship of the state. We've been playing seven years. Right now I'm making important changes in the swing style."

Herald News Nightlifer (Aug. 5, 1939): "His was one of the bands that should have gone places, but failed for some reason."

Tiny Prince: "Frank had a society band. They played simple tunes—what the older folks liked—waltzes and fox trots that everybody could dance to."

Gibson, Danny Drummer. Born in Newark, June 29, 1913; son of Alfred C. (Pop) Gibson, who owned Radio Inn, barnlike upstairs nightclub on Halsey Street, and was dominant political figure of old Third Ward and one of city's first black politicians; got first set of drums as Christmas present when he

was 13; taught by "Mr. Kirschner, who had a store on Springfield Avenue"; first club date with Harold (Hal) Mitchell and Joe Crump's Band of 1,000 Themes; joined Savoy Dictators (1930s); recorded on Savoy with Dictators (1939) and on Manor with Deek Watson and Brown Dots (1946); led groups including Del Mar Boys at Del Mar Bar (1945); in combo with Al Cooper and Grachan (Brother) Moncur (1946).

Gibson, Herman Guitarist and banjo player (1920s–30s). Worked in rathskeller of Kinney Club with Joe Crump, George Cooper, and Carl McIntyre (c1932); played with Duke Richardson Orchestra (1932).

Leon Eason: "He was the best I ever heard—in the category of Walter Barnes and, later, Charlie Christian."

Giles, John Trumpeter. Played in Frank Gibbs Orchestra (1934).

Gilmore, Artie Saxophonist; became bartender and club manager.

Gilmore, Irving Emcee. Often compared to Rudy Vallee because he used megaphone; played Kinney Club (1930s).

Givens, Clifford Singer. Newarker who replaced Hoppy Jones with Ink Spots; subsequently joined Golden Gate Quartet.

Gonzales, Babs *See* Brown, Lee.

Goode, Bill Singer and drummer. Got his start in Works Progress Administration (WPA) Federal Theater Project; formed Four Shades with Danford (Larue) Jordan, Joe Gregory, and Babs Gonzales (1939); sang and played piano at Picadilly (1941); resumed career after Army stint as emcee at Grimsley's, Dodger's, and other local clubs; recorded "With the Wind and Rain in Your Hair" for Savoy (1947); with his Four Bars and a Melody, packed them in at Picadilly (1947); emcee at Meeker Avenue's Downbeat Club (1949); led Bill Goode Quartet at Caravan Club (1949); noted for his tender voice; deceased.

Gordon, Flash Dancer. Headliner at Kinney Club as star of Reese LaRue's *Tropical Revue* (1947); also danced regularly at Lloyd's Manor.

Bill Roberts: "They called her the black

Marlene Dietrich, 'cause she had a helluva shape."

Gordon, George (Fats) Composer, arranger, and pianist. Born in Newark June 10, 1916; as child, sneaked into New York clubs to hear Art Tatum; by 14, was playing at house rent parties; played solo and with trios; recorded on Prestige; centered life's work on perfecting vocal arrangements and accompanying his three children, George Jr., Honi, and Richard, who sang backgrounds as the Gordons for Eddie Jefferson and recorded on Debut with Charles Mingus; died Dec. 26, 1982.

Meredith Gordon (widow): "George started Honi, George, and Richard singing when Richie was about six or so. It was fun for them. Honi sang when she was a baby."

Gordon, Louise Torch singer and dancer. Performed at Boston Plaza and Dodger's (mid-late 1930s); appeared in many shows with Emma Hawkins and Billie Sermond, billed as Three Regular Girls; became ill and returned home to Kansas City (1939) following gala farewell party at Boston Plaza.

Gordon, Olive Dancer. Described as "The Flash Queen" in Kinney Club review (1939); appeared that year in *Take Me Back to School* at Kinney.

Gregory, Joe Singer, dancer, drummer, and emcee. Born Aug. 4, 1918 in Hartford, N.C.; moved with family to Morristown, N.J. when he was 18 months old; parents musical (father played guitar; mother was "a pretty good piano player"); started dancing at local clubs and taverns with Thomas Collins and Bub Martin; hitchhiked to New York, where he and Collins got job at Harlem Cave; hired by Miss Cleo Wilson for carnival show at New York's Hubert's Museum (1930s); won $5 first prize at amateur hour at Saul's Tavern, Newark (1937); danced at Dodger's (early 1938); emcee at Saul's, Waverly, Picadilly, and Alcazar (1938–41); teamed with Abe (Snakehips) Moore as Slip and Slide and with Anna May Hall as Bread and Butter; played Kelly's Stable on 52nd Street in New York (c1940s); teamed with Slappy White and Clarence (Red) Scheffey as Slip, Slap, and Slide, playing Montreal

for 9 months (1942); early TV appearance at Wright's Hotel in Schenectady, N.Y.; played piano and sang at Atlantic City's Paddock Club (1942–45); toured with Doles Dickens Quartet (1945–52).

Hacksley, Crackshot One of country's top black-faced comedians; first name unknown. Teamed in 1943 with straight man Monte Hawley, opening at Apollo Theater in New York; veteran funnyman in revues at Dodger's (1940s); teamed (late 1940s–early 1950s) with Roscoe Dyla doing skits on order of Pigmeat Markham, e.g., climbing ladder while drunk; husband of singer Doris Rheubottom.

Haley, Marshall Singer. Trained in opera; appeared in Kinney Club revues (late 1930s); one of his numbers "More"; died 1986.

Hall, Anna May Dancer. Regular at Nest Club and Kinney Club (1930s–40s); one of Brown Dots with George Rollins and Bill (Robinson) Chapman; also teamed as Bread and Butter with Joe Gregory; appeared in *Back Streets of Harlem* revue at Boston Plaza (1942); toured with USO (1945); performed at Sonny Carroll's Downbeat Club (1946); wife of dancer/emcee Arthur (Prince) Hall; worked as school crossing guard until health failed; died in South Jersey nursing home (1978) after suffering stroke.

Hall, Arthur (Prince) Emcee and tap dancer. Husband of Anna May Hall; performed at Saul's Tavern with Mousie and His Cats (1938), Nest Club (1944), and Kinney Club (1945–46); died in Nov. 1946 while in *Memphis Bound* on Broadway.

Hall, Jimmy Trumpeter (1920s)

Leon Eason: "Jimmy was an old World War I trumpet player who told me some good things, like how to warm up my horn. He was with [a group led by] Bam Holman."

Hamlette, Norma Sweet singer. Appeared in Dodger's floor shows (1944–45); had New York's Lenox Rendezvous rocking with her blues (1946); performed at Twinlite Tempo Room (1945); died May 25, 1988.

Miss Rhapsody: "She was just a fine, good singer."

Hannah, Hazel Dancer and singer. Star of

Parade of Stars at Dave and Maney's (1939); played Montreal clubs (1938); deceased.

Hardy, Buster Trumpeter; first name unknown. Traveled road for many years before returning to Newark; played with Benny Carter (1930s) and possibly Jimmie Lunceford (n.d.).

Hardy, Earl Trombonist. From Newark; responsible for much of Teddy Hill's popularity with New Jersey fans; played for time with Alabams (early 1930s); subsequently played with Cab Calloway.

Hardy, Elwood Pianist. From Kinston, N.C.; toured with Miss Rhapsody and Her Three Sportsmen of Rhythm (mid 1940s); became postal worker; returned to Kinston, where he died.

Harris, Lester Blues singer. From Paterson, N.J.; played with Arthur Terry and His Grand Rascals at Lloyd's Manor (1946); emcee at Dodger's (1946); lead singer with Ray-O-Vacs, whose hit was "I'll Always Be in Love With You"; stayed with group until his death in 1951.

Harris, William (Buster) Pianist. Performed at house rent parties (1930s); played some gigs at Golden Inn.

Harvest, Richard (Dick) Bassist. Born in Newark, Feb. 27, 1918; took lessons from Ernie Ransome so he could replace Al Henderson on Henderson's off night; studied trombone with Newark Elks' Professor Burke and bass with Albert Best; first gig at Orange's 42nd Club with Coates brothers (1930s); played with and recorded on Savoy with Four Bars and a Melody (1947); arranged "It Couldn't Happen to a Dream."

Hastings, Lowell (Count) Tenor saxophonist. Played with Frank Gibbs Orchestra (1934), Al Henderson Orchestra (1936), Savoy Dictators (1939–40), and Pancho Diggs Orchestra (1930s); recorded on Savoy with Dictators (1939); toured with Tiny Bradshaw (early 1940s); headlined Bradshaw's *King of the Jitterbugs* show with Billy Ford at Howard Theater, Washington, D.C. (June 1945); believed to be tenor soloist on "Bradshaw Bounce" (1944); recorded with Louis Jordan and His Tympany Five (1954), including "Messy Bessy," "I Seen Watcha

Done," "A Dollar Down," and "Hurry Home."

Hawkins, Eldridge Saxophonist. Played with Frank Gibbs Orchestra (1934).

Hawkins, Emma Singer. "Queen of the Nightclubs"; mainstay at Dodger's and Boston Plaza (mid 1930s–early 1940s); known for renditions of "I Let a Song Go Out of My Heart" and "My Blue Heaven"; deceased.

Florence McIntyre: "Emma came to the Orpheum Theater in 1928; she'd slap this fellow in the face and he'd slap her while she sang 'After My Laughter Came Tears.' "

Hawley, Monte Actor and comedian. Straight man for Crackshot Hacksley; won fame as a movie actor in 21 "colored" and 12 "white" films.

Hayes, Billie Singer. Featured with Melba Smith (Bonnie Davis) and Skippy Williams at Dodger's (1943); performed with Ernie Phipps Orchestra at Savoy Plaza (1944).

Hayes, Genora Singer. Songbird at new Twinlite (1944).

Hayes, Gus Trumpeter. Played with Melmore Stompers (early 1930s); brother Marvin also in band.

Hayes, Marvin Saxophonist. Played with Melmore Stompers (early 1930s); brother of trumpeter Gus Hayes.

Haynes, Cyril Pianist. Played with Savoy Sultans (c1940).

Albert McCarthy (*Big Band Jazz*): "Pianist Cyril Haynes was not allocated much solo space on record [with the Sultans], but is an effective member of the rhythm section."

Heard, Gladys Blues singer. Performed at Twinlite and Hi-De-Ho Club (mid 1940s); sang with Pancho Diggs Orchestra; once billed as "The Sweetest Voice This Side of Heaven"; mother of author Nathan Heard.

Hember (or Himber), Richard Bandleader. One of Newark's earliest black bandleaders; played in Kinney Club rathskeller (c1920s).

Henderson, Al Bandleader, bassist, and tuba player. Born in Troy, Ala., July 5, 1913; moved to Newark before entering school; played house rent parties as teenager with Bobby Plater; employed during Depression with Works Progress Administration (WPA) Federal Music Project; played tuba in Duke

Richardson's Orchestra (1932) and Frank Gibbs Orchestra (1934–35); led band for walkathons starring Red Skelton (1936); formed Savoy Dictators (c1938), whose theme song was "Sleep"; took band into Harlem on Hudson, nightclub along Jersey Palisades (1938–39) when Frank Sinatra was "working down the way in a roadside tavern and would come up and sing with our band during intermission"; led Dictators on first Savoy record, "Heyfus Geyfus" (1939); formed Picadilly Pipers with Clem Moorman and Ernie Ransome (early 1940s); left music and became Newark's most noted black photographer; died Jan. 30, 1989.

Henderson, Frank (Slim) Saxophonist. Played in band that included Gus Young (drums), Wes Clark (bass), Herb Scott (trumpet), and Vernon Biddle (piano) at Hi Spot (1943); there when Bennie (Red) Robinson came in later that year; toured South with Buddy Johnson's band (c1942).

Henderson, Lucille Dancer and singer. In revues at Dodger's with Emma Hawkins, Herb Pugsley, and Louise Gordon (1938); opened one show dancing to Harlem dance "The Scronch" with Hawkins and Gordon; sang ditty called "You're an Education."

Henderson, Tit Dancer. From New York; performed at Kinney Club, where she "shakes everything except her boss for a raise" (1939 *Herald News* review); played clubs in Elmira with Gertrude Turman (early 1940s).

Hensen, Herb Saxophonist. Played with Chick Webb; played mostly at Kinney Club, where his wife, Ann, was waitress (late 1930s–early 1940s); headed groups at Pat and Don's and Tony Galento's in Orange, N.J.; led a 5-piece band at Howdy Club (1947).

Herbert, Frances Shake dancer and chorus girl. Performed at the Nest Club (early 1940s); described in *Afro* review as "crawling around the floor."

Hickman, Floyd Violinist. Led the Orpheum Theater pit band (late 1920s–mid 1930s); influenced many younger musicians; performed in band led by Will Vodrey (1920s) that played in Lew Leslie productions; deceased.

Highe, Lillian Singer. Slim beauty who started out in Lew Leslie's *Blackbirds* (1925); sang "Wagon Wheels" and gave "a new interpretation" of "On the Sentimental Side" at Dave and Maney's in Orange, N.J. (1938); performed at Washington's Crystal Caverns and Club Bali (1940s); featured at Dodger's (1946).

Hodge, Bob Drummer. Played with Pancho Diggs's band and with Corporal Brady Hodge's civilian unit.

Hodge, (Corporal) Brady Trumpeter and bandleader. Led an orchestra after World War II; played Savoy Palace, Graham Hall, and Lloyd's Manor, mostly for dances; also engaged in "Battles of Swing" at Graham's.

Hoeffler, Margaret Petite singer. Shared bill with Miss Rhapsody at Dodger's (1946).

Holder, Gene Pianist. Performed with Sonny Murray and Alabams (early–mid 1930s); Leon Eason's roommate on road; played earlier dates with Eason at Bungalow, Giddy's in Mountainside, N.J., and Lenox Avenue Club in New York (mid 1930s); played at Park Rest, Blue Goose, and Club Miami (1936–37).

Holley, Joe Pianist and bandleader. Played with Eddie Wells' band (c1930) and Joe St. John's band (c1932); also led own band (1930s).

Holloway, Joe Trombonist. Played in Pancho Diggs Orchestra (late 1930s–early 1940s).

Holman, Bam Altoist. Played in small, local groups; had Selmer sax, which few other musicians could afford; friend of many jazz greats, including saxophonist Sidney Bechet and arranger Jimmy Mundy, who often congregated at his West Kinney Street home; died 1955.

Howard, Freddie Bandleader. Billed as "The Sepia Benny Goodman"; played Fisher's Tavern with Freddie Howard and His Swingsters (1939), with Grace Smith handling vocals.

Howard, Thad (Chuck) Singer, dancer, and emcee. Born in Shellman, Ga., Oct. 29, 1912; moved with family to Newark in 1920; first job with Lucky Louie Anderson at Shady Rest Country Club, where he emceed show and closed it by "singing eight songs for a dollar and a half"; frequently played with John (Smoky) Jones (1934), including WNEW broadcast on which he sang "Red Sails in the Sunset"; known for falsetto until severe cold dropped his voice to baritone; played Club Miami, Saul's Tavern, Kinney Club, Dodger's (2 years), Alcazar, and Love Nest in Vauxhall section of Union, N.J., before moving to upstate New York (c1940); with wife, Annetta, performed as dance team appropriately named Maniacs; died in July 1990.

Gertrude Turman: "He sang like Orlando Robeson."

Hoyt, Mildred Sweet singer. Performed at Hydeaway (1944).

Hughes, Calvin Trumpeter. Played with Don Linton Orchestra (mid 1940s).

Hutchinson, Myrtle Dancer. Born in Newark, 1916; got start touring (early 1930s) with Bill (Bojangles) Robinson, Buck and Bubbles, and Noble Sissle in *Harlem on Parade* (early 1930s); toured Canada before returning to Newark to play Nest Club; sang and danced at Charlie's Paradise in Passaic, N.J. (1938); toured with USO during World War II; billed as "Queen of Taps"; deceased.

Ike Drummer; real name unknown. Frequently played with stride pianist Donald Lambert (1930s).

Irving, Joseph Singer. Singing waiter at Nest Club (1944).

Jackson, Frances High velocity shake dancer. Performed at Kinney Club (1940–46); described in *Afro* as having "torso movement with a stacatto tempo that caused her body to vibrate all over."

Jackson, Jig-Saw Contortionist. From New York; did dance for W. C. Handy's 65th birthday party celebration at New York's Cotton Club (1938); performed at Boston Plaza (1943).

Jackson, Johnny Bandleader and promoter. Led Johnny Jackson and His Society Orchestra (early 1940s–50s) that forged to front of dance circles by setting scorching rhythms; played dances for all city's major clubs, including Craftsmen, Swanksmen, bartenders, beauty shop owners, and Oldtimers; rallied to boost purchase of war stamps at Savoy Plaza (1944).

Jackson, Torchie Sweet singer; first name unknown. Performed at Boston Plaza (1943) and Dodger's (1945); lyrical voice.

James, Joe One-armed trumpeter. Played with Pancho Diggs Orchestra (late 1930s) and Tiny Bradshaw (c1940–42); top-notch arranger and writer whose specialty was writing for acts.

Jarrett, Bobby Saxophonist and bandleader. Played with Barons of Rhythm (later 1930s–early 1940s); formed dance band (mid 1940s) that played club dances, fashion shows, and other social events.

Jenkins, Cecil Saxophonist. Played with Melmore Stompers, predecessors of Alabams (c1930s).

Jenkins, Harold Saxophonist. Played with Melmore Stompers (c1930s); brother of saxophonist Cecil.

Jenkins, Pat Trumpeter. Played with Savoy Sultans; talent obscured because Sam Massenberg got most good parts.

Albert McCarthy (*Big Band Jazz*): "[Jenkins] possessed an attractive full tone and was extremely agile with the mute."

Jenkins, Tony Singer. Performed with Andy Kirk's band; wowed crowds at Dodger's and Picadilly, setting feminine hearts aflutter when he sang "Begin the Beguine" (1946); appeared at Picadilly with Redd Foxx (1946).

Jennings, Fortune (Fats) Comedian. Born Oct. 9, 1914 in Sumter, S.C.; teamed with Jackie Mandeville as Nacki Sacki Fats and Jackie, one of Newark's top comedy acts (1930s–40s); kept working no matter what the economy; traveled as far as Rockhead's Paradise in Montreal; after retirement from show business worked for Newark Housing Authority; died Sept. 19, 1983.

Jennings, Inez Singer. Born Nov. 25, 1920; sister of Fortune; had style resembling Billie Holiday; moved with family from Sumter to Newark (1922), where mother hosted house rent parties featuring 3-piece band when family lived at 159 Pennsylvania Avenue (1929); sang on WHBI; danced in amateur shows at Paramount Theater; sang and danced as amateur for first time at Villa

Maurice (1936); got into Alcazar as teenager by forging note from her mother to sing "for nothing"; sang at Dodger's, Nest Club, and Freddy's, club in Ironbound area of Newark (1938); played Utica, Troy, and Albany, N.Y. clubs (1940); married piano player in Pete Diggs's band (1941); ran La Coral Beauty Shop (1960s); retired employee of Newark Violations Bureau.

Johnson, *Bobby* Teenage tap dancer. Performed with sister Winnie (Wini) at Nest Club (late 1930s) when they were so young their parents had to accompany them to shows.

Johnson, *Ducky* Emcee. Performed at Eagle Bar and Howdy Club (early 1950s).

Johnson, *James P. (Jimmy)* Legendary stride pianist. Born in New Brunswick, N.J. in 1891; played at Kinney Hall (1914); replaced Willie (The Lion) Smith at Randolph's (1914); died Nov. 17, 1955.

Johnson, *William Lee (Willie or Bill)* Guitarist and banjo player. Born in Dothan, Ala., Feb. 22, 1915; came to Newark as child; became interested in music while working as candy boy at Orpheum Theater; took up ukelele, tenor banjo, and guitar at age 17; teamed with Alphonso Burford and Connie Cabell, playing Saturday night house rent parties; played with Bill Mackey's Orchestra, Mandy Ross and His Walkin' Rhythm, Frank Gibbs Orchestra, Savoy Dictators, Barons of Rhythm, and Leon Eason's band (1930s–1940s); accompanied Jubilaires on Arthur Godfrey Show on CBS-TV; led quintet at Picadilly (1947–50); recorded on Savoy with Dictators (1939); became policeman and stationary engineer for City of Newark; owned new Alcazar on Sixteenth Avenue in Irvington, N.J., just over Newark border (1980s).

Johnson, *Winnie (Wini)* Dancer, actress, and singer; married name Brown. Started in show business as dance duo with her brother Bobby at Nest Club; chosen with 16-year-old Lena Horne as youngest girls in New York's Cotton Club chorus line in *Tan Town Topics* revue (1941), produced by Irvin C. Miller and performed by James P. John-

son's band at New York's Apollo Theater; turned to acting and singing; supposedly married actor Stepin Fetchit, who claimed union was bogus in widely publicized court case and denied fathering her son; featured with Lionel Hampton (late 1940s–early 1950s); sang "Gone Again" and "Bewildered" at Jersey City (N.J.) Armory in military show (1950).

Jones, *Albennie* Blues singer. From New York; recorded on Savoy and Decca; sang at Alcazar, Dodger's, Nest Club, and Picadilly (early–mid 1940s); died June 24, 1989.

Miss Rhapsody: "She was a heavy, dark brown-skinned girl who could sing. I got her to follow me into a club in Chattanooga for a hundred and fifty dollars a week. They kept her twelve weeks. She was no big name, but she could sing!"

Jones, *Audrey (Celeste)* Singer. Born May 31, 1908 in New York City, where her mother and stepfather owned Riverlette between 136th and 137th streets on Seventh Avenue, which often had live music; sometimes sang there; came to Newark in 1937; sang first at Dodger's, where "everybody had a chance to get up and do something"; appeared frequently at Dodger's, Pat and Don's in Harrison, N.J., and Dave and Maney's in Orange, N.J. (late 1930s); performed at Omega Bar and Grill in Roselle, N.J. (early 1940s); called "The Girl With the Mockingbird Voice"; noted for operatic-like soprano and renditions of "Trees" and "Indian Love Call"; died July 27, 1990.

Jones, *Frank* Altoist, clarinetist, and flute player. Born in 1910; from Montclair, N.J.; lead alto in Banjo Bernie's band (c1937–38) at 101 Ranch at Lenox Avenue and 138th Street in New York; played Lake George and Saratoga Springs, N.Y., with Three Brown Buddies; played in many local pick-up groups, sometimes with Leon Eason.

Jones, *James (Chops or Jimmy)* Trumpeter, bassist, and drummer. Born in Newark, Aug. 18, 1916; original member of Barons of Rhythm, playing first trumpet (1930s); couldn't read a note, but faked well enough not to be discovered for 2 years; influenced largely by Roy Eldridge and Dizzy Gillespie; played in Army bands at Fort Greene and Fort Lee in Virginia; joined Ame Garrison's band at Boston Plaza after 1943 discharge; played for Mandy Ross's Walkin' Rhythm; employed as assistant music director for Newark Division of Recreation and Cultural Affairs (1980s–early 1990s).

Jones, John (Smoky) Pianist; also nicknamed "Wheatstraw." Took his Swingsters into Saul's Tavern (1939).

Thad Howard: "I played a lot of jobs with him back in 1934–35."

Leon Eason: "We used to hire him on gigs when we couldn't get a good one."

Jones, Mary Bandleader. Led Mary Jones and Her Rhythm Band at Boston Plaza (1944).

Jones, Milton (Prince) Trumpeter. Played with Sultans of Swing (c1940) and Jimmy Stanford's group (1946).

Leon Eason: "He was the first guy I heard play bebop. He used to come into the Alcazar and say, 'C'mon, man; let me play a tune.' When I went into the Army, it was swingin'; when I came out, they were beboppin'. He played it real early—before Babs [Gonzales] and them—before it caught on."

Jones, Roscoe (Rosie) Bandleader. Had the band at Radio Inn on Halsey Street, one of first black-owned clubs (late 1920s), with Buster Tyler on drums, Brownie on trumpet, and Cecil Jenkins on sax.

Jones, Sammy (Smilin') Emcee. Performed at Villa Maurice and Dodger's (1938); known for personality and ability to make friends.

Jordan, Danford (Larue) Pianist, arranger, and combo leader. With Babs Gonzales, a major innovator of bebop; artistic genius who also created the band's backdrop mural at Newark's Savoy Ballroom; influenced by idols Jimmie Lunceford and Duke Ellington; made a 5-and-10-cent store record of "Fallin' in Love" (1940) with Gertrude Turman, Bill Goode, and Babs Gonzales as Three Notes and a Staff; played with Two Notes and a Tempo, bebopping at Lloyd's Manor (1947); deceased.

Leon Eason: "Ray Charles said Larue was a genius."

Hal Mitchell: "He could play Lunceford chord for chord."

Jordan, Shirley Comedian; known as Snowball. From Montclair, N.J.; top-rate professional; played New York's Cotton Club; deceased.

Kato, Billy See Cato, Billy.

Kee, Gene Pianist, bandleader, and arranger. Worked with Sultans of Swing out of Montclair, N.J.; played with Leon Eason at Park Rest (c1937) and Saul's Tavern (c1940) and with Brother Kelly and Jabbo Smith at Howdy Club (1943); booked his Deep Rhythm Orchestra into Lincoln Hall, Orange, N.J. (1945); secretary of the Musicians' Staff Club (1946); later backed Gladys Knight and Pips.

Keith, Madeline Sweet singer. Appeared in *Back Streets of Harlem* and *Big Plantation* revues at Boston Plaza (1941); emceed there (1943); called "The Girl With 1,000 Songs."

Kelly, Charles (Charlie, Brother, or Drummer) Drummer. Regular drummer with Alabams and groups led by Leon Eason at Blue Goose, Park Rest, and Club Miami (1936–37); considered Newark's main show drummer; performed at Villa Maurice (1938), Howdy Club (1943), Twinlite (1944), and Hi-De-Ho Club (1946); deceased (c1952).

Kent, Vernon Trombonist and bandleader (early 1930s).

Kid Noisy Banjo player. House rent party musician who played 4-string banjo.

King, Jimmie Emcee. Performed at Golden Gate (1944) and Hi-De-Ho Club (1946).

Kinney, Leoparte (Chink) Saxophonist. Played with Ray-O-Vacs, who recorded popular tune "I'll Always Be in Love With You."

Kirk, Roebie Singer. Discovered as amateur (1939) at Dodger's; sang blues with Jimmie Lunceford; brought down house with "I Surrender, Dear"; trumpeter Billy Ford's cousin.

Lambert, Donald Newark's legendary stride pianist whose powerful left hand wove tunes with the right. Born in Princeton, N.J. in 1904; supposedly couldn't read a note, although his mother taught piano; musical genius sought out for "cutting contests" by James P. Johnson, Art Tatum, and Fats Waller; preferred obscurity of local taverns to concert halls and fancy clubs; played for house rent parties (1920s–30s); fixture at Angeline's, Newark after-hours joint (early 1930s); hired Harold (Hal) Mitchell for duo at 95 Prince Street (early 1930s); played at Nest Club (c1936); led trio at Fisher's Tavern (1938); played at Pat and Don's (1938), Howdy Club (1945), Jock's Room in Harlem with Maxine Sullivan (1946), Town House in Montclair, N.J. (late 1940s), and Star Bar (1950s); for last 14 years of his life (1948–62) played at Wallace's High Tavern, West Orange, N.J.; recorded for Bluebird (1941) and Solo Art (1951); "took the show" from Fats Waller and Eubie Blake at 1960 Newport Jazz Festival; died in Newark's Martland Hospital, May 8, 1962 after suffering stroke.

Bob Queen (*Afro-American*): "He didn't read or write music, but was considered to be a genius. He never received the publicity warranted by his artistry, but led a fruitful life. He was always willing to lend a hand to some struggling vocalist or pianist and played numerous benefits."

Frank R. Wallace: "He was a genius. He could play 'Malaguena' with the left hand and 'Temptation' with the right."

Lang, Floyd (Floy Floy or Papa Stoppa) Pianist. Born in Gainesville, Fla.; a natural piano talent; could replicate whatever he heard; came to Newark at age 17; played Vanderpool Bar on Frelinghuysen Avenue for many years (1940s); traveled cocktail circuit playing hotels and motels at vacation spots (1950s–60s); preferred playing "white spots" where "you don't have to kill yourself"; played on and off at Hoboken's Clam Broth House (1980s).

LaRedd, Cora Singer and dancer. Raised on Broome Street; Broadway musical star (late 1920s–early 1930s); appeared in *Messing Around* with music by James P. Johnson at New York's Hudson Theater (1929) and Hamtree Harrington and Alberta Hunter in *Change Your Luck* (1930); in her heyday,

known for splashing her money around; led band in New York at one point; toured Europe several times; when her star fell, returned to Newark, playing Golden Inn and other clubs; according to *Herald News* reviewer (1939), "fell into Dodger's and had everyone in stitches with her funny exchanges . . . a real trooper"; deceased.

Joe Gregory: "In our eyes, she was a star."

Wesley Clark: "She had a beautiful body; she danced like a man. She was tough—a top dancer to come out of Newark."

Bill Roberts: "She was very much a black woman who lavished her money on younger men. That's what took her down."

Jonah Jones (*The World of Swing*): "We [Jimmie Lunceford's band] had a chance to come down to New York [from Buffalo] and try out for a job, but we missed it because a girl called Cora LaRedd (primarily a vocalist) had a band they liked better."

LaRue, Reese Interpretive dancer and choreographer; real name Albert Jones. Born in Newark's Ironbound section; attended East Side High School; began career as creative dancer at 16 in Apollo Theater's male chorus; danced all over world; served in Army; returned to Newark (mid 1940s) and took up residency at Kinney Club, where he teamed with shake dancer June Fletcher; put on shows including *Tropical Revue* and *Gay Paree* at Kinney (1947); known for torrid terpsichore; died Aug. 8, 1985.

Lee, Goldie Singer. Sang blues at Hi-De-Ho Club (1947).

Lee, Johnson Singer. Sang with Ernie Phipps (1944); described as "solid hometown sender" while engaging in swing battle opposite Billy Eckstine (with Georgie Auld's band) at Laurel Garden (1944).

Leonardo, Earl Singer. Known for renditions of "Little Sir Echo" and "Umbrella Man"; performed at Dodger's (1944), Twinlite (1944), and Forbes Beach (1952); appeared with comic Freddie Toler at Famous Door on Bedford Street (late 1940s).

Lester, Baron Singer. Sang with Al Henderson Orchestra (late 1930s); also did some emcee work; performed at Villa Maurice and Carnegie Hall, Vauxhall, N.J. (1938); inducted into Army (1941).

Lewis, Anna May Lundy Organist and pianist extraordinaire. Born in Jacksonville, Fla., July 25, 1916; as child "just sat down at the piano and started playing"; featured in church productions at age 8; came to Newark as teenager to live with her father, Dick Lundy, famous ballplayer who became manager of Newark Eagles of old Negro League; played Dodger's, Picadilly, and long stint at Hydeaway (early–mid 1940s); recorded gospel music on several labels; minister of music at New Point Baptist Church for more than 55 years; grandmother of teenaged tap dancing sensation Savion Glover.

Lewis, William (Billy) Organist, pianist, and singer. Born Sept. 9, 1913 in Gates, Pa.; began entertaining in tavern in Pawtucket, R.I., where he was raised; sold bootleg beer and whiskey for $3 a pail; influenced by tenor Orlando Robeson; played most popular white clubs on Broad Street (1940s–50s); toured with Ben Smith and other bands; recorded (1960s) on Flo-Lou label ("Won't Tell a Soul What You Did to Me" and "Stool Pigeon Baby"); played and sang on Bill Cook's "Stairway to the Stars" television program (mid 1950s); former husband of Anna May Lundy Lewis.

Lightning Pianist; real name unknown. Blind 1920s house rent party piano player.

Lindbergh, William (Bass Byrd) Bassist. Performed with Joe St. John's band on road with Jean Calloway (1931); played with Joe Crump's Band of 1,000 Themes (1936–37) and at Hydeaway (1943) and Omega Bar and Grill (1943–44); toured with Miss Rhapsody and Her Three Sportsmen of Rhythm (1944–45); also played saxophone, clarinet, and tuba; deceased.

Little Marguerite Dainty Oriental dancer. Danced in chorus with Sadie Matthews and Mae Darling at Nest Club (1943).

Little Rita Singer. Sang with Savoy Sultans at Graham Auditorium, pounding out "Hey Lawdy Mama" (1943).

Lomax, Louis (Doc) Terrific ballroom dancer.

Worked at Nest Club (1945); also was emcee there.

Louis, Babe Bandleader. Led a band that performed in Kinney Club rathskeller (before 1920); also played at Palace Lucille.

Love, Ruby Dancer. Mainstay in Kinney Club chorus line (late 1930s).

Lucas, Emory Bandleader (1930s). Strove for perfection; influenced many younger musicians.

Clyde Bernhardt: "If somebody in the band was weak, he was on them."

Willie Johnson: "He could play everything. He played mostly with white bands. He was a great teacher. He called me in and asked, 'What the hell are you doin'? Are you readin' or are you bullshittin'? You've been in this band all this time and you can't read? I ought to kick your ass. You could have spoiled everything.' Then he told me to come to his house the next day and started me on music. I didn't know nothin' and he caught me dead to rights. He told me to go out and get a teacher."

MacDonald, Marion Bandleader (late 1940s–early 1950s).

MacIntosh, Henry Trumpeter.

Afro-American (June 29, 1946): "Brooklyn lad who blows so much trumpet with Joe Crump."

Mack, Clarence Bassist. Played with Barons of Rhythm (early 1940s), Arthur Terry and His Grand Rascals at Lloyd's Manor on and off (1940s), and Togge Smythe at Picadilly (1947); recorded with Wynonie (Mr. Blues) Harris on New York session (1947) that included "Wynonie's Boogie" and session in Cincinnati (1954) that included "K Christina."

Mack, Lottie Chorus girl. Appeared in *Just a Kid Named Joe* at Kinney Club (1939).

Mackey, Bill 1930s bandleader.

Madame Porkchops Comedienne. Performed at Kinney Club (1930s) in act on order of Phyllis Diller; wore big, long shoes and raggedy clothes and told crazy jokes.

Madison, Bingie Tenor saxophonist, clarinetist, pianist, bandleader, and arranger. Born in Iowa (1902); joined Bobbie Brown's

Quartet in Canada (1921); rejoined Brown's group in Newark (Aug. 1922), remaining until 1925; led own groups; played briefly with Sam Wooding and Luis Russell; joined Louis Armstrong (1940), then Edgar Hayes; led small band at New York's Tango Palace (1947–53).

Majors, Clement Trombonist. Played in band out of New York (1930s); father of Yolanda (Princess Margo) Majors.

Majors, Yolanda (Princess Margo) Exotic dancer. Performed her "Dance of the Seven Veils" at Club Caverns in Washington, D.C. (1941); occasionally sang; performed at Twinlite (1944), Eagle Bar (1951), and Silver Saddle (1951); toured South (1952) with Crackshot Hacksley, Roscoe Dyla, Larry Darnell, and Wynonie (Mr. Blues) Harris; worked at Newark City Hall (1980s).

Mandeville, Jackie (Little Jackie) Comedian and dancer. With partner Fortune (Fats) Jennings showstopping tap dancing comedy team known as Nacki Sacki Fats and Jackie, the top comedy act out of Newark (1930s–40s); teamed earlier with Little Black Jimmy (Fairbanks); emcee at Picadilly, Kinney Club, and Melody Club, including long stay at Pic (1942–45); got lots of applause with his comic rendition of "I Can't Get Started With You" at Cameo Club (1947); "Pennies from Heaven" another of his hits; died Dec. 26, 1989.

Manhattan Paul Dapper singer and producer of shows. Wore a big diamond, tails, and top hat; cosmopolitan performer who sang sentimental tunes; appeared at Dave and Maney's (1939) and Picadilly (1945); staged Manhattan Paul's Revue (1952) at Newark Opera House, starring Pancho Diggs, Crackshot Hacksley, Edna McGriff, and Joe Holliday and His Orchestra.

Mann, Russell Tenor saxophonist and altoist. Led Russell Mann and His Royal Ambassadors, 1930s forerunner of Savoy Sultans, with Erskine Butterfield on piano and Larry Ringold on saxophone, a band heard regularly on WHBI radio in Newark.

Marrero, Carrie Singer. Cuban songbird in Kinney Club revues (1938–39); had ladies dabbing their eyes with rendition of "Marie."

Marshall, Sonny Early 1930s bandleader. Often played at Mom Jeanie's in Passaic, N.J.

Martinez, Cynthia Singer and dancer. Performed at Kinney Club (1945); described in *Afro* (Nov. 24, 1945) as wearing "a costume composed only of two G-strings with some frills on them."

Mason, Ruby Pianist, accordionist, and saxophonist. Played in Orpheum Theater pit band (1920s).

Massenberg, Sam Trumpeter. Played in Frank Gibbs Orchestra (1934); subsequently joined Savoy Sultans.

Al Henderson: "I nicknamed him 'Bluey.' He could play some beautiful passages, then he'd play a 'bluey' [a sour note]."

Albert McCarthy (*Big Band Jazz*): "Massenberg was a musician, who, like [Rudy] Williams, could easily have held down a job in one of the major big bands, his solo work being notable for its power and freshness."

Massey, William (Duckey) Pianist and bandleader. Played with Leon Eason's band at Alcazar (1939–40); led Duckey Massey and His Ducklings at Lloyd's Manor (1951–52); played Howard Bar with Arthur Terry (1952); died Jan. 2, 1958 at age 41 after getting sick New Year's Eve at Club 83 on Warren Street.

Matthews, Amanda (Mandy) Blues singer. Born Feb. 2, 1912 in Philadelphia; sister of Sadie Matthews; performed at Villa Maurice and other local clubs (1930s); died young.

Matthews, Charlie Lean, tall, and broad-shouldered emcee, singer, and dancer. Born in Daleville, Ala., April 20, 1917; came to Newark from Philadelphia at age 10; trained as fighter; took up tap dancing as youth; did number one night at Colony Club and started going on gigs with Bill Chapman; first club date at Glockie's in Harrison, N.J., then Pat and Don's "for white audiences"; star at Dodger's (1936–37) and Nest Club (1935–40); member of Works Progress Administration (WPA) Theater Project (1936–37); played featured role in *The Trial* *of Dr. Beck* and appeared with actor William Bendix; subsequently entered Democratic politics; elected Third Ward leader (1945–54), Essex County's first black freeholder (1954), and first black freeholder director (1966); died March 30, 1990.

Matthews, Leslie (Dick) Bandleader and saxophonist. Had house band at Dave and Maney's in Orange, N.J. with Gene Ballard on piano, Freddie Ballard on tenor banjo, Carl McIntyre on saxophone, and Bill Bonner on drums (late 1930s).

Matthews, Sadie (Little Poopsie) Dancer and singer. Born April 19, 1915 in Philadelphia; started dancing at Elks Club in Philly; with sister Dorothy won amateur contest at Standard Theater, singing "Porkchops"; with Dorothy and sister Mandy, formed trio and sang "Moanin'" as one of their main numbers; singing waitress in North Philadelphia; moved to Atlantic City (early 1930s) to sing with Banjo Bernie's band, performing on Boardwalk and traveling with band for shows in Baltimore and Washington; moved to Newark (1935); danced, sang, and did "bits" at Nest Club; also worked at Dave and Maney's and Saul's Tavern; put on floor shows at Orpheum Theater; played upstate New York clubs in Albany, Utica, and Troy (c1940); known for her rendition of "Little Sir Echo," first song she learned as a girl.

Maurice, Billie Singer and dancer. Star at Nest Club (1939); described in 1944 *Afro* review as "The Girl Wonder With a Million Dollar Talent"; her dancing wowed the boys at Fort Dix during the war when she sang "Moonlight and Shadows"; confined at Essex County Sanitarium in Verona, N.J. (1947).

McAllister, James, Jr. (Smokey) Popular emcee and dancer; also known as "Mr. Touch." Headlined shows at Kid Eddy's south of New Brunswick, N.J., the Kinney Club, and many north Jersey clubs (early 1940s); also ran barber shop on South Orange Avenue (late 1940s); teamed with Roland Morse (1947) to form eccentric dance team at Cameo Club; host at Lloyd's Manor (1947); emcee at Rahway's Palace Blue Room (1951); played Lloyd's, Tyler's Chicken Shack in Avenel, N.J., and former Picadilly (1952); after long period on road, including club dates in Montreal, played first New York jobs at Small's Paradise and Baby Grand (1952).

McCrae, Otis Singer. Sang with Ernie Phipps Orchestra at Savoy Plaza (1943).

McCraw, Leatha Sweet singer. Known for her renditions of "You Can't Tell the Difference After Dark" and "'Round Midnight"; performed at Fisher's Tavern and Dodger's (1938) and Hydeaway (1942); niece of comedienne Carrie Adams.

McDaniel, Evelyn Emcee. Performed at Lloyd's Manor with Arthur Terry and His Grand Rascals (1947).

McDonald, Alice (Madame) Pianist. Popular piano player at house rent parties; hired musicians to create big bands for local dances (after World War I).

Charles Sowell: "She'd send to New York and get different musicians. One time she played at the [Newark] armory."

Willie Johnson: "She was a stout, brown-skinned woman who could read anything, and she drank plenty of whiskey."

McIntyre, Carl Altoist. Born in Charlotte, N.C., Feb. 10, 1910; raised by aunt in Montclair, N.J.; attended Johnson C. Smith College with intention of becoming doctor; played first with Joe Crump on New Year's Eve at Roseville Armory; "best teacher" Larry Ringold; also studied with Bobby Plater; first regular job with Crump at Kinney Club; other jobs at Passaic County's Bungalow; joined Heat Waves, 12-piece band that played locally, at New York dance schools, and 6 summers in Catskills (c1928–34) after band "broke down into six pieces"; joined Leon Eason as tenor player (c1940–43); played 42nd Club (1943–48) with Clarence Coates; played Elks Lodge on weekends until 1955 "with the same guys"; left music for factory job in 1955; husband of Florence (Hall) McIntyre.

McIntyre, Florence Dancer; maiden name Hall. Born in Montclair, N.J., Aug. 31, 1912; danced with group of girls including Hazel

Hannah, Myrtle Hutchinson, Doryce Bradley, and Helena Turman who put on shows choreographed by Johnny B. Gardner (early 1930s); toured East Coast (1930–32) with Danny Smalls' *Harlem on Parade* before marrying Carl McIntyre.

McNeal, James Tenor saxophonist. Played tenor saxophone with Savoy Sultans.

McQueen, Anna Mae Captivating contralto. Sang at Dodger's (1943–44); dubbed "The Mocking Bird of Sweet Songs" at Roselle's Omega Bar and Grill (same period).

McQueen, Jackson (Flap) Bassist. Born in Cincinnati, Ohio, July 21, 1916; began playing banjo, 4-string guitar, and ukelele with Proctor, alto sax player from Newark; played Bergen Street bars with Proctor for tips while attending Central High School; original bassist with Pancho Diggs Orchestra (1934–35); played in Army's 369th Regiment Band overseas and in Honolulu (1941–43); formed Ray-O-Vacs out of Lloyd's Manor (late 1940s) and toured with group for 14 years; recorded on Coleman, Decca, Josie, and Jubilee, including Ray-O-Vacs' 1947 hit, "I'll Always Be in Love With You"; headlined Apollo Theater; owned Tippin' Inn, Newark bar, for many years; worked at Jersey City Public Library (1980s).

Medlin, Joe Singer. Known as "The Sepia Sinatra"; featured on Buddy Johnson's "Baby, Don't You Cry"; played club and theater dates with Johnson at many Newark clubs (1940s); from Paterson, N.J.

Merritt, Miles Trumpeter. Played with Alabams.

Miller, Ala Mae Pianist. Born in Georgia, Oct. 5, 1915; brought to Newark in infancy; grew up in Bloomfield; started playing on pump organ and was hit of neighborhood; took classical piano lessons; self-taught jazz musician; first paid job at 18 at Cohen's Rhythm Club in West New York, N.J. in band led by drummer Dee Douglas; led trio at Omega Bar and Grill in Roselle (mid 1940s); wife of saxophonist Bobby Plater.

Ala Mae Miller: "I played the Boston Plaza, Fisher's Tavern, the Nest Club, Picadilly, and 42nd Club on Parrow Street in Orange. Just jazz. I played a lot of gigs with Grace Smith and Sadie Matthews. They used to say I swung. Then I was in the church, and I was swinging in there, too. Real shoutin' tunes. I was a true chord player—followed the melody and played the chords. And when I played for a singer, I played for the singer, not for me. When it came time to swing or jam with a band, I'd do my little thing, and they'd say, 'Take two, Ala Mae.'"

Miller, Clarence Trumpeter (1940s).

Miller, Lawrence Singer, dancer, and emcee. Polished singer who "took all the women's hearts"; first black to perform with all-white band at Newark's Branford Theater, appearing with Ted Lewis; longtime favorite at Waverly Tavern (1938), Nest Club, Cotton Club, and other top spots (late 1930s); smooth stylist who made a lot of money at tables singing "My Mother's Eyes," "Outside of Paradise," and "Call Me Darling"; died in fall 1971.

Gertrude Turman: "Lawrence was in a bracket with Billy Eckstine. We were his family. When he died, his body laid in the morgue five weeks. Finally, we buried him."

Miller, Mamie Blues star and comedienne. Performed at Kinney Club (1942–44); sang risque numbers and often danced with Johnny Fussell; expert at doing "ups."

Millinder, Lucius (Lucky) Bandleader; better known to Newarkers as Doc Wilson, advice columnist and fortune teller for *New Jersey Herald News*, black weekly. Born in Anniston, Ala., Aug. 8, 1900; colorful figure who sold herbs and potions by mail order; fronted Mills Blue Rhythm Band (1934–38); occasional singer and dancer, but did not play musical instrument; according to *Newsweek* (Sept. 7, 1942), Al Capone "bought him a band"; had house band at New York's Savoy Ballroom for 12 years; died in New York, Sept. 28, 1966.

Mischieux, Oliver Top trumpeter. Settled in Newark; played with Tiny Bradshaw's band (c1943–46); deceased.

Willie Johnson: "He played like a tornado from Haiti."

Miss Rhapsody   *See* Wells, Viola Gertrude.

Mitchell, Alex (Razz)   Drummer. Played with Savoy Sultans (1930s–40s); appeared in film *Caldonia* in band led by Louis Jordan (1945); according to Albert McCarthy in *Big Band Jazz*, toured Philippines, Japan, and other Pacific areas with the Jeter-Pillars band (1946); died young.

Mitchell, Harold (Hal)   Trumpeter. Born in Newark, Jan. 28, 1916; first job at Freeman Hall in Newark with William (Buddy) and Huzzy Schenck (early 1930s); as teenager played in duo with Donald Lambert at 95 Prince Street; played Tango Palace, "dime a dance" joint in New York, with Duke Richardson's Orchestra (c1934); organized Joe Crump and His Band of 1,000 Themes (1936–37); played walkathons featuring Red Skelton in Hagerstown, Md. (mid 1930s); joined Al Henderson's Orchestra; led Savoy Dictators (late 1930s); traveled with Tiny Bradshaw (1941); played Apollo Theater in New York, Royal in Baltimore, and Howard in Washington, D.C.; joined Benny Carter's band and played famous Salt Lake City Ballroom (which later burned down) on way to Los Angeles with Carter's band; on sound track for films *Thousands Cheer* and *Stormy Weather*; toured Canada with Jimmie Lunceford; played brief engagements at small clubs on 52nd Street in New York; moved uptown to Small's Paradise with Chris Columbus Orchestra; played 20 RKO theaters with Louis Jordan and Will Mastin Trio; joined Ted McRae's relief band at New York's Club Zanzibar; short stint with John Kirby Orchestra; toured with Eddie Durham.

Mobley, Danny   Pianist and arranger. Played with Jerry Bogar's Royal Club Orchestra (1940s–50s); arranged "I'll Never Walk Alone" for singer Roy Hamilton; cousin of tenor player Hank Mobley.

Mobley, Hank   Tenor saxophonist and noted composer. Born in Eastman, Ga., July 7, 1930; as teenager played Newark area clubs; ran jam sessions at Picadilly (late 1940s); played with Jerry Bogar's Royal Club Orchestra (late 1940s); joined Max Roach (early 1950s); subsequently played with Dizzy Gillespie; founded Jazz Messengers with Art Blakey, Horace Silver, and Kenny Dorham (later replaced by Miles Davis), famous jazz group that toured worldwide for three decades and played at White House (1981); in recent years has led own groups.

Moncur, Grachan (Brother)   String bassist. Born in Miami, Fla., Sept. 2, 1915; mother played concertina and piano; half-brother of Al Cooper, who led Savoy Sultans; started out playing trombone and tuba; played tuba on stage at Miami's Ritz Theater in first job; started gigging "around Newark" with Cooper (1933–34), mostly playing clubs Down Neck (Ironbound section); then played for long while with Matinee Idols, who broadcast over WHBI in Newark and whose theme song was "Let Us Bring Our Happiness to You"; discovered by CBS's John Hammond, who signed him to record with vocalist Mildred Bailey and Red Norvo, Billie Holiday, Mary Lou Williams, Johnny Hodges, and Bunny Berigan; remained with Sultans for "about twenty years," including 12 at New York's Savoy Ballroom; traveled extensively with Sultans; played Lloyd's Manor (1947); recorded with Deek Watson and Brown Dots; formed Grachan Moncur and His Strollers (late 1940s), playing Picadilly, Howdy Club, Eagle Bar, and other Newark clubs and dance halls; returned to Miami (1950s); father of avant-garde trombonist Grachan Moncur 3rd.

Moody, James   Tenor saxophonist, altoist, and flutist. Born in Savannah, Ga., March 26, 1925; graduate of Newark's Bruce Street School for the Deaf; first professional work at Lloyd's Manor in Newark (1946) after serving in Air Force; belongs to group of musical innovators who moved focus from swing to bop in 1940s; first big break with Dizzy Gillespie (1947); also composes and sings; his vocalese on "Moody's Mood for Love," takeoff on "I'm in the Mood for Love," became jukebox favorite among black Newarkers; played at Grimsley's Tavern (1947); toured overseas extensively, playing Paris Jazz Festival (1949); teamed with Arnett Cobb, Art Blakey; rejoined Gillespie (1959–62); led own groups, ranging in size from trios to septets, for 15 years; returned to New York club scene (late 1970s) after 6-year stay in Las Vegas.

Moore, Abe (Snakehips) Dancer and emcee. Participated in Works Progress Administration (WPA) Federal Theater Project (mid 1930s); nicknamed for hip-wiggling routine that delighted fans at Colony Club; regular at Nest Club (late 1930s), teaming with Charlie Matthews and Ernie Ransome; paired with Joe Gregory as Slip and Slide; made "comeback" in *Memphis Bound*, 1945 show featuring Ethel Waters and Bill (Bojangles) Robinson; played Caravan Club (Dodger's) (1949); became preacher; died 1983.

Moore, Billy Guitarist. Led quartet at Picadilly (1946) with Albert Best on bass and Thelma (Moorman?) on piano; their rendition of "Poor Butterfly" reportedly "rocked the house."

Moore, Ethel Mae Advertising manager and social columnist for *New Jersey Afro-American*. Former wife of dancer Abe (Snakehips) Moore.

Moorman, Clement (Clem) Singer, pianist, organist, and arranger. Born in Newark, March 20, 1916; from musical family; brother of Hazel, who played and taught piano, Thelma, a professional pianist, and Hoffman (Mixie), who played alto sax and led small combos; started playing at house rent parties with Mixie while in high school; played with Frank Gibbs Orchestra (1934) and Al Henderson Orchestra (1936); joined Works Progress Administration (WPA) Federal Music Project (1935); at Reservoir Club with Russell Mann (c1936); arranger for Barons of Rhythm and Savoy Dictators; recorded on Savoy with Dictators (1939); also made several recordings with Bunny Banks Trio on Savoy, featuring his wife, Melba (Bonnie) Davis, including hit tune, "Don't Stop Now"; influenced by styles of Erskine Butterfield, Emory Lucas, his teacher for a

while, and Ike Quebec, when Quebec played piano; formed Picadilly Pipers (1941) with Henderson and Ernie Ransome, playing long stints at Pic and in Atlantic City and Philadelphia into mid 1940s; reformed group and continued to tour into 1950s; long stint as pianist/singer in residence at Martha's Vineyard, Clifton, N.J. (1975–84); toured South with Della Reese (1984) and Eartha Kitt (1985) in *Blues in the Night*; plays piano and sings at suburban restaurants and cocktail lounges, most recently at Colucci's in Haledon, N.J.

Moorman, Hazel Pianist and piano teacher. Sister of Mixie, Thelma, and Clem Moorman.

Moorman, Hoffman (Mixie) Popular altoist. Played at house rent parties (late 1920s–30s); played in Bill Mackey's band; played a "big spot" on Branford Place (mid 1930s); opened Tile Tavern in Paterson (1937), leading Mixie's Red Hots; deceased.

Moorman, Thelma Pianist. Played piano at Newark area clubs (1930s–1940s); sister of Mixie, Hazel, and Clem Moorman.

Moreland, Mantan Broadway comedian of 1930s. Appeared in 1930 version of Lew Leslie's *Blackbirds* with Ethel Waters, Buck and Bubbles, Flournoy Miller, and Berry Brothers; teamed with Jackie (Moms) Mabley, Dewey (Pigmeat) Markham, and Tim Malone in *Blackberries of 1932*; also in *Yeah, Man* (1932) with Eddie Rector and Leigh Whipper, which closed after four performances, and in *Shuffle Along of 1933* with Edith Wilson and Noble Sissle; featured in many Hollywood movies, including *Cabin in the Sky* with Louis Armstrong (1942); lived in Newark and performed locally in comedy team; deceased.

Morris, Walter (Phatz) Trombonist and arranger (1930s–40s).

Morse, Roland Dancer. Had eccentric act with James (Smokey) McAllister that was hit with Cameo Club patrons (1946).

Moses, Marsha Nell *See* Avant, Kitty.

Mouse *See* Fulford, Clarence.

Mundy, Jimmy Tenor saxophonist and top-notch arranger. Born in Cincinnati, Ohio,

June 18, 1907; started playing violin at 6; also learned several other instruments; played tenor in bands led by Carroll Dickerson and Erskine Tate (1926–31); played in Eddie White Orchestra in Newark and upstate New York (c1929–31); arranged scores for Earl Hines and Benny Goodman (beginning in 1935), including "Sing, Sing, Sing" (hit of Goodman's 1939 Carnegie Hall jazz concert that won Mundy induction into the National Academy of Recording Arts and Sciences), for Count Basie (late 1930s–early 1940s), including "All of Me" and "My Old Flame" for singer Lynne Sherman, for Harry James, and for Lionel Hampton; one of best-known arrangements was "Tune Town Shuffle," on which Buddy Tate has tenor solo; died April 24, 1983.

Leon Eason: "He played tenor with Eddie White's band. Shad Collins and Jeff, a little dark fellow, were in it then. He wrote arrangements for the Alabams—a good arranger like Fletcher Henderson, Lee Blair, and Benny Carter. All their arrangements were good. We went down to Texas and cut everybody. If you pulled those arrangements out, you gonna get 'em! We had a battle of music in Houston, playin' a theater. They invited us to play against this band out of New Orleans. We started playin' them New York arrangements and the people went wild."

Murphy, Collins Pianist. Played house rent parties (1930s); took part in Works Progress Administration (WPA) Federal Music Project (1930s); played with Dick Matthews' band at Dave and Maney's (late 1930s) and with Jerry Bogar's Royal Club Orchestra (1940s–early 1950s).

Murray, Sonny Guitarist. Led Melmore Stompers, forerunner of Alabams.

Wesley Clark: "His big band used to play at an upstairs dance hall on Mulberry Street and another one on Washington Street where the men used to pay to dance with the ladies. That was way back in the late 1920s."

Napier, Jane (Janie) Dancer. Danced at Cabin LaBlanche (1937) and was regular when it became Nest Club (late 1930s–mid 1940s); on summer bill with Miss Rhapsody at Frank Napolitani's New Deal in Asbury Park (1940–41).

Nelson, Earl Drummer. Played with Frank Gibbs Orchestra (1934) and Al Henderson Orchestra (1936–37), playing walkathons in Hagerstown, Md.; joined Savoy Dictators (1938–39); played with Barons of Rhythm (1940); featured with Ernie Phipps on bill starring Billie Holiday at Savoy Plaza (1944); joined Jimmy Stanford's band (1946).

Nelson, Lindsey Trumpeter. From Elizabeth, N.J.; toured with Buddy Johnson's Orchestra (c1942); formed Billionaires, who played until recently at spot near City Hall in Elizabeth; also plays piano and electric piano.

Billy Anderson: "A lot of musicians, especially trumpet players, play piano. They work with their horn at their side. Piano is related to all instruments. It is the key to all instruments."

Nelson, Willie (Coot or Little Willie) Unheralded trumpeter. Played with Barons of Rhythm and then with Buddy Johnson's Orchestra; got little recognition for beautiful solo work.

Jimmy (Chops) Jones: "He could play Roy Eldridge note for note."

Nesbitt, Howard Tenor saxophonist and Hawaiian guitarist. "Gig man" who played Saturday night affairs with Leon Eason and had own groups; cabinetmaker and piano repairman.

Nolls, Bill (Willie) Drummer. Played with Bobbie Brown's Society Orchestra (1920s) and locally in small combos (1930s).

O'Laughlin, Joe Saxophonist. Brother of Stash O'Loughlin; played first alto with Buddy Johnson's Orchestra (mid 1940s) and locally with Brady Hodge's Orchestra (1940s).

O'Laughlin, Stanley (Stash) Pianist. Played with Millard Trio at Diamond Jim's on North Fifth Street (1946) and with Brother Kelly's band at Hi-De-Ho Club (1947); died in Dec. 1984.

Old Man Mose Bandleader; real name unknown. Performed at Reiff's Bar and Grill, 94 South Orange Ave., with his Swingsters and Joe Durham's Trio (1939).

Herald News (June 7, 1939): "We're glad to see Old Man Mose get a break starring at Reiff's. He's another one of those performers who always does his best and usually brings down the house."

Outcalt, James (Chippie, Mr. Chips) Trumpeter and arranger. Born Nov. 29, 1912 in Newark; grew up in Asbury Park, N.J.; at age 8 took 2 lessons on trumpet from Old Man (Frank) Wheeler, who had a marching band; played house rent parties with Mickey Waters; first job with Trenton Night Hawks (c1929–30); at age 20 returned to Newark; stayed 2 years, playing on and off with Joe Crump at Colony and Kinney clubs—"all the little joints"—and with "Bernie [?] out of Elizabeth who played a lot of ofay [white] gigs"; played 101 Ranch in New York City (c1933–34); joined dancer Floyd Ray (1934), who formed band of college boys: "When they finally got it together we went out on the road with *Harlem on Parade* all the way to California [as Floyd Ray and His Harlem Dictators]"; after returning to Newark joined Pancho Diggs Orchestra and arranged band's most popular number, "Swanee River"; joined Al Henderson's Orchestra, which became Savoy Dictators (mid 1930s); joined Tiny Bradshaw (1940–42); arranged for Lionel Hampton, Luis Russell, Don Redman, and Billy Eckstine (1944–45); jammed at Lloyd's Manor with Diggs (1949); moved to Detroit (early 1950s); deceased (c1989).

Padgette, Henry (Patches) Bassist. From Philadelphia; played with Pancho Diggs; took Al Henderson's place with Picadilly Pipers (mid 1940s).

Paige, Elsie Singer. Performed regularly at Nest Club; top chirp, who also sang at Villa Maurice (1936) and Tyler's Chicken Shack in Avenel, N.J. (1938).

Parham, Duke Pianist. Original piano player with Pancho Diggs Orchestra; recorded on Decca (1946) with Frank Humphrey's Orchestra playing arrangements by Eddie

Durham of "After You're Gone" and "Lonesome Mood"; deceased.

Patterson, Omar Songwriter. Wrote "Give Love Another Chance," recorded by Deek Watson and Brown Dots on Decca (1945).

Payne, Mary (Sugar) Dancer and singer. From Baltimore, Md.; as child, supposedly danced on street corner with Honi Coles, who became famous dancer; reportedly "stranded in Newark with a carnival"; in chorus line at Nest Club with Sadie Matthews and Frances Herbert (1938); performed at Carnegie Hall in Vauxhall (Union), N.J. (1938); in *Back Streets of Harlem* revue at Boston Plaza (1942); mother of Mary Barnett, who became a choreographer for Alvin Ailey; died Jan. 20, 1991 in Baltimore hospital.

Clem Moorman: "A petite miss and frantic little entertainer who was very cute and bubbly."

Payton, Harry Popular house rent party pianist.

Pease, Anna (Mom) Singer. Sang at Palace Lucille (1920s); described by bartender Bill Roberts as "tall, slim, and classy."

Pease, Morty Pianist. Played by ear and performed with Joe St. John; played Radio Inn (1925–26); his brother Edward supposedly played with Fats Waller.

Perry, Nettie Singer. Sang on order of Emma Hawkins and Miss Rhapsody; played Club Alabam (c1930); worked with Charlie Matthews at New World in Orange, N.J. (c1935); appeared at Kinney Club (late 1930s).

Lucille (Dorsey) Morton: "She was a gentleman's lady, like Mae West. All the men wanted her. She had a very pretty body and face."

Persip, Charli(e) Famous bebop era drummer. Born in Morristown, N.J., July 26, 1929; studied under Pearl Brackett in Springfield, Mass.; first paid jobs in Newark with Billy Ford Orchestra and with Joe Holliday; played with Tadd Dameron (1953), Dizzy Gillespie (from Sept. 1953 until group disbanded in Jan. 1958), and Harry James band (April to May 1959); led own groups since 1959.

Phipps, Ernie Bespectacled jazz pianist and bandleader. Born in Newark, Feb. 14, 1923; older brother of Gene Phipps; first job at YMCA on Court Street (1939); formed Monarchs of Rhythm, top swing band that played Dreamland Academy (1941) and Savoy Plaza (1943–44), including date with Billie Holiday and Sunday night dances for capacity crowds; toured Washington, Virginia, and West Virginia (1943); joined Gene Phipps Orchestra upon return from military duty (1946); appeared at new Caravan Club with vibes band (1949); played Bobaloo Club, Howard Bar, and Orange's Diamond Mirror (1952).

Phipps, Gene, Sr. Alto and tenor saxophonist. Born in Newark, Dec. 7, 1927; younger brother of Ernie Phipps; cousin of musicians Nat and Billy Phipps; played in high school with Barringer Blue Jackets; took over Monarchs of Rhythm when Ernie entered service; recorded "G & R Blues" on Regis (1944); pitted against Corporal Brady Hodge's band in a "Big Battle of Swing" at Graham Auditorium (1945); played "All-Star Victory Show" at Mosque Theater (1945); after stint in service traveled with Hot Lips Page and Billy (Longhorn) Thompson; played with Gus Young (1951–52) at Washington Cafe and with brother Ernie at Howard Bar (1952); occasionally appears with son Gene Jr., who plays reeds and flute at Newark clubs.

Phipps, Nat Bandleader. Led group that appeared with Nat King Cole and Bunny Briggs at Newark Opera House (1951); with his society orchestra played many dances at Terrace Ballroom (1950s).

Pie Trumpeter; real name unknown. Brother of Sport, who played piano; once lived in same house on Boyd Street as Donald Lambert.

Pittman, Milton Club owner, manager, pianist, composer, and affable emcee. Native of Florida; played Villa Maurice (1938–39); birthday party in his honor given at Boston Plaza, where he was host and led band (1939); organized Monday and Wednesday jams at 7 of city's major clubs; brought jam sessions to Union County; opened Hyde-away on Halsey Street (1942); among many generous acts, spearheaded drive for funds for Millie Williams' funeral (1941) and effort to buy instruments for Charlton Street School Drum and Bugle Corps (1944); owned Pitt's Place, 285 West Market Street; past president of Newark Tavern Owners' Association and president of Bethany Baptist Church Men's 400 Club; father of Milton Jr., who plays keyboards, often teaming with Gene Phipps Jr.

Plater, Robert (Bobby) Altoist. Born in Newark, May 13, 1914; also played clarinet and flute; first professional work with Duke Richardson's Band (1934); joined Al Henderson's Orchestra, which segued into Savoy Dictators (1937–39); went with Tiny Bradshaw when Dictators broke up (1940–42); scored hit with his composition "Jersey Bounce"; led Army's 93rd Division Band (1942–45); played briefly with Cootie Williams (1946), then joined Lionel Hampton (1946–64), where he was top-notch arranger and gifted soloist except for recovery period after breaking his legs in 1955 band coach accident; joined Count Basie (1964); died Nov. 20, 1982 in Lake Tahoe, Nev., while touring with Basie band.

Plinton, Hollis Bassist. Played with Barons of Rhythm (1940); became Union County undertaker.

Plowden, Tat Chorus line girl. Performed at Nest Club with Laura Reilly, Sugar Payne, and Christine Northington (late 1930s).

Polite, Henry Singer. Often performed at Roselle's Omega Bar and Grill (early 1940s); married Una Coleman, sister of Coleman Brothers; deceased.

Leon Eason: "He tried to sound like Lawrence Miller."

Porter, Sam Pianist. From Detroit; house rent party piano player specializing in boogie woogie and blues; self-taught; died (mid 1970s) in his 90s.

Powell, Ernie Tenor saxophonist. Played with Joe St. John's and Joe Holley's bands (early 1930s), Earle Howard's band (summer 1933), Al Jenkins (c1937), and Oran

(Hot Lips) Page's big band (1938); recorded on Vocalion with Benny Carter (1939); appeared in (1943) film *Stage Door Canteen* with Count Basie's Orchestra.

Clyde Bernhardt: "He had a brother [Bobby], who played trumpet with white bands (possibly Chick Webb's). Bobby was a mulatto and looked like an Italian. He switched over to black bands in the 1930s."

Price, Helen Singer. Performed occasionally at local clubs, mostly at amateur shows.

Joe Gregory: "I liked the way she phrased on 'I Understand.'"

Princess Margo *See* Majors, Yolanda.

Proctor Saxophonist; first name unknown. Played with local groups.

Pryor, Jesse Singer. Favorite at Orpheum Theater; had voice that sounded like he was crying when he sang.

Prysock, Arthur Famous singer. From Paterson, N.J.; became one of nation's top vocalists in 1940s; performed at Kinney Club (late 1940s).

Prysock, Wilburt Bandleader. With his orchestra, backed *Tropical Heat* revue at Kinney Club, featuring Reese LaRue (1947); brother of singer Arthur Prysock.

Pugsley, Herbert (Herb) Comedian. Performed side-splitting sketches as regular at Dodger's (1939–43); moved to Nest Club (1943); became Democratic leader in old Third Ward (1945); deceased.

Purnell, Louis (Slim) Cornetist and trumpeter. Played with Pancho Diggs Orchestra; died (1938) at Newark City Hospital after undergoing emergency appendectomy.

Quallo Trumpeter. Orpheum Theater pit band musician. Influenced many younger musicians; left Newark to live in upstate New York.

Quebec, Danny Saxophonist. Nephew of Ike Quebec; died young.

Quebec, Ike (Jim Dawgs) Tenor saxophonist and pianist; real name Ike Abrams. Born in Newark, Aug. 17, 1918; gigged as teenager at Dave and Maney's in Orange, N.J.; danced in traveling show *Harlem on Parade*; member of Pancho Diggs Orchestra; first professional work on sax with Barons of Rhythm (1940); worked with many small bands including those led by Frankie Newton, Benny Carter, Coleman Hawkins, Trummy Young, and Hot Lips Page (1940s); developed bebop theme known as "Mop Mop" with Kenny Clarke at Kelly's Stable in New York (1941–42); played on and off with Cab Calloway (1944–51); performed at Graham Auditorium with Sarah Vaughan (1947); led combos (1950s), including one that played Picadilly and Washington Bar (1952); won several *Esquire* magazine top jazz ratings; died of lung cancer in New York City, Jan. 16, 1953; buried in Woodland Cemetery, Newark.

Rainey, Ruby Singer and dancer who played piano and drums. One of city's most versatile entertainers; handled vocals at Club Del Rio on Washington Street (1939) and Hydeaway (1942).

Rainier, Buck Saxophonist. From Vauxhall (Union), N.J.; self-taught; played with band led by Roscoe (Rosie) Jones.

Wesley Clark: "He couldn't read a note, but he could play in any key. I never knew anyone who could play like that. I took him to New York and Ike [Quebec] said, 'Where'd you get him?' I said, Out of the woods."

Ransom, Daniel Singer. First tenor with Southern Imperiale Quartet; joined Southern Sons (1945).

Ransom, Eddie Altoist. Played with Pancho Diggs Orchestra; became New Brunswick postal worker.

Ransome, Ernie (Skeets) Guitarist and tipple player who also sang. Described by reviewer as "the Sepia Bing Crosby"; Works Progress Administration (WPA) Federal Theater Project act with Charlie Matthews; starred in shows at Nest Club (1938) and Dave and Maney's (1939); formed Picadilly Pipers with Clem Moorman and Al Henderson (1941).

Ravenue, Hubert Bandleader (early 1930s). From Montclair, N.J.; originally from West Indies.

Raymond, Fun Banjo player and guitarist; first name unknown. Played with Frank Gibbs Orchestra (1934).

Reeves, Eurlee Club owner. Born in Pelham,

Ga., Feb. 19, 1898; owned Nest Club on Warren Street, one of Newark's major black nightclubs offering full-scale musical revues (late 1930–40s); died Feb. 1, 1990 in New Community Nursing Home, Newark.

Rennick, Andrew Altoist. Played with Hubert Ravenue's band (early 1930s); played area clubs including the Bungalow in Passaic County, N.J.

Rheubottom, Doris Singer. Wife of comedian Crackshot Hacksley.

Count Basie (*Good Morning Blues*): "She sang ballads and popular show songs like 'Indian Love Call,' 'Somebody Loves Me,' and with her great voice and stage personality she could break the house up every time. She was something else. She was also Crackshot's girlfriend."

Richard and Kat Dance team at Twinlite (1944).

Richards, Kenny Drummer. Played with Leon Eason's band at Alcazar (1940).

Richardson, Duke Bandleader. Played trombone with Heat Waves when the band had 12 pieces and after it became a 6-piece unit, playing dime-a-dance halls in New York; led band whose personnel included Bobby Plater, Cornelius Chinn, and Al Henderson (1934).

Richardson, Jazzlips Comedian; first name unknown. Featured regularly in revues at Boston Plaza and Dodger's (1942–43).

Rico, Rita Cuban songstress. Performed at Picadilly (1943); starred in *It's Groovy, Like a Movie*, show promoted by Tiny Prince.

Ringold, Larry Saxophonist and clarinetist. Played in Boston (1930) with band led by pianist Earle Howard; played with Russell Mann's group at Fatty Harris's place upstairs on Halsey Street with Leon (Cateye) Roberts on trumpet, Brother Moncur on bass, and Erskine Butterfield on piano; took his Sultans of Swing into Dodger's (1939); played at Charlie's Tavern, 35 Sussex Avenue (1941); led swing band, the Mellowtones, at Victoria Hall on Thursday nights (1941); with Gus Young and Alexander (Buster) Stothoff, recorded "The Alcazar Jump" on Decca (1943); led 7-piece band at Alcazar (1944) and swing combo at Twinlite (1945);

strongly influenced many Newark musicians; talented arranger who also could play piano and trumpet; deceased.

Clem Moorman: "He was one of the best talents this area has ever known. He played alto, tenor, trumpet, and a little piano and was one of the best arrangers I've ever met."

Leon Eason: "He taught us all."

Roberts, Henry Saxophonist. Had a band with Buster Stothoff.

Roberts, Judy Risque singer. Performed at Kinney Club; also performed at Dodger's (1946).

Roberts, Leon (Cateye) Trumpeter. From Passaic, N.J.; played with Larry Ringold and with Bill Mackey band (1930s).

Al Henderson: "He was a note man."

Robinson, Bennie (Red) Saxophonist and clarinetist. Born in Bluefield, W. Va. in 1907 to "a family of musicians" in which father played mandolin, guitar, and flute, mother played piano, and brother Ikey became well-known banjo player and bandleader in Chicago; played carnivals, minstrel shows, including Florida Blossom Minstrel Show, and theaters in Baltimore for 3–4 years, including show featuring Nicholas Brothers; came to New Jersey with vibraphonist Pete Diggs, playing summers in Asbury Park with Diggs (early 1940s); in Army band for 3 years during World War II; led band at Hi Spot (1947–49); retired from music after becoming amputee.

Robinson, Peggy Chorus line girl. Regular at Kinney Club with Goldie Simpson and Ruby Vincent; also sang (late 1930s).

Robinson, Robert (Butch) Saxophonist and clarinetist. Played small clubs, including Blue Goose and Park Rest, with Leon Eason (1936–37); played with Pancho Diggs Orchestra (late 1930s); considered "a loner."

Robinson, Satchel Dancing emcee and comedian. Often teamed with Pal Williams; teamed with Myrtle Hutchinson (1938) in Nest Club revue; performed at Dodger's and Dave and Maney's (1938); became waiter at Jersey shore and in Florida when jobs were scarce (1941); played Boston for a year (1942); performed at Pat and Don's (1942) and Club Bali, Washington, D.C.

(1943); toured Canada and upstate New York (1943); considered "Hollywood-bound" after 2-week engagement in Philadelphia (1944); opened for Marva Louis, wife of boxing champ Joe Louis, at New York's Apollo Theater (1945); suave dancer with Deek Watson and His Band at Club Bali (1946); played Murrain's in Harlem (1947).

Rodgers, Johnny Tenor saxophonist. Often worked with Leon Eason; retired electrician.

Roebuck, Robert Drummer. Original member of Pancho Diggs Orchestra.

Rollins, George Tap dancer. From theatrical family; one of 12 children of Rose Rollins, who lived to be 100; sister of fashion designer Emily Miles and brother of saxophone player and organist Pop Pop Rollins; toured internationally with Cab Calloway's *Cotton Club Revue;* appeared before king and queen of England; played New York's Apollo Theater, teaming with Little Black Jimmy (Fairbanks) as Two Turbans; starred at Boston Plaza and Dodger's (1938–42); enrolled in Newark's Apex College of Beauty (1946); died at age 49.

Rollins, Harold (Pop Pop) Saxophonist and organist. Younger brother of George Rollins; got nickname because he could make his horn "pop"; toured worldwide with Redd Foxx and Sammy Davis Jr.; played behind Ruth Brown, Dionne Warwick, and other singers; subsequently formed organ combo; played local clubs including Lloyd's Manor and Fredericks' Lounge.

Ross, Mandy Bandleader and trumpeter. Led Mandy Ross and His Walkin' Rhythm, which played swing matinees, band battles, dances, and beauty pageants; played Victoria Ballroom in North Newark (1941), YMHA Ballroom at Kinney and High streets and Campus Terrace (1943), Savoy Plaza (1944), and Graham Hall (1944–46); "accepted" at Atlantic City's Cliquot Club, a white spot (1945), after southern tour marred by Jim Crow incidents; played at Diamond Jim's in North Ward (1946); played swing battle against Corporal Brady Hodge at Graham's (1946); led New Man-hattan Sextet in Morristown, N.J. (1947); deceased.

Bob Queen (*Afro-American*, May 17, 1980): "Like Pancho Diggs, he had a coveted Savoy Ballroom gig in Harlem [early in his career], then moved downtown to the Lincoln Center Ballroom, a small dance hall on the site of the Lincoln Center cultural center."

Royster, Clarence (Gee) Saxophonist and bandleader. Led Swingsters at Saul's Tavern (1942); played third alto with Alabams and with Leon Eason (late 1930s) at Park Rest, Club Miami, and Alcazar.

Russell, Helen Talented singer from Georgia. Had a good repertoire; played floor shows at Dodger's (1943–45).

St. John, Joe Tenor saxophonist and bandleader. Led band that played at New York's Savoy Ballroom (1929–30).

Clyde Bernhardt: "His band used to play at the Savoy Ballroom [in New York]. He played a lot of hotel jobs for white people. They always had two bands—one black and one white."

Salley, Leo Trumpeter and arranger. Born in Newark, May 29, 1921; given trumpet and lessons as mascot for Elks Lodge, of which his father was member; subbed for "regular musician" at tavern and got fired from first job because he "only knew five or six numbers"; original member of Barons of Rhythm at age 14, playing second trumpet; played one-night gigs regularly with Gus Young and Leon Eason; also played with Bobby Jarrett, Mandy Ross, Al Terrell (1930s–1940s), and his own aggregation, Leo Salley Orchestra (c1965), which played at dance halls and for some club and tavern dates; for 30 years, a claims supervisor at Newark Post Office; died Sept. 4, 1987.

Sawyer, Bill Saxophonist and clarinetist. One of first musicians to play Colony Club on Broome Street as saxophonist for Joe Crump's Band of 1,000 Themes.

Hal Mitchell: "He was like a farmer. He used cellophane wrappers for pads on his horn, but he knew how to play. He amazed us all."

Scheffield Harmonica player; first name unknown. Played at house rent parties and got jobs for other musicians.

Schenck, Huzzy Drummer; first name unknown. From Paterson, N.J.; brother of saxophonist and clarinetist William (Buddy) Schenck.

Schenck, William (Buddy or Bill) Reed player. Brother of drummer Huzzy; from Paterson, N.J.; played tenor with original Barons of Rhythm (mid 1930s); joined Jimmy Stanford's group (1946).

Scoodlelum Guitarist; real name unknown. Made early 1930s record entitled "Come on Baby, Let's Scoodlelum."

Scott, Bernice Dancer. Teamed as act with emcee Cliff Buchanan; billed as "Queen of Swing" at Dave and Maney's in Orange, N.J. (1939); showed off her frenetic jitterbugging skills in Kinney Club shows.

Scott, Herbert Lee (Herb or Scotty) Trumpeter and singer. From Trenton, N.J.; moved to Newark (mid 1930s) after playing with bands in Midwest; comic talents became apparent at Dodger's, where he sang "I Can't Give You Anything but Love" in such rapid-fire fashion he had patrons in stitches; known for comic solo "Mrs. Skeffington"; played with Doles Dickens Quartet (from mid 1940s), touring East Coast; died July 1980; Billy Ford and Clem Moorman played "Memories of You" at funeral service in Clinton AMEZ Church in Newark.

Scott, Howard (Sadiq) Fine trombonist. Original member of Pancho Diggs Orchestra and Savoy Dictators; played with Billy Eckstine's band (1945) and Heat Waves (late 1930s).

Scott, James Trombonist (late 1940s).

Scott, Jimmy (Little Jimmy) Famous singer known for his falsetto. Born in Cleveland, Ohio, July 17, 1925; began professional career on bills with comedian/dancer Jockey Gray and comedian Tim McCoy; traveled South with *Caldonia's Revue*, starring Estelle (Caldonia) Young, comedienne/contortionist; appeared at Baby Grand in New York and Gambie's in Baltimore; toured with Lionel Hampton (late 1940s) and recorded half-dozen tunes, including "Everybody's Somebody's Fool," "I've Been a

Fool," and "I Wish I Didn't Love You So"; popular recording artist (late 1940s–50s) best known for Roost release "The Masquerade Is Over"; billed at Newark's Cafe Society (1949) and Teddy Powell's Holiday Inn (1958); remained active musically into 1960s, performing at small clubs; on comeback trail (mid 1980s), performing at New York clubs, has 6 albums to his credit, including 4 on Savoy, one on Atlantic, and 1990 release *Doesn't Love Mean More*; featured in tribute to trumpeter Harold (Hal) Mitchell at Essex County College in Newark (April 1985); formed Jazz Expression quartet, which backs him (1990); played Center Grill of Roosevelt Hotel in Los Angeles (1990).

Sermond, Billie Singer; married name Hall. Born in Newark, 1910; became enchanted by show business after seeing *Shuffle Along* when she was about 13; ran away to New York's Lafayette Theater (1924); started singing in vaudeville show in New York with Mamie Smith as teenager, then ran away to Pittsburgh with *Checkers' Revue*; got stranded, but worked her way back to Newark (c1930) by forming act with friend Dorothy Bryant; faced discrimination as mulatto because of light skin; known for rendition of "Smoke Rings"; sang mostly at white clubs on Broad Street (late 1930s–early 1940s), including Silver Ball off Lincoln Park; married man-about-town Eldridge Hall; teamed with Henry (Bobby) Walker to play Palm House in Vailsburg section and Cottage on Heller Parkway in North Ward; stopped singing in early 1960s.

Celeste Jones: "She could swing. She could sing a sweet number, too. She's what I'd call an all-round singer."

Shavers, Charlie Saxophonist; not to be confused with well-known trumpet player of same name. Played with Pancho Diggs Orchestra.

Simpson, Goldie Chorus girl. Performed at Kinney Club with Ruby Love and Peggy Robinson (late 1930s–mid 1940s).

Sims, Horace Guitarist and singer. Performed with Mandy Ross's Walkin' Rhythm (early 1940s), with which he toured South;

served in Army; performed with Ross at Diamond Jim's in North Ward (1946); husband of singer Lu Elliott; occasionally accompanied her in small combos.

Sinkford, Clarence Trombonist. Played in Orpheum Theater pit band; influenced many younger musicians; deceased.

Slade, Billie Chorus girl. Waitress at Ted Adams' luncheonette on Barclay Street (late 1930s); occupied end position in chorus at New York's Club Sudan (1946).

Slater, Chester (Chet) Organist supreme. Once led group called Harlemaires; ensconced at Dwyer's Elbow Room on Broad Street for 22 months (1950–52); appeared at Holiday Inn in Hoboken (1952), Edison Lounge and Century Lounge in Newark, Baltimore's Comedy Club, and Omega Bar and Grill in Roselle, N.J.; disabled in later years by series of strokes.

Slip and Slide *See* Gregory, Joe *and* Moore, Abe.

Smalls, Julius (Geech) Trumpeter and trombonist. Product of Jenkins Orphanage Band, Charleston, S.C.; settled in Newark; played in 1920s and 1930s bands; asthmatic; found dead (1977) in his rooming house after failing to appear for recording date for G & R Records in Newark.

Smith, Cladys (Jabbo) Legendary trumpeter. Born in Pembroke, Ga., Dec. 24, 1908; raised at Jenkins Orphanage in Charleston, S.C., where he learned trumpet, trombone, alto, and baritone saxophone; inspired by trumpeter Gus Aiken; worked in Chicago with various bands after being stranded (1928) with James P. Johnson's show *Keep Shufflin';* followed Leon Eason into Alcazar, where he led his own trio at first and then played with Larry Ringold's group (c1942–45); revived career as soloist in off-Broadway production *One Mo' Time* (1979); died in New York, Jan. 16, 1991.

Al Henderson. "He could play figures behind a ballad singer, and it was the sweetest stuff."

Smith, Grace Torch singer. Born in Columbia, S.C., Jan. 1, 1908; came to Newark at age 14; started as chorus girl at Nest Club; often billed as "Miss Grace Smith, Queen of the Blues"; known for her renditions of "Easy Living," "I Cried for You," and "Them There Eyes"; sang at Celebrity Club in New York; one of all-time favorites at Newark clubs (1930s–1940s), including Rin Tin Inn (1938), Fisher's Tavern (1939), Nest Club (1943), Picadilly (1944), and Kinney Club (1945); dubbed "Bahama Mama" after touring islands (c1940); stole show during USO tour (1945) with routine with comic Johnny Berry; toured with Wynonie (Mr. Blues) Harris; played Norfolk's Big Track club (1946); drawing card at Small's Paradise, Kelly's Stable, and Baby Grand in New York City; played upstate New York and Canadian clubs (1946); back home at Cafe Superior (1947), Nitecap (1951), Rahway, N.J.'s Blue Room (1951), and Silver Saddle (1951); spent winter performing in Miami with Joe Gregory and Anna May Hall (1952); turned to gospel music (1970s); member of Abyssinian Baptist Church Choir in Newark; died Oct. 26, 1989.

Smith, Jabbo *See* Smith, Cladys.

Smith, Melba (Bonnie) Singer; recorded as Bonnie Davis. Alabama college girl; came north with Erskine Hawkins to join Teddy Hill's orchestra in New York; played engagement with Leon Abbey Quartet at Newark's Picadilly (1942); married pianist Clem Moorman; became vocalist for Picadilly Pipers, for whom Moorman played piano; recorded on Savoy as Bonnie Davis, including hit "Don't Stop Now" (1942); played local clubs with Pipers and toured East Coast spots, including gigs in Philadelphia, Atlantic City, and Baltimore, into 1950s; mother of singer/actress Melba Moore; deceased.

Smith, Ted (Big Ted) Part-time pianist. Born in 1916; went into Wallace's High Tavern in West Orange, N.J. to sub for Donald Lambert when Lambert became ill and was hospitalized; popular house rent party musician; became a longshoreman.

Smith, Willie (The Lion) Stride piano legend. Born in Goshen, N.Y., Nov. 25, 1897; stepbrother of club manager/drummer Melvin Smith and club manager Bobby Smith;

one of most colorful stride pianists of his era; served with distinction with 350th Field Artillery in World War I; decorated for "heroism under fire"; known for his $50 derby and stogie; accompanied Mamie Smith on "Crazy Blues," 1920 Okeh recording that sold 75,000 copies in one month and a million in first year; ruled Harlem, working "small cellars from 125th to 140th Streets" (1920s); braggadocious master of cutting contests; got Fats Waller first paid job as his replacement when he quit Leroy's in Harlem; later ensconced at New York's Rhythm Club; took trio into Newark's Picadilly (1943) with Benny Carter's wife, Inez Lester, as vocalist; made many records on Decca (1935–40); played White House reception for President Richard Nixon (1969); died in New York City, April 18, 1973.

Leonard Feather (*Book of Jazz*): "One of the subtlest of the stride pianists"; played "lacy, springy, airy themes."

Smothers, Joe (Mother Smothers) Song and dance man. Performed with singer Billy Daniels at Picadilly (1942–43).

Smythe, Togge Saxophonist. Born in Richmond, Va., Dec. 21, 1912; came to Newark at 18; "turned on" by violinist Stuff Smith, so started playing violin; switched to sax, taking lessons in New York from Walter (Foots) Thomas; for first gig, at friend's tavern in Orange, N.J., got $2.50 a night (1938); worked at Kinney Club for 3 years with Elmer Chambers (late 1930s); played "every club in Newark, sometimes two at a time"; began singing jazz and "ran round vocalizing with George Gordon"; led Togge Smythe and Four Sounds (1945–46); played with Hal Mitchell's Savoy Dictators, Dud Bascomb, Tiny Bradshaw, and Eddie (Cleanhead) Vinson (1941–47); retired from music in 1954 and moved to Willingboro, N.J. to go into nursing.

Snow, Hattie Singer. Popular out-of-town performer who played many times at Orpheum Theater (late 1920s).

Snowball See Jordan, Shirley.

Snowball One of city's top lindyhoppers; real name unknown.

Sparrow, Mr. Pianist; first name unknown. Played at house rent parties.

Spence, Bill Drummer.

Spo-De-O-De Comic singer; real name unknown. Played Newark clubs when things got tough in New York (mid 1940s); frequently appeared at Picadilly; known for his renditions of "You Can't Get That No More" and "I'll Be Glad When You're Dead, You Rascal You."

Sport Pianist; real name unknown. Played at house rent parties (1930s); brother of trumpet player Pie.

Stalks, Hazelwood (Woody) Saxophonist and bandleader. Led group that won many dance dates (late 1940s); entertained nightly at Cameo Club and new Hi-De-Ho (1947).

Standard, Ann Pianist and singer. Performed with Ame Garrison's Sirens of Swing on Sundays at Boston Plaza (1938); played piano with Smoky Jones's band at Saul's Tavern (1939); featured vocalist at Charlie's Tavern with Larry Ringold's band (1941).

Stanford, James (Jimmy) Saxophonist. Born Aug. 8, 1922; started playing sax at age 13; teachers included Charlie Shavers and Lowell (Count) Hastings; considers Walter (Gil) Fuller his mentor; "baby" of Barons of Rhythm as teenager attending Arts High (mid 1930s); joined Buddy Johnson's band after serving in Navy (1942–46), traveling southern circuit; with Johnson, played opposite Billy Eckstine's band in Rocky Mount, N.C. "when Diz and Bird and all those guys were in it"; after war tried unsuccessfully to revive Barons; joined Four Chucks at Howard Bar, replacing Ame Garrison (1947–58); also played T-Bar and boxer Charlie Fusari's club across from City Hall during same span; stopped playing in 1964 because of illness; worked for Navy; lived for many years in Mechanicsburg, Pa., where he was transferred and lived until retirement; returned to Newark (1988).

Stothoff, Alexander (Buster) Pianist, bandleader, and arranger. From Belleville, N.J.; often played with Gus Young and Larry Ringold's groups; backed Nest Club revue featuring Lawrence Miller, Miss Rhapsody, Satchel Robinson, Myrtle Hutchinson, and Abe (Snakehips) Moore (1939); recorded "The Alcazar Jump" on Decca (1943); died in Clara Maass Hospital, Belleville, N.J., Jan. 13, 1976.

Willie Johnson: "He was such a good musician—always in demand, always with the big shots."

Strange, Mary Cabaret singer. Brought by emcee Honey Boy Thompson into Kinney Club (late 1930s), where patrons would request her peppy renditions of songs like "You're Nobody 'til Somebody Loves You."

Strickling, Ella Sweet singer. From Belmont Avenue; performed at Picadilly (1942); moved to Florida.

Struttin' Sam Dancer; real name unknown. Specialty "The Cane Dance" done to tune "Shine"; described by reviewer as "twirling blur on dancing toes, flashing his cane"; appeared often at Dave and Maney's (late 1930s).

Styne, Sadie Popular late 1940s singer.

Sutton, Frank (Gersh) Altoist. Traveled to upstate New York with Joe St. John's Orchestra (c1932); played with Al Henderson Orchestra (1936–37).

Swangin, Thomas O. (T. O.) Saxophonist and clarinetist. Born in Newark, Nov. 23, 1918; joined Queen of Angels church band as a teenaged clarinet player; started playing alto sax with Barons of Rhythm while attending South Side High School (mid 1930s); attended Seton Hall College (1937–39); served in 353rd ASF Band while stationed in Wyoming in Army (1944), when Sammy Davis Jr. was cadre man who sang with unit and bassist George Duvivier was band member; entered Newark Police Academy after discharge; played tuba in police band; retired Newark cop; died April 23, 1990.

Tabbs, Lawrence Trumpeter. Played with local bands (late 1940s).

Tanner, Jimmie Piano player (1940s).

Taylor, Bob (Lance) Singer, real name Bob Holmes. Silvery-voiced crooner with "terrific range"; entertained at Dodger's, Nest Club, and Alcazar (late 1930s–mid 1940s); known for staples including "Marie," "Dark Eyes," "Prisoner of Love," and "Let Me Dream"; dreamed of starting "a Negro theater group" (1938); member of Works Progress Administration (WPA) Federal Theater Project; sang with Johnny Jackson's band (1944); left to take role in Broadway production of *Anna Lucasta;* appeared in films and television dramas as Lance Taylor.

Leon Eason: "He used to sing my tune, 'Beverly.'"

Thad (Chuck) Howard: "I saw him on TV in a police episode."

Taylor, Edna Blues singer. Performed at Kinney Club (1938).

Taylor, Haywood Piano player. Played with Barons of Rhythm (1940).

Terrell, Al Guitarist. Played with Barons of Rhythm (c1940).

Terry, Arthur Piano-playing comic, hoofer, and emcee. Popular emcee at Boston Plaza, Nest Club, Dodger's, and Waverly Tavern (late 1930s); style described as "breezy," his handling of acts, "clever"; performed in Miami and Nassau (1941); emcee at Picadilly and Hi Spot (1942) and 42nd Club in Orange, N.J. (1943); toured Canada with Grace Smith (1944); performed at Dodger's (1944–46); formed Arthur Terry and His Grand Rascals for long stay at Lloyd's Manor (1946); emcee for Monday night jams; played Howard Bar (1951–52); died in Jersey City, N.J. in 1970.

Afro-American (Feb. 15, 1947): "A pint-sized entertainer who's still carryin' on; no one will forget his takeoff on the guys who earned $30.25 every two weeks leaning on a shovel for the WPA."

Thomas, Flo Comedienne. Born Jan. 10, 1909 in King Fisher, Okla.; raised by grandmother in St. Louis; daughter of William Riley, Newark photographer with studio on Prince Street; chorus girl in Kansas City; married black-face comedian Dyke Thomas and teamed with him (1928); played theaters "all over the United States and Canada," including Orpheum; came to Newark after her husband died to work Kinney

Club; stayed 7 years doing comedy; known for her risque number "Old Man Mose Is Dead"; married a customer, Ahmed Hassan (1939); teamed with Smokey McAllister at Picadilly (1952); entered burlesque; quit show business (1955); died Sept. 6, 1988 in St. Mary's Hospital, Orange, N.J.

Herald News (July 23, 1938): "Her comedy number is the climax of the new Kinney Club revue. Dressed in an 1880s costume, she Virginia reels and prances through a ballad about an ill-fated 'Nancy Green from the hills of West Virginia'; it's a swinging number leading to 'Turkey in the Straw' that rolls 'em in the aisles."

Thompson, Buster Singer. Singing waiter at Boston Plaza (1939); sang "My Buddy" at funerals and interesting version of "Sunrise Serenade"; described in *Herald News* review (1939) as "the best male singer in town."

Thompson, Dicky (Duke) Left-handed guitarist. Played with Doles Dickens Trio at Picadilly (1946) and New York's Club Zanzibar (1947); moved to Honolulu.

Thompson, Edith Blues singer. Performed at Dodger's (1946).

Thompson, Honey Boy Top-notch emcee and dancer. Performed at Kinney Club (early 1940s).

Thompson, Lloyd Singer. Savoy recording star; played Melody Club with Gus Young (1946) and Eagle Bar (1951).

Thorpe, Obie Guitarist (late 1940s).

Thorpe, Ulysses (Bubbles) Saxophonist. Born in Macon, Ga., 1922; from Elizabeth, N.J.; played in Kinney Club band (1947) and other local gigs; played in Buddy Johnson's reed section; deceased.

Thurmond, William (Sonny) Drummer. Played with Jerry Bogar's Royal Club Orchestra (late 1940s).

Timmons, Joe Singer. Smooth, syncopated, romantic style that made ladies swoon; performed at Alcazar (1942) and Nest Club (1943); former tenor with Golden Gate Quartet; moved to Nashville to start business.

Toler, Freddie Comedian and song and dance man. Born May 11, 1914; began entertaining in "all the theaters on Springfield Avenue" as teenager; handled intros at Dodger's (1939); played Twinlite (1944); fixture at Famous Door on Bedford Street; teamed with singer Earl Leonardo (early 1950s); appeared in World War II USO shows; moved to California in 1950s; deceased (c1988).

Tolson, Charles Eugene (Gene) Drummer. Born in Newark; played with Skeeter Best, Buddy Terry, Eddie Blackwell, Duke Anderson, and Little Jimmy Scott (1948–80s); headed Gene Tolson and Rhythm Kings; worked at Bendix Aerospace in Teterboro, N.J. for 31 years, retiring in 1981; died Jan. 1, 1991 at age 59.

Tucker, Robert (Bobby) Pianist, arranger, and composer. Born Jan. 8, 1923 in Morristown, N.J.; began performing at 14; member of Los Casanovas, Newark club that booked bands (Babs Gonzales was another member); played Mt. Royal Hotel, Montreal (early 1940s); studied at New York's Institute of Musical Art; accompanied Mildred Bailey, then Billie Holiday until 1949; accompanist of singer Billy Eckstine for more than 30 years; featured in Quincy Jones film *Listen Up! The Lives of Quincy Jones* (1990).

Turman, Geneva Singer. Born in Plainfield, N.J. settled in Newark at age 6; started singing with her brother Buddy; played New York's 101 Ranch, Four Towers, Meadowbrook in Cedar Grove, N.J., where famous big bands played, and Canadian clubs, including Rockhead's Paradise and Montmartre in Montreal; billed (late 1930s) at Dave and Maney's in Orange, N.J.; brought down house with "Call Me Darling"; played Omega Bar and Grill in Roselle, N.J. and Dodger's (early 1940s); toured Washington, D.C. with USO on bill co-starring Grace Smith (1945); played weekend dates in Pittsburgh and Washington, D.C. (1947).

Turman, Gertrude Interpretive dancer and occasional emcee; married name Brown. Born March 6, 1919; daughter of owner of "gutbucket joint" on Broome Street, where Donald Lambert played piano and she danced for coins as child; sister of Buddy, Helena, and Geneva, who "already were in the business"; played Nest Club (1944–45); traveled most of her career, playing upstate New York, including 10 years in Elmira at Green Pastures, and Canadian spots like Rockhead's Paradise; member of Three Notes and a Staff with Larue Jordan, Babs Gonzales, and Bill Goode.

Turman, Helena Dancer. As teenager, danced in shows produced by Johnny B. Gardner; toured for several years with Danny Smalls' *Harlem on Parade;* joined brother Buddy and sister Geneva as act after they won an amateur show at Orpheum Theater; played Nest Club (1938); became nurse's aide at Essex County Hospital; was Central Ward district leader (1960s); died in 1969 at age 56 in Beth Israel Hospital, Newark.

Turman, Isaac (Buddy) Emcee, hoofer, and comedian. Brother of dancers Helena and Gertrude and songstress Geneva; terrific showman in days when Newark nightlife drew scores of patrons from New York; often on Colony Club bill; played Mt. Royal Hotel in Montreal (early 1940s); member of Los Casanovas, a group of local guys, including Babs Gonzales, who booked bands for dances; steel company employee and active trade unionist; died in July 1981.

Turner, Irvine C. Singer and ukelele player. Born in Newark; studied for ministry; attended New York School of Journalism; on staff of *New Jersey Guardian* and former co-editor and publisher of *New Jersey Record,* black newspapers; often called on to warble "Besame Mucho"; nicknamed "Ukelele Ike" because he supposedly sent notes to emcees requesting him to perform; Newark's first black councilman (1954–70); related to Count Basie; died Sept. 9, 1974 at age 59.

Turner, Merle Singer. Former singer with Erskine Hawkins Orchestra; sang and tended bar at Picadilly (1941); served in Army; entertained at Twinlite and Three Deuces, where "Cherry," which he recorded, was his big number; played Fredericks' Lounge (1946); also sang at Kinney Club.

Turp, Demon Tap dancing emcee; Demon probably a nickname. Performed in Kinney Club shows (late 1930s).

Tyler, Buster Drummer. Inspired Herman Bradley; played with Bobbie Brown's band in Newark (c1922–25), with Rosie Jones at Radio Inn, and with Larry Ringold (late 1920s–early 1930s); deceased.

Underhill, Harold (Hal) Guitarist. Toured with Banjo Bernie's band (early 1930s), starting long association with Miss Rhapsody, with whom he played Kansas City for 14 months at height of Basie era (1937–38); returned to Newark (1938); played Fisher's Tavern (1938) and Omega Bar and Grill in Roselle, N.J. (early 1940s); male vocal on Savoy recording "Night Before Judgment Day"; sergeant-at-arms of Musicians' Staff Club (1946); deceased.

Van Horn Tenor player, first name unknown. Played (1930s) with group led by Russell Mann, including George Carey and Buck Ranier; band considered forerunner of Savoy Sultans.

Van Pelt, Harold Baritone saxophonist. Born in Newark, April 5, 1930; as teenager played with Mandy Ross and His Walkin' Rhythm (1948) at Graham Hall, Club Harold, Terrace Ballroom, Wideway Ballroom, Kinney Club, Nest Club, and Lloyd's Manor; while serving in military, played with Elvin Jones and Dwike Mitchell (late 1940s).

Van Slyke, Myrtle Risque comedienne in her 60s or 70s who wore funny costumes when she entertained at Kinney Club (late 1930s).

Vaughan, Sarah Lois Singer. Born in Newark, March 27, 1924; also played piano and organ; only child of musical parents (her father played guitar and sang for fun and her mother sang in Mt. Zion Baptist Church Choir); at age 8 accompanied choir; first manager supposedly Frank Tucker, neighbor and insurance agent who booked her at local clubs like Halsey Street's Hydeaway; signed by Earl Hines (1942) after winning Apollo Theater amateur show; *Esquire* and *Downbeat*'s "Queen of All Chirps" (1940s); played Graham Hall with Billy Eckstine

(1946), Terrace Ballroom with Illinois Jacquet (1948), and Adams Theater with Boyd Raeburn (1949); guest artist at Caravan Club (1949); honored at testimonial benefit to raise funds for Christian Education Building for Mt. Zion (1954); first million-selling record, "Broken Hearted Melody," on Mercury (1959); toured Great Britain with Count Basie Band (1963); performed at White House dinner for President Lyndon B. Johnson (1965); performed Gershwin program with New Jersey Symphony in Newark's Symphony Hall (1975); last Newark engagement with New Jersey Symphony Orchestra (1988) at Symphony Hall; brought Newark international acclaim as its premier gift to entertainment world; considered most important singer to emerge from the bop era; died of cancer, April 3, 1990; funeral service at Mt. Zion attracted 2,000 fans and celebrities, including Al Hibbler, Ralph Cooper, and Sylvia Sims.

Tiny Prince: "When Sarah first started going to New York I used to run affairs at the Picadilly Club and she used to come in and sing once in a while. If I had listened to George [Haber] and Roddy [Rodberg], who ran the place, I would have put her under contract."

Walker, Henry (Bobby) Pianist. Played with Duke Richardson's Orchestra (1934) and subsequently Heat Waves; also sang; teamed with Billie Sermond at Newark clubs (early 1940s).

Walker, Mack Bassist. Played with Gus Young at Kinney Club (1930s).

Warren, Elmer Guitarist. Vocalized a bit, adding sparkle to Hi-De-Ho Club bill (1947); deceased.

Washington, Ernestine Singer. Gained national fame (1943) for her Regis recordings.

Washington, Inez (Lady) Singer. Billed at Picadilly (1943–44); South Plainfield's Belmonte Jazz Club (1961).

Washington, Kenny Drummer.

Washington, Robert (Wash or Bob) Trombonist. Original member of Barons of Rhythm, (1930s–early 1940s); in Army's 92nd Division Band; tried with Jimmy Stanford to revive Barons (1946); turned to acting, starring in Freddie Roach's *Soul Pieces* and its revival by George (Fats) Gordon (early 1980s).

Waslund, Raymond Novelty rope tap dancer. Performed at Kinney Club (1948).

Waters, Emzey Singer. Fronted Pancho Diggs Orchestra at Skateland; rendition of "Swanee River" a big hit (late 1930s); led Emzey Waters and His Del Mar Boys at Del Mar Bar (1945); died June 1985.

Waters, Mickey Alto saxophonist. From Asbury Park, N.J.; performed at Radio Inn (early 1930s); with brother Wally played with Al Henderson Orchestra (1936–37); played with Savoy Dictators (1939) and with band that accompanied Miss Rhapsody at New Deal in Asbury Park (1940–41); major influence on younger musicians in Newark area.

Waters, Wally Trumpeter. With brother Mickey, played in Al Henderson Orchestra (1936–37).

Watson, Joe Bassist. Performed at Howard Bar with Frank Brown on piano, Danny Gibson on drums, and Jimmy Stanford on tenor (1951).

Watson, Rita Starred with Reese LaRue in *Tropical Revue* at Kinney Club (1947).

Watson, Sid Drummer. Led 5-piece band at Pete's on Spruce Street (1937); led bands in Elizabeth, N.J.; played weekend jobs.

Webber, Harry Journalist. Advertising manager of *New Jersey Herald News*, black weekly; wrote column called "After Hours," then founded nightlife magazine of same name (late 1940s); photographer for weekly *New Jersey Afro-American* for many years before its demise in 1980s; resident of Newark Extended Care Facility, Newark nursing home, since suffering stroke in late 1980s.

Webster, Gladys Singer. Performed in Kinney Club revues, including *Take Me Back to School* and *Take Me Out to the Ballgame* (1939).

Lucille (Dorsey) Morton: "She was a real

money-picker-upper. She wore beautiful gowns and talked a lot of stuff to the men. She sang songs like 'You Got the Right Key but the Wrong Keyhole.' She'd say, 'Don't put quarters on the table; put dollars.'"

Wells, Eddie Bandleader and drummer. Played with Matinee Idols, who broadcast each Sunday on WHBI radio (mid 1930s); only Newark drummer at time to use temple blocks.

Wells, Viola Gertrude (Miss Rhapsody) Singer. Born in Newark at 21 Scott Street, Dec. 14, 1902; toured as teenager with Salika Johnson Glee Club under direction of Ruth Reid, choir director at 13th Avenue Presbyterian Church; first professional job, Miner's Theater on Washington Street (c1920); toured as far south as Georgia with Banjo Bernie's band (early 1930s); worked carnival show with Mighty Sheesley; toured with blues singer Ida Cox; 14-month stay at Kansas City's Sunset Palace (1937–38); performed at Fisher's Tavern (1938), Apollo Theater with Bunny Berigan, Erskine Hawkins, and Claude Hopkins orchestras (1939–40), and New Deal, Asbury Park, N.J. (summers 1940–41); broadcast each Sunday on network radio from New York as regular on "The Sheep and Goat Show" (1940); "Brown Gal" (her theme song) and "Bye, Bye, Baby" favorites at Dodger's and Roselle's Omega Bar and Grill (early 1940s); played Kelly's Stable on New York's 52nd Street (1940–44); recorded 12 sides on Savoy label (1944); played Club Bali, Washington, D.C. (1943–46); toured with her trio, Three Sportsmen of Rhythm, and as solo at clubs in Chattanooga, Detroit, and Cleveland (mid 1940s); performed at Pitt's Place, West Market Street (1950s–60s); recorded and toured Europe with Harlem Blues and Jazz Band (mid–late 1970s); made TV programs in Paris about her life and music (1975); after amputation, resumed career (1980), playing 53 weeks at New York's Ginger Man with Ram Ramirez on piano and Al Hall on bass; died Dec. 22, 1984 in Clara Maass Hospital, Belleville, N.J.; buried in Heavenly Rest Cemetery, East Hanover, N.J.

White, Bob Bassist (late 1940s–early 1950s).

White, Eddie Bandleader and pianist. Led 12-piece band (late 1920s–early 1930s) that spent winter residency at Roseland dance hall on Market Street across from Bamberger's and Orhbach's department stores.

White, Evelyn Singer. Sang with Savoy Sultans (1942).

White, Johnny Saxophonist. Played with Lundy-Lewis Trio at Hydeaway (1943).

White, Leslie Dancer. Kinney Club entertainer who danced with fire.

White, Melvin (Slappy) Dancer and comedian. Born in Baltimore, Md., Sept. 27, 1921; moved to Newark (c1938) as teenager to seek work; claims he was "stranded" when train conductor called out "New-ark" and he got off, thinking he was in New York; worked first at Saul's Tavern, then at Nest Club, Boston Plaza, Kinney Club, Picadilly, Hour Glass, and Pat and Don's in Harrison, N.J.; toured Montreal with Joe Gregory and Clarence (Red) Scheffey (1942); joined Cetlin and Wilson carnival (early 1940s) and got stranded in Albany, N.Y. "when the guy ran out of money"; met comedian Redd Foxx while Foxx was playing Gambie's in Baltimore; with Foxx has performed for 30 years, most recently at Hacienda Hotel in Las Vegas.

White, Princess Blues singer. Born in Philadelphia, Jan 14, 1881; star of *Silas Green from New Orleans* minstrel show (early 1920s–1938), dispensing blues and pretty ballads; toured with *Irvin C. Miller's Brownskin Models;* moved to Newark (1950s); resumed career in 1975 at age 94, sharing vocals with Miss Rhapsody and Harlem Blues and Jazz Band; performed at Connecticut Jazz Club show, Meriden, Conn. (June 1975), New York Overseas Press Club Jazz Club show at New York City's Roosevelt Hotel (1975), and outdoor concert in Mamaroneck, N.Y. (1975); recordings include "Sittin' on Top of the World," "Every Woman's Blues," and "Peepin' in the Wrong Keyhole" on album entitled *Clyde Bernhardt and the*

Harlem Blues and Jazz Band (Barron, 1975); died performing at Emelyn Theater, Mamaroneck, N.Y., March 21, 1976.

Whitey *See* Wilson, Whitey.

Wilcox, Norman Terrific banjo player and guitarist. Born in Cincinnati, Ohio; encouraged by mother to play piano, which she played, but preferred string instruments; filled in (late 1920s) with Eddie White's Orchestra at Newark's Roseland dance hall; organized Matinee Idols (c1930), popular musical group heard on Sundays on WHBI radio; after Depression became post office employee; died in 1978.

Williams, Art Bassist (early 1950s).

Williams, Belle Shake dancer; known as "The Gorgeous Huzzy." Performed at Dodger's and Waverly Tavern (1939).

Williams, Bobby Big band trumpeter. Born Feb. 11, 1914 in Capps, Ala.; started playing with Melmore Stompers, neighborhood group in East Orange, N.J. (1929), forerunner of Alabams; toured with Alabams until 1935; played with brother Varis's band at Newark's Club Miami "when Jackie Gleason was the emcee"; performed with Savoy Sultans at Cotton Club on Lenox Avenue in New York, then went with Luis Russell, Don Redman, Willie Bryant, Benny Carter, Roy Eldridge, Edgar Hayes, Fats Waller, and Ovie Alston (until 1947); played with Cab Calloway's Orchestra for next 18 months, crisscrossing country; toured Europe annually with Harlem Blues and Jazz Band (1970s–80s) as leader/arranger.

Williams, Connie *See* Woodruff, Connie.

Williams, Courtney Trumpeter. Born in Asbury Park, N.J., March 29, 1916; began studying violin at 8; took up trumpet in teens; traveled with Al Henderson Orchestra (1936); first chair with Savoy Dictators; played in bands led by Fats Waller and Hot Lips Page (1930s) and orchestras of Benny Carter, Claude Hopkins, and Noble Sissle (1940s); recorded with Louis Jordan (1935) and Buddy Johnson (1941) on Decca; took civil service job in New York (1947); continued arranging.

Williams, Donald Singer. Sang with Carl McIntyre's band at Alcazar (1942).

Williams, Edward (E. J.) Saxophonist. Brother of Bobby and Varis (Vay) Williams; played with Alabams (1930s).

Williams, Howard (Humpy) Banjo player. Brother of Rudy Williams; toured South with blues singer Ida Cox (late 1920s); hunchback.

Leon Eason: "The best banjo player I ever heard."

Williams, Johnny Peg-leg pianist. Got Herman Bradley his first job at hall in Paterson, N.J. (late 1920s); played with Dick Matthews' band (1938).

Carl McIntyre: "He was a buddy of Cora LaRedd, who played with us up in the Catskills (early 1930s). She called him 'Johnny Stick.'"

Williams, Josephine Singer. Performed at Melody Club with Gus Young's band (1946).

Williams, Larry Late 1940s–early 1950s entertainer.

Williams, Millie Dancer and singer. Born in Florida in 1885; starred with (Bert) Williams and Walker Show; after moving to Newark, worked every major club; one of oldest entertainers on Newark's swing scene (late 1930s); gave "June frolic" at Dodger's (1939), featuring Lawrence Miller as emcee and Pittman's Plaza Four; according to entertainers, ran brothel; died Feb. 10, 1941 of stroke at Newark's Community Hospital.

Herald News (obituary): "Millie lived the life and loved the life she lived. She was always a free spender and ever willing to give the other fellow a break. She made plenty of money, but when she breathed her last she had nothing of the world's goods. It was necessary for her friends to raise the money to put her to rest, showing that nitelifers take care of their own. To Milton Pittman goes our everlasting respect for heading up the committee to raise the funds, and to those who so freely contributed must also go plenty of credit. One fellow in the community must certainly feel like a heel for failing to contribute and not even attending her funeral—a local emcee who called Millie 'mother.' She took care of the guy for three years when he wasn't on the turf. He has a good job and a little of the material life, but those who knew him in this case feel that any person who was as good as she was to him deserved a better treatment from him in death."

Williams, Pal Dancer. With Satchel Robinson, half of handsome dance team in white tie and tails; staged jams at Kinney Club (early 1940s); man-about-town who moved to New York.

Williams, Paul Singer and dancer. Popularized song and dance "The Hucklebuck"; played Graham Auditorium (1949) and Teddy Powell's Holiday Inn (1950).

Williams, Rudy (Bones or Looney) Altoist. Born in Newark in 1919; brother of banjo player Howard (Humpy) Williams; mother and sister Myrtle played piano; began playing sax and clarinet at 12; star of Savoy Sultans (1937–43); played with Hot Lips Page, Luis Russell, and Chris Columbus (1943); formed Rudy Williams and His Orchestra (1944), appearing at Newark's Campus Terrace; short spells with Dud Bascomb (1944) and John Kirby Sextet (1945); led own band at Minton's Playhouse in Harlem (mid 1940s); toured Far East in USO shows with Oscar Pettiford (1945–47); took his band to Boston (1949–50), playing at Hi Hat; drowned in swimming accident in Massachusetts in Sept. 1954.

Dizzy Gillespie (*To Be or Not to Bop*): "[Al Cooper] was the leader [of the Sultans], but the main cog was Rudy. Without being the bandleader, he was the leader in spirit. His style line was based on Willie Smith; he had that kind of fire. He wanted to play like Charlie Parker."

Williams, Skippy *See* Corley, Mary.

Williams, Varis (Vay) Bassist. Older brother of Bobby and Edward (E. J.) Williams; fixture in (1930s) local groups; traveled with Alabams (mid 1930s); deceased.

Williams, Woodrow (Fats) Trombonist. Played with Pancho Diggs Orchestra; drove Cadillac when band traveled; like his buddy, Louis Purnell, died young.

Williamson, Herbie Lee Trumpeter. Played with Duke Richardson's Orchestra and Heat Waves (early 1930s); performed at Nest Club with Hal Mitchell and Danny Gibson (1930s).

Al Henderson: "He ruined his lip doing a Louis Armstrong."

Willis, Frances Dancer. With brother George, half of brother-sister team hired to dance outside Herman Lubinsky's record shop in 1942 "to put Bonnie Davis's 'Don't Stop Now' before the public in the shortest time."

Willis, George Dancer. Hired with sister Frances to plug Savoy recording "Don't Stop Now" at Herman Lubinsky's record shop (1942).

Willis, Luther (Gates) Trumpeter; got nickname from old friend and it "stuck." Born March 10, 1911 in Fitzgerald, Ga.; moved to Newark at 13; started playing jazz in junior high school to support family; first job at "old dance hall on High Street" with June Cole and Buster Tyler; got into jazz combos with help of "an elderly man who took me to Newark to play in the Reindeers," a marching band; played trumpet and mellophone in Pancho Diggs Orchestra; also played piano; played virtually all of city's clubs with Diggs, Johnny Jackson Orchestra, Grady Thomas, and Larry Clark; recorded on Savoy with Mandy Ross's band; became factory worker and casino employee; moved to Las Vegas (mid 1970s).

Wilson, Nate Singer. Sang at Dodger's on bill with Geneva Turman (1942).

Wilson, Speedy (Beans) Ace black-face comedian. Went over big at Charlie's Paradise in Passaic, N.J. (1938) and Dave and Maney's in Orange, N.J. (1939); former RKO Proctor star who frequently worked with Struttin' Sam.

Wilson, Whitey Trombonist; first name unknown. Played trombone with Joe St. John's and Larry Ringold's bands (c1930) and Al Henderson Orchestra (1936–37).

Wing, Harold (Chink) Drummer and pianist; also known as Chink Williams. Born in Newark; began composing songs at 9; took lessons from drummer Herman Bradley; "adopted" by Charlie (Brother) Kelly, who taught him to "play shows" at 13 and allowed him to sit in; worked in bands led by Billy Ford, Leon Eason, Larry Ringold, Gene Phipps Sr., and Billy Harris; influenced by percussion effects of Art Blakey; recorded on Savoy, Decca, and Blue Note; frequently performed with Erroll Garner, who sang his number "Cologne"; wrote and recorded "I Wonder What Kind of Guy You'd Be" with Ella Fitzgerald; made two albums with James Moody and Sonny Stitt; performed with Charlie (Brother) Kelly's band at Hi-De-Ho (1947); had house band at Teddy Powell's Holiday Inn on Meeker Avenue (early 1950s), playing behind Orioles and other top acts; long stint on road with James Moody; one-time music director for Newark Department of Recreation and Parks.

Woodruff, Connie (Williams) Pianist and journalist. Born October 24, 1921 in New Rochelle, N.Y.; grew up in Newark; studied piano for 12 years in childhood with intention of becoming concert pianist; as teenager at South Side High School, became original piano player with Barons of Rhythm (c1938), playing mostly at a storefront on Fairview Avenue and at Shady Rest Country Club; former editor and nightlife columnist for *New Jersey Herald News*, black weekly; became union official and Democratic national committeewoman; retired administrator, Essex County College; president (1984–86), National Association of Commissions for Women.

Woodyard, Sam Drummer. Born Jan. 7, 1925; from Elizabeth, N.J.; self-taught; sat in locally in Newark and around north Jersey until he joined Paul Gayten Trio (1950); with saxophonist Joe Holliday (1951), Roy Eldridge (1952), and Milt Buckner's Organ Trio (1953–55); joined Duke Ellington, who considered him one of his top drummers (an opinion disputed by critic Leonard Feather, who thought he sometimes handled "every number as if he were breaking rocks"); recorded with vocalists Gayten and Annie Laurie (late 1940s–early 1950s).

Wortham, Merrille Guitarist. Original member of Pancho Diggs Orchestra (late 1930s–early 1940s).

Wright, Edward (Eddie) Guitarist. From White Plains, N.Y.; learned guitar from his mother, Olive Tucker, who was still playing regular gigs in her eighties in White Plains; nephew of Joe Rivers, banjo player heard on early radio programs; played with Arthur Terry and His Grand Rascals at Lloyd's Manor (1946) and Dick Harvest Trio at Orange, N.J.'s Diamond Mirror (1952); came to Newark in 1946 after serving in Navy to join Don Linton's Orchestra.

Miss Rhapsody: "I don't know how it was possible, but he always said his mother played more guitar than him. He worked with me in Eatontown [at the Greenbriar] maybe a year or more."

Wright, Florence Singer. Born in Orange, N.J., Aug. 28, 1928; mother was missionary who sang and played tenor saxophone; as teenager, sang at Hotel Suburban in East Orange, N.J.; married guitarist Willie Wright (1946); played one-night stands with Pancho Diggs Orchestra (1947); performed at Lloyd's Manor (1947), Dodger's with Herb Scott (1947), and Caravan Club (1950); managed by Bill Cook; made several hit records and played Silver Saddle on Clinton Avenue (1951); catapulted to fame with her recordings of "Deal Me a Hand" and "The Game of Broken Hearts."

Wright, Linn Singing maestro. Led a band at Lloyd's Manor (1947).

Wright, Louis Saxophonist. Played in Milton Pittman's band at Boston Plaza (1939).

Wynn, Freddie Tenor saxophonist. Often performed with Gus Young (early 1940s); inducted into Army (1942).

Young, Gus Drummer. Born in Jacksonville, Fla., Sept. 16, 1916; formed dance team at age 10 with Ace Harris, who became pianist with Erskine Hawkins Orchestra; came north with Blue Pheasants; joined Walter Johnson's band in central Jersey at age 14; settled in Newark area after band broke up while playing Broome Street's Colony Club; played Kinney Club on and off for decade, starting late 1930s; formed band with Teddy Brannon and Frank (Slim) Henderson (1941); joined Buddy Johnson's band (1943); recorded "The Alcazar Jump" on Decca with Larry Ringold and Alexander (Buster) Stothoff (1943); played and sang "When a Woman Loves a Man" on Coleman label (late 1940s); played at Dodger's and Lloyd's Manor (late 1940s), Howard Bar, Silver Saddle, and Washington Cafe (early 1950s); did a great deal of vocalizing with his bands; influenced so many young musicians he was revered as "Mr. World"; deceased.

Eurlee Reeves (Nest Club owner): "When I started [the club] I had Gus on drums and Joe Crump on piano—just the two of them."

Zazu Twisting, supple-limbed Oriental shake dancer. Headlined at Dave and Maney's in Orange, N.J. (1938); performed in revues at Boston Plaza (1942); traveled East Coast circuit few years later with partner as Zazu and Jellyroll.

Newark Bands, 1925–50

Afro Cubanaires Horace Sims, guitar; Garnett Donaldson, marimbas; Ulie, small drums; Mai Gordon (Jelly Belly), congas; Mavis Donaldson, vocals (1950).

The Alabams Sonny Murray, guitar/leader; Marvin Hayes, Leon Eason, and Bobby Williams, trumpet; Cecil Jenkins, cornet; Earl Hardy, trombone; Eddie (E. J.) Williams, Harold Jenkins, and Clarence (Gee) Royster, alto; Marvin Hayes and Robert (Butch) Robinson, tenor; Charlie (Brother) Kelly, drums; at various times, Roosevelt Durham, piano, and Billy Butler, drums (early 1930s).

Al Henderson Orchestra Al Henderson, bass; Clem Moorman, piano; Earl Nelson, drums; Arthur (Fergie) Ferguson and Howard (Sadiq) Scott, trombone; James (Chippie) Outcalt and Harold (Hal) Mitchell, trumpet; Bobby Plater and Lowell (Count) Hastings, saxophone (c1936–37).

Al Henderson Trio Al Henderson, bass; Johnnie Bell, piano/vocals; Roy Coleman, electric guitar; at Picadilly and Dodger's (1943).

Ame Garrison's Sirens of Swing Ame Garrison, saxophone; Ann Standard, piano; Sunday matinees at Boston Plaza (1938).

Anna May Lundy Lewis Quartet Anna May Lundy Lewis, organ; Billy Lewis, Solovox; Al Burwell, vocals; William (Bass Byrd) Lindbergh, bass; at Hydeaway (1943).

Arthur Terry and His Grand Rascals Arthur Terry, piano; Eddie Wright, bass/guitar; Nate Brown, vocals; at Lloyd's Manor (1946).

Arthur Terry Trio Arthur Terry, piano; Herb Scott, trumpet; Albert Best, bass; at Hydeaway (1944) and Al Cook's Grill (1948).

Barons of Rhythm Conrad Butler, leader/trumpet; Leo Salley, Sam Cureton, and James (Chops) Jones, trumpet; Jimmy Stanford, Bobby Jarrett, and T. O. Swangin, saxophone; Robert (Wash) Washington, trombone; Connie Williams and Robert (Bobby) Tucker, piano; various other musicians, including Ike Quebec, saxophone; Hollis Plinton, bass; Walter (Gil) Fuller, arranger (late 1930s–early 1940s).

Billy Anderson Orchestra James (Billy) Anderson, leader/bass; at various, times, Ike

Quebec, Lloyd Wheeler, ? Roundtree, Coy Shockley, Joe Holliday, William Hamilton, and Joe Perfumo, saxophone; Lou Jones and Leo Salley, trumpet; Al Terrell, guitar; Corky Caldwell and June Cole, piano; Bob Washington, Howard Scott, and Phatz Morris, trombone; Harold Showers, drums; (Little) Joe Alexander, Edith Caldwell, Jinni Gregory, and Billy Matthews, vocals (late 1940s–50s).

Billy Moore Four Billy Moore, guitar; Thelma (last name not known), piano; Albert Best, bass; at Dodger's (1946).

Billy Van Dunk Orchestra Billy Van Dunk, guitar; Lloyd Tillman, drums; Togge Smythe, Danny Quebec, and Eddie Ransom, saxophone; Howard (Duke) Anderson and Bobby Tucker, piano; on WHBI radio (1936–39).

Blue Rhythm Syncopators Julius (Geech) Smalls, trumpet; Walter Purdy, alto; Irving Coates, tenor; Herman Tisdale, dancer/fronted band; Howard (Duke) Anderson, piano; Jimmy Hamilton, guitar; Freddie Lee, bass; James (Jimmy) Butler, drums (1934–37).

Bobbie Brown's Syncopators (also known as Bobbie Brown's Society Orchestra) Bobby Stark, Shorty Stanford, and A. Jenkins, trumpet; Herb Gregory, trombone; Happy Caldwell, tenor/clarinet; Ed Burrows, bass horn; Goldie Lucas, banjo/violin; Buster Tyler, drums; also Johnnie Johnson, Walter Johnson, Bill (Willie) Nolls, and Andrew James (1922–25), according to *Big Band Jazz*. Early 1920s band whose leader/saxophonist was from Newark; most prominent musician to emerge from the group was trumpeter Rex Stewart.

Clarence (Gee) Royster and His Swingsters At Saul's Tavern (1941).

Dave McDuffie Orchestra Dave McDuffie, trumpet/leader; Earl Watson, tenor; Harold Ford, piano; Harold Underhill, guitar; Bub Clark, bass; Eddie (Fats) Williams, drums; at Palm Gardens, Asbury Park, N.J. (summer 1949); Palace Blue Room, Rahway, N.J. (1949).

Del Mar Boys Tony Allen, piano; Danny Gibson, drums; Emzey Waters, saxophone; at Del Mar Bar (1945).

Dick Matthews and His Swing Band Leslie (Dick) Matthews, alto/tenor/leader; Johnny Williams and Gene Ballard, piano; Freddie Ballard, tenor banjo; Carl McIntyre, saxophone; house band at Dave and Maney's in Orange, N.J. (late 1930s).

Doles Dickens Trio Doles Dickens, bass; Teddy Brannon, piano; Dicky Thompson, guitar; at Picadilly (1942); trio became a quartet with June Cole, piano; Herb Scott, trumpet; Thompson and Dickens; at Picadilly (1946).

Don Linton Orchestra Dave Burns, Calvin Hughes, and Willie (Coot) Nelson, trumpet; Alfred Lawson, Mayhon Hobson, and Bobby Jarrett, alto; Don Linton, tenor; Chuck ?, piano; Ben Williams, bass; Sam Bailey and Sam Woodyard, drums (mid 1940s).

Drummer (Charlie) Kelly's Band Charlie (Brother) Kelly, drums; Gene Kee, piano; Jabbo Smith, trumpet; other personnel unknown; at Villa Maurice (1939); also at Howdy Club (1943), Twinlite (1944), Hi-De-Ho Club (1946–47).

Duckey Massey and His Ducklings William (Duckey) Massey, piano; at Lloyd's Manor (1951) and Howard Bar (1952).

Duke Anderson Orchestra 19 pieces, including Howard (Duke) Anderson, leader/piano; Eddie Ransom and Eddie Smith, alto; Harry Porter and Billy Wright, tenor; James (Brownie) Brown, Al Armstrong, Prince Jones, Ray Copeland, and Dave Andrews, trumpet; James (Chippie) Outcalt and Chiefie, trombone; Pete Fields and Charlie (Brother) Kelly, drums; James (Billy) Anderson, bass; Eddie Wright, guitar (1947–57).

Duke Richardson's Orchestra Henry Walker, piano; Al Henderson, tuba/bass; Dee Richardson, drums; Herbie Lee Williamson, trumpet; Robert (Bobby) Plater, alto; Duke Richardson, trombone (early 1930s).

Eddie White's Orchestra 12-piece aggregation from Philadelphia; Warren Jefferson, trumpet; Harry White, trumpet/trombone/alto; Jimmy Mundy, tenor; Eddie White, piano; Mason Hawkins, guitar; ? Booth, tuba/

string bass; Tommy Myles, drums (1927–33, *Big Band Jazz*); at Roseland dance hall on Market Street (winters late 1920s–early 1930s). The most famous musician to emerge from the group was arranger Jimmy Mundy.

Four Bars and a Melody Edward (Eddie) Wright, guitar; Stanley (Stash) O'Laughlin, piano; Bill Goode, conga drums; Richard (Dick) Harvest, bass; Margaret Hoeffler, vocals (mid 1940s).

Frank Gibbs Orchestra Allen Gibbs and Eldridge Hawkins, alto; Lowell (Count) Hastings; tenor; Frank Gibbs, Sam Cureton, Sam Massenberg, and Johnny Giles, trumpet; Whitey Wilson, trombone; Fun Raymond, banjo/guitar; Ann Standard, piano; Al Henderson, bass; Nathaniel (Fats) Ennis, drums; Clem Moorman, piano (c1934).

Freddie Howard and His Swingsters At Fisher's Tavern with vocalist Grace Smith (1939).

George Gordon Quartet George Gordon, piano; Frank Verdell, bass; Earl Nevius, guitar; Togge Smythe, vocals/saxophone.

Gus Young's Band At Nest Club with Joe Crump on piano (1938), Kit Kat (1941), and Kinney Club (1942–46); jamming at Dodger's on Mondays, (1945); at Dodger's (1946–47) and Silver Saddle (1951–52).

Gus Young's Miami Club Orchestra Herb Scott, trumpet; Frank (Slim) Henderson, tenor; Humphrey (Teddy) Brannon, piano; Wesley Clark, bass; Gus Young, drums.

Hal Mitchell Trio Harold (Hal) Mitchell, trumpet; Humphrey (Teddy) Brannon, piano; Wes Clark, bass; at Hi Spot (1942).

Harold Ford Quartet Harold Ford, piano; at Picadilly, Lloyd's Manor, and Club Theresa (1946–49).

The Heat Waves Gus Young, founder/drums; Henry Walker, piano; Bobby Plater, bass; Rudy Williams, alto; Howard Scott, trombone; Herbie Lee Williamson and James (Brownie) Brown, trumpet; Cornelius Chinn, saxophone; Albert Best, bass (1939); later, Humphrey (Teddy) Brannon, piano; at Picadilly (1942).

Herb Hensen's Band 5-piece group led by Hensen on sax at Howdy Club (1947). Earlier Hensen headed groups at Pat and Don's in Harrison, N.J. and Tony Galento's in Orange, N.J.

James Moody Trio James Moody, saxophone/vocals; Harold (Chink) Williams, drums; Larry Goines, bass; at Wideway Ballroom (1952).

Jerry Bogar's Royal Club Orchestra Jerry Bogar, bass/leader; Collins Murphy and Danny Mobley, piano; Joe Brakes and William (Sonny) Thurmond, drums; Count Branch and Hank Mobley, saxophone; Kitty Brooks, vocals; organized c1940; at Three Towers, Somerville, N.J. (late 1940s) and Carnegie Hall, Vauxhall, N.J. (c1950); house band at Caravan Club, which Bogar owned (1953–54).

Nancy Bogar (wife): "I did all the driving and I had to sit up all night as they arranged their songs on the way to wherever we were going. They were one of two bands that played at Carnegie Hall, the featured band, and they were the house band at the Caravan Club after we bought the place in 1953."

Jimmy Scott's Wailers and Their Clique Jimmy Scott, alto/leader; Al Armstrong, trumpet; Willie Wright, tenor; Gene Kee, piano; William Windbush, drums; Henry King, bass; at King Hiram Craftsmen's Center (1948).

Joe Crump's Band of 1,000 Themes Joe Crump, piano; Harold (Hal) Mitchell, trumpet; Bill Sawyer and Cornelius Chinn, saxophone; at Colony Club (c1936).

Joe Holley's Orchestra Billy Lewis and Herbie Lee Williamson, trumpet; Whitey Wilson, trombone; Ernie Powell and Frank (Gersh) Sutton, alto; Joe Holley, piano; William (Bass Byrd) Lindbergh, bass/tuba; Buster Tyler, drums; Larry Ringold, alto (early 1930s).

Joe St. John's Orchestra Joe Holley, piano; William (Bass Byrd) Lindbergh, bass; Buster Tyler, drums; Billy Lewis, Leon Eason, and Ernie Powell, trumpet; Whitey Wilson, trombone; Frank (Gersh) Sutton, alto; Joe St. John, tenor (1932).

Johnny Jackson and His Society Orchestra
Clem Moorman, piano; George Hyman, drums; Merle Turner, vocals; Johnny Jackson, tenor; Allen Gibbs and Eldridge Hawkins, alto; Sandy Williams, trombone; Charles Coursey and Lawrence Maddox, trumpet; Varis (Vay) Williams, bass; at times, Ken Billings, piano; Al Henderson, bass; Herb Barney, drums; Jim Price and Joe Richards, trumpet; Katherine Thompson and Bob Taylor, vocals (1939–41).

Kinney Club Orchestra Elmer Chambers, trumpet; Al Williams, alto; Gene Ballard, piano; Pete Fields, drums (late 1930s).

Larry Ringold and His Sultans of Swing Larry Ringold, saxophone/clarinet/arranger; at Dodger's (1939) and Charlie's Tavern (1941); at Victoria Hall on Thursday nights (1941); 7-piece band at Alcazar (1944).

Leon Eason's Band Leon Eason, trumpet/vocals; William (Duckey) Massey, piano; Carl McIntyre, saxophone; Albert Best, bass; Willie Johnson, guitar; Kenny Richards, drums (late 1930s).

Madhatters Linwood Proctor, piano; Don Banks, guitar; Gary ?, bass; popular group at Picadilly (1946–47).

Mandy Ross and His Walkin' Rhythm Luther (Gates) Willis, Lindsey Nelson, Milton (Prince) Jones, and Billy Seymour, trumpet; Mayhon Hobson and William Hamilton, alto; George Lewis and Bobby Jarrett, tenor; Horace Sims, guitar; Scotty ?, piano; Fritz Pollard, bass; Sam Woodyard, drums (1947).

Mary Jones and Her Rhythm Band Fronted by vocalist Mary Jones at Boston Plaza (1944).

The Matinee Idols Teddy Cole, piano; Clarence (Mouse) Fulford, trumpet; Norman Wilcox, banjo/guitar; Eddie Wells, tenor; Grachan (Brother) Moncur, bass; George Cooper, drums; broadcast Sunday afternoons on WHBI (early–mid 1930s). Wilcox toured upstate New York with group or its forerunner (c1926).

Melmore Stompers Sonny Murray, guitar/organizer; Leon Eason, Bobby Williams, and Gus Hayes, trumpet; Clarence Coates, drums; Marvin Hayes, saxophone; Varis (Vay) Williams, bass; Gene Holder, piano. Forerunner of Alabams (c1930).

Mixie Moorman's Red Hots Mixie Moorman, sax; Beans, piano; at cabaret on Branford Place (mid 1930s); at Tile Tavern opening, Paterson, N.J. (1937).

Musical Belles All-girl band at Picadilly with singer Ruth Brown (1949).

Old Man Mose and His Swingsters At Reiff's Bar and Grill (1939).

Omega Trio Ala Mae Miller, piano; Earl Davis, saxophone; William (Bass Byrd) Lindbergh, bass; at Omega Bar and Grill (1944).

Pancho Diggs Orchestra Duke Parham, piano; Jackson (Flap) McQueen, bass; Robert Roebuck, drums; Merrille Wortham, guitar; Billy Ford and Joe James, trumpet; Robert (Butch) Robinson, Charlie Shavers, Eddie Ransom, Luther Smith, and Pancho Diggs, saxophone. In late 1940s, Jay (June) Cole was pianist.

Picadilly Madcaps Ed Terry, piano; Dave Erwin, guitar; Wes Clark, bass; at Picadilly (1943).

Picadilly Pipers Clem Moorman, piano; Al Henderson, bass; Ernie Ransome, tipple/guitar; Jewel Collins, succeeded by Melba Smith (Bonnie Davis), vocals; at Picadilly (1941–42). Henderson was replaced on bass by Henry (Patches) Padgette.

Pittman's Plaza Four Milton Pittman, piano; Frank Cross, drums; Louis Wright, saxophone; Julius (Geech) Smalls, trumpet; at Boston Plaza (1939).

The Ray-O-Vacs Joe Crump, piano; Leoparte (Chink) Kinney, saxophone; Jackson (Flap) McQueen), bass; Lester Harris, vocals.

Roscoe (Rosie) Jones Jones, piano/leader; Buster Tyler, drums; James (Brownie) Brown, trumpet; Cecil Jenkins, saxophone; at Radio Inn (late 1920s–early 1930s).

Russell Mann and His Royal Ambassadors Russell Mann, tenor/alto; Erskine Butterfield, piano; Larry Ringold and Rudy Williams, alto; Pat Jenkins and Leon (Cateye) Roberts, trumpet; Larry Clark, piano;

William (Bass Byrd) Lindbergh, bass (c1933). Mann also was part of a group that featured George Carey and ? Van Horn, tenor, and Buck Ranier, trumpet.

Savoy Dictators Clem Moorman, piano; Al Henderson, bass; Danny Gibson, drums; Harold (Hal) Mitchell and James (Chippie) Outcalt, trumpet; Bobby Plater, alto; Lowell (Count) Hastings, tenor; Willie Johnson, guitar; Howard Scott, trombone; Walter (Gil) Fuller, arranger (late 1930s–early 1940s).

Savoy Sultans Al Cooper, leader/clarinet/saxophone; Grachan (Brother) Moncur, bass; Alex (Razz) Mitchell, drums; Oliver Richardson and Cyril Haynes, piano; Pat Jenkins and Sam Massenberg, trumpet; Rudy Williams and James McNeal, saxophone; Jack Chapman, arranger/guitar (late 1930s–1940s); sometimes joined by tenor saxophonist Lonnie Simmons or George Kelly.

Scotty and His Frani-Kats Herb Scott, trumpet; Bill Goode, drums; Eddie Wright, guitar; Al Best, bass; Frank (Red) Brown, piano.

Sid Watson's Band 5-piece band; Sid Watson, drums; Luther (Gates) Willis, trumpet; Bobby Jarrett, tenor; at Pete's on Spruce Street (1947).

Smoky Jones and His Swingsters John (Smoky) Jones, piano; Clarence (Gee) Royster, alto; George Cooper, drums; at Saul's Tavern (1939).

Sultans of Swing Gene Kee, piano; Sam Debnam, bass; Herb Barney, drums; Clarence Hatchett, Bill Bynum, and Solomon (Moose) Satterwhite, trumpet; Lloyd Wheeler and Rolin Bynum, saxophone; Sam Taylor, alto; Fenton Carey, tenor; George Chapman, saxophone/vocals; Evelyn White, vocals; subsequently, Prince Jones, trumpet; at NAACP dance at Skateland (1942). Early 1940s band out of Montclair whose members were "too young to play in nightclubs"; theme song: "I May Be Wrong, But I Think You're Wonderful"; organized in 1939; disbanded when the members volunteered or were drafted for World War II military service.

Three Blue Notes June Cole, piano; Joe Durham and Al Best, bass; Harold Underhill and Dave Erwin, guitar; at Omega Bar and Grill, Roselle, N.J. (1942–43).

Three Chicks and a Chuck Ame Garrison, saxophone/leader; at Howard Bar (1949). "Mule Train" was one of their big numbers.

Three Guys Named Moe Swing trio at Picadilly (1943).

Three Tempos At Picadilly (1945).

Togge Smythe and the Four Sounds Togge Smythe, saxophone; Corky Caldwell, piano; Milton Hayes, drums/vocals; Curley Bell, bass; at Marble Rail (1947) and Howard Bar (1951).

Two Beats and a Sound Joe Manning, piano; Curley Bell, bass; Red Walcott, drums; Tony Jenkins, vocals; at Cafe Society (1950) with Jenkins singing Manning's "Here Is My Heart."

Two Notes and a Tempo Danford (Larue) Jordan, piano; Danny Gibson, drums; Tony Alexo, tenor; at Lloyd's Manor (1947).

Velvetones Vocal combo composed of Madison Flanagan, Walter Dawkins, Enoch Martin, and Sam Rucker, guitar/first baritone; at Picadilly (1945–46). All were South Side High School graduates except Martin, the arranger, who attended Wilberforce University.

Woody Stalks and His Band Opened Cameo Club (1947); at new Hi-De-Ho Club (1947); played club dances.

Big Band Appearances in Newark

1942

August 22 Laurel Garden. Jimmie Lunceford, Ella Fitzgerald; Labor Day Dance sponsored by Royal Enterprise Association.

October 17 Laurel Garden. Tiny Bradshaw versus Doc Wheeler's Sunset Royal Orchestra; Orlando Robeson, vocalist; Ralph Cooper, emcee/judge.

October 29 Laurel Garden. Andy Kirk and His Clouds of Joy; June Richmond, vocals.

November 14 Laurel Garden. Earl Hines.

November 29 Laurel Garden. Erskine Hawkins; Victory Dance sponsored by the Spring War Service Committee.

1943

January 9 Laurel Garden. Andy Kirk and His Clouds of Joy.

January 16 Laurel Garden. Jay McShann and Walter ("Confessin' the Blues") Brown, vocalist.

February 13 Laurel Garden. Statewide jitterbug contest with "big cash prizes."

March 13 Laurel Garden. Erskine Hawkins.

April 3 Laurel Garden. Louis Jordan; basketball game and dance featuring Johnny Jackson's Orchestra.

April 24 Laurel Garden. Jimmie Lunceford.

May 15 Laurel Garden. Buddy Johnson.

June 26 Laurel Garden. Ink Spots, Lucky Millinder, Sister Rosetta Tharpe, sponsored by Lincoln Civic Association.

June 19 Laurel Garden. Coleman Hawkins.

July 24 Laurel Garden. Ella and Buddy Johnson, offering their hits, "Baby, Don't You Cry" and "Let's Stop Pretending."

October 16 Laurel Garden. Count Basie.

November 20 Laurel Garden. Milton Larkins and His Band.

November 27 Laurel Garden. Lucky Millinder.

December 11 Laurel Garden. Cab Calloway.

December 25 Laurel Garden. Jimmie Lunceford.

1944

January 15 Laurel Garden. Erskine Hawkins.

January 22 Laurel Garden. John Kirby.

February 5   Laurel Garden. Benny Carter; Savannah Churchill, vocals.

February 12   Laurel Garden. Ernie Phipps Band, directed by Gene Phipps, and International Sweethearts of Rhythm.

March 4   Laurel Garden. Louis Jordan.

April 1   Laurel Garden. Gene Phipps (Johnson Lee, vocals) versus Georgie Auld (Billy Eckstine, vocals).

May 14   Laurel Garden. Golden Gate Quartet.

June 24   Laurel Garden. Duke Ellington.

July 15   Laurel Garden. Buddy Johnson; vocalists Ella Johnson and Joe Medlin.

August 15   Laurel Garden. Lucky Millinder.

August 22   Laurel Garden. Lionel Hampton.

October 21   Laurel Garden. Roy Eldridge.

November 4   Laurel Garden. Jean Park and Her All-Girl Orchestra.

November 11   Laurel Garden. Luis Russell, featuring Nora Blunt.

November 18   Adams Theater. Louis Jordan and His Tympany Five.

November 25   Orange Armory. Benny Carter, Savannah Churchill, and Nat King Cole Trio.

December 16   Laurel Garden. Andy Kirk.

December 25   Laurel Garden. Jimmie Lunceford.

1945

January 27   Adams Theater. Benny Carter and Nat King Cole Trio.

May 12   Orange Armory. Lionel Hampton with Dinah Washington and Rubel Blakely.

November 24   Laurel Garden. Erskine Hawkins.

December 29   Laurel Garden. Don Redman.

1946

March 2   Orange Armory. Luis Russell.

April 6   Orange Armory. Woody Herman.

April 13   Orange Armory. Lucky Millinder and Slam Stewart.

November 2   Laurel Garden. Jimmie Lunceford.

December 14   Adams Theater. Buddy Johnson's Orchestra and Johnny Moore and His Three Blazers.

1947

May 3   Laurel Garden. Buddy Johnson.

December 4   Adams Theater. Illinois Jacquet, Sarah Vaughan, and Buddy Johnson.

1948

February 2   Laurel Garden. Lionel Hampton.

November 22   Adams Theater. Nellie Lutcher.

1949

January 17   Orange Armory. Sarah Vaughan and Boyd Raeburn.

February 5   Adams Theater. Mills Brothers.

February 12   Laurel Garden. "Miss Sepia America Beauty Contest," featuring "25 beauties"; Lucky Millinder with Annisteen Allen, vocals.

April 2   Laurel Garden. Lionel Hampton.

May 28   Laurel Garden. Dizzy Gillespie.

December 31   Laurel Garden. Buddy Johnson.

1950

January 21   Adams Theater. Lionel Hampton.

March 11   Laurel Garden. Ravens, Dinah Washington, Cootie Williams.

1951

February 2   Orange Armory. Nat King Cole and Buddy Johnson's Orchestra, presented by Teddy Powell.

Clubs, Theaters, Halls, and Hangouts

Adams Theater 26–30 Branford Place. Built in 1913 as Kinney's; renamed Shubert; staged plays as tryouts for Broadway (1920s); stage show theater until it was renamed Adams (1939) and began offering stage and screen shows; home of big bands (1940s); home to Minsky's burlesque until city crackdown (1957); closed (1986); two-story structure enhanced by a variety of stylized Greek revival details; facade dominated by projecting art moderne marquee; featured stars (1940s) such as Abbott and Costello, Tommy and Jimmy Dorsey, Cab Calloway, Count Basie, Fats Waller, Guy Lombardo, Milton Berle, Mills Brothers, Erskine Hawkins, Woody Herman, Louis Prima, Lionel Hampton, Nat King Cole, Pearl Bailey, Sarah Vaughan, Louis Jordan and His Tympany Five, Benny Carter, and Buddy Johnson.

Afro Club Quitman Street. James Fultz, owner; Rocky Morris, bouncer; became Owl Club (1946).

Alcazar 72 Waverly Avenue. One of leading "colored-owned" clubs (late 1930s–early 1940s); Iva (Pop) Durham, owner; Dewey Payne, manager (1943); 96-foot room featuring mammoth double horseshoe bar and music every night; Leon Eason's band and Matty Alston, the emcee, top attractions (late 1939s–early 1940s).

Big Ale Halsey Street. Tavern of questionable reputation opposite Hi Spot; target of criticism by many prominent citizens; under scrutiny of Alcoholic Beverage Commission (1943).

Blue and Silver Tavern Norfolk and Warren streets. Ed Henry, owner (1930s); along with Fredericks' Lounge, 570 Club, Corprew's, and Vanity Club (1940s), one of 5 clubs offering Original Blue Monday jam sessions.

Bluebird Ballroom and School of Dancing 842 Broad Street. Rose Gonnell, owner; featured Mandy Ross's band 6 nights a week (1945).

Blue Mirror 275 Clinton Avenue. Opened to blacks (1947) after a 13-year "all whites" policy; 400 seats, dancing, and round bar; hangout for gangsters and "big numbers people"; became Silver Saddle (1951) and Club Bolero (1953).

Boston Plaza 4–6–8 Boston Street. Owned

by 5 Berry brothers; Elie (Bert) Berry, president, and William (Son) Berry, manager; shows booked by Milton Pittman, who doubled as pianist and leader of Pittman's Plaza Four; Bill Roberts, bartender (late 1930s); small, but jammed, with one door leading to bar, another into club that offered 2 floor shows on Thursdays, Saturdays, and Sundays plus Sunday matinees starting at 4 P.M. (late 1930s). Son, Bert, and Jimmy bought Greenbriar in Eatontown, N.J., Jersey shore's premiere black nightclub (1938).

Cabin LaBlanche 241 Warren Street. Later Nest Club; Blanche Henry, whose husband Edward owned Blue and Silver Tavern, original owner; taken over (late 1930s) by Eurlee Reeves and renamed Nest Club; club where Joe Crump and His Band of 1,000 Themes was launched and where Grace Smith, one of Newark's top blues singers, started as chorus girl (early–mid 1930s).

Cafe Society 14 Belmont Avenue. Featured acts such as Jimmy Scott and His Band, singer Tony Jenkins, and Wailer and His Chick (1939).

Cafe Superior New name for Cedar Gardens, nightclub area of Graham Auditorium (1947); reopened with Eddie Durham's band and Warren Evans on vocals; Monday band nights (1947) featuring Howard (Duke) Anderson, Alton (Pancho) Diggs, Togge Smythe, Harold (Chink) Williams, and Jimmy Stanford; Bill Cook's broadcasting base on WHBI (1947).

Cafe Zanzibar 171 Howard Street at Court. Featured Ink Spots (1944) with Newark vocalist Cliff Givens, regular with Southern Sons, filling in for Orville (Hoppy) Jones.

Cameo Restaurant 252 South Orange Avenue. Featured "Iron Jaw" Jackson and His Band (1945); reopened (1946) by Theresa Williams and Jerry Battles, featuring Brownie's Club Royal Orchestra.

Campus Terrace 100 Belmont Avenue. Hall where many holiday and club dances were given (1940s).

Caravan Club 8 Bedford Street. Former Dodger's Bar and Grill, redecorated for 1949 "grand reopening" featuring Roscoe Dyla as emcee; all-star slate of guest artists (Dec. 1949) such as Buddy Johnson, Sarah Vaughan, Illinois Jacquet, Arthur Prysock, George Shearing, and Al Hibbler; bought by bandleader Jerry Bogar and his wife, Nancy, (1953); spot where Billie Holiday was booked (1953) and where Chuck Willis sang "Hang Up My Rock and Roll Shoes" a week before his death (early 1950s).

Casa Blanca on Broad Street, near Kinney Street. Opened by Georgie Haber, who ran Picadilly (1943); Rabbit Rodberg, manager; featured Clem Moorman on piano as opening act.

Charlie's Tavern Passaic, N.J. Member of Big Six jam session group (1939).

Charlie's Tavern 35–37 Sussex Avenue (at Boyden Street). Featured Larry Ringold's band and vocalist Ann Standard (1941).

Clinton Manor 104 Clinton Avenue. One of key locations for dances staged by social set during war years; dances often sponsored by Captivators: Lacey Brannic, Major Taylor, and Johnny Jackson, bandleader.

Club Alabam opposite Kinney Club on Barbary Coast, no address. Owned by Joe (King) Broadus, who played violin; spot where trombonist Clyde Bernhardt played first Newark job in 8-piece band led by Richard Cheatham (1928); Jackie (Moms) Mabley also on bill; singer Nettie Perry one of regulars.

Club Del Rio Washington Street. Jumped to vocalese of Estelle Bailey and Ruby Rainey (1939).

Club Harold 71 Bloomfield Avenue. Ballroom featuring Billy Harris and His Afro Cubanaires (late 1940s–early 1950s); offered "jukebox jamboree" on Wednesdays (1953).

Club Miami 118 Clinton Avenue. Isadore Kaplan, owner; restaurant and tavern where comedian Jackie Gleason gained recognition (mid 1930s).

Club Theresa Howard and Mercer streets. Offered jam sessions and amateur hours on Tuesdays (1949); also featured Harold Ford and His Piano Orchestra (late 1940s).

Coleman Hotel 59 Court Street. Offered regular entertainment in Musical Lounge (1946–early 1950s); Bill Cook's "Candleglow Show" broadcast on Sunday (midnight–12:45) from lounge on WHBI; Robert Banks at Hammond organ Thursdays.

Colony Club Broome Street at Sussex Avenue. Mob spot; Lucky Louie Anderson, wearing white tails and tie, emcee (1937); home of Joe Crump and His Band of 1,000 Themes (1936–37).

Cook's Bar and Grill 333 Orange Street. Featured Arthur Terry and His Rascals (1948).

Corprew's Tavern 272 Springfield Avenue. One of 5 taverns taking part in Original Blue Monday jam sessions (1940s) besides Fredericks' Lounge, Vanity Club, 570 Club, and Blue and Silver Tavern.

Cotton Club few steps beyond Kinney Street at Washington Street. Tavern where Lawrence Miller enchanted female patrons with his silvery voice (late 1930s).

Cotton Club 88 Waverly Avenue. Opened with revue (1951) featuring Ike Gary and His Recording Reigners.

Dave and Maney's 120 Parrow Street (at Central Place), Orange, N.J. Featured Dick Matthews and His Swing Band (1939) and Satchel Robinson's *Parade of Stars* (1939); boasted "the largest bar in New Jersey" after grand reopening (Aug. 1939); remodeling patterned after Moulin Rouge, popular Atlantic City supper club; Roland Jett, proprietor (1942).

Del Mar Cocktail Bar Howard and Mercer streets. Featured Danny Gibson and His Del Mar Boys (1945); Nacki Sacki Jackie (Mandeville), emcee, and Grace Smith, vocals (1945).

Dodger's Bar and Grill 8 Bedford Street. One of city's leading nightclubs (1935–46); previously Paradise Club; subsequently Caravan Club; offered fast-paced floor shows on weekends; plain grill when Ma and Pa Frazier owned it (1937); sold (1939) to Gus Campisi; packed for Guy Gordon's amateur nights (1939); remodeling (1943) included installation of huge, oval bar surrounded by 150 red-topped chromium stools; Jack Gayle, manager (1943).

Doelger's Hall Morris and Springfield avenues. Hall where dance bands including Cootie Williams' (1943) played; name changed to Sokol Hall.

Downbeat Club 149–53 Meeker Avenue, opposite Weequahic Park. Bill Goode, emcee for its opening (1949), and Ruth Brown, featured attraction; parking for 300 cars; site of "After Hours Musician of the Year" awards (1950), honorees being Sarah Vaughan, Ike Quebec, Bobby Plater, Babs Gonzales, and Bill Cook.

Dreamland Academy Beacon Street. Dance hall that became Lloyd's Manor; mecca of jitterbugs (late 1930s); featured Barons of Rhythm at Sunday jam sessions and Mousie and His Cats on Mondays (1938); also used for events sponsored by followers of Father Divine, leader of religious cult.

Eagle Bar 255 Mulberry Street. Ducky Johnson, emcee; among those featured (1951), blues singer Kitty Madden, Carrie Adams, Princess Margo, Savoy recording star Lloyd Thompson, and Brother Moncur's Strollers.

Empire Theater *See* Miner's Theater.

Famous Bar 268 Market Street. Featured drummer Dolly Gordon and Gladys Easter Trio (1950); amateur nights on Wednesdays; house band led by Gus Young (1951).

Famous Door Bedford Street. Featured comedian Freddie Toler and singer Earl Leonardo (c1940).

Fisher's Tavern 192 Newark Street. "So small the waiters had to pass over the drinks"; owned by Ike Fisher (mid 1930s); taken over by Pat Patterson as manager (1939); featured regular entertainers like Donald Lambert, Grace Smith, Miss Rhapsody, Leatha McCraw, Freddie Howard and His Swingsters, and Roosevelt Durham's band.

Flamingo Room 324 Springfield Avenue. Earl Baker featured during 1951 opening; blues singer Gladys Heard billed (1951).

Forbes Beach Route 35 near Laurence Harbor, N.J. Resort offering full-scale revues during summer months (late 1940s–early 1950s).

42nd Club 157 Parrow Street, Orange, N.J. John Butler, manager (1943); Arthur Terry, emcee, and Little Sadie Matthews, vocalist (1943); jam sessions every Monday, Tuesday, Thursday, Saturday, and Sunday night (1944–46).

Frank and Eddy's 570 Club 570 Market Street. The only "colored establishment" below Penn Station; owners, Frank Nealy, who formerly owned National Theater in Toledo, Ohio, and Eddy Burton; George Howard, bartender; club enlarged, murals and carvings added to decor (1945).

Fredericks' Lounge 4 Boston Street. Old Boston Plaza; purchased by Fredericks brothers (1946), Otto, John, and Bill, who had been bartender (1942) at Little Johnny's Tavern on Montgomery Street; with 4 other clubs (Blue and Silver, 570 Club, Corprew's, and Vanity Club) presented Original Blue Monday jam sessions on musicians' night off (1940s).

G & R Records 162 Prince Street. Promoted unknown talent; billed Gene Phipps' "G & R Blues" as a war hit.

Golden Gate Casino 81 Hayes Street, near Fifteenth Avenue. Mrs. A. Beaty, proprietor; featured Joe Crump and His Band, "four sweet songbirds, two dancing boys" (1944); jams on Thursday nights with Jimmie King as emcee.

Golden Inn Bar and Grill 150 Charlton Street. Owned by Mom and Pop Anderson, two of first black tavern owners in old Third Ward; William (Buster) Harris featured on piano; opened Honeydripper Room (1946).

Graham Auditorium 188 Belmont Avenue. Site of many Swing Era dances; featured top bands including Ike Quebec's (1940s); favorite hangout of Sarah Vaughan; in recent years national headquarters for Prince Hall Masonic Order, largest black Masons' group in U.S.

Grand Hotel 78 West Market Street. William L. (Bill) Derricks, owner; famous for its jam sessions (late 1930s), which were resumed in 1943; Betty Cobbs and Billie Sermond among featured vocalists (1939); Johnny B. Gardner and Allen Drew kept crowd in stitches (1943); hangout for ballplayers and politicians (1946).

Greenbriar Country Club Eatontown, N.J. Advertised as "The Dream Palace of the Jersey Shore"; opened (1938) by Berry brothers; had cabins on grounds, where guests could stay; offered fast-stepping New York floor shows on Saturdays and Sundays and Sunday matinees; William (Son) Berry, owner, with his brothers Elie (Bert) and Jimmy; Jim Rhett, manager; Harold Lincoln, assistant manager.

Gridiron Club Washington Street, across from Orpheum Theater. Mid 1930s haunt for musicians; upstairs gambling hangout.

Grimsley's Tavern Pacific Street. Chauncey Grimsley, owner; Bill Goode, emcee (1946); offered weekend entertainment (late 1940s).

Guiliano's Recreation Center North Sixth Street and Davenport Avenue (in Victoria Hall). Featured Don Linton and His Band (1942).

Happy Hour Club 50 Howard Street, near Thirteenth Avenue. Opened (1946) with Collins Murphy on piano; Horace James, saxophone; Andrew Brown, guitar; Lindsey Brown, trombone.

Hi-De-Ho Club 89 Springfield Avenue. Big spot that had its grand opening April 20, 1946, boasting one of largest circle bars in city and red and black motif; offered Chinese food; featured Charlie (Brother) Kelly on opening night; advertised as "strictly for refined persons who want to go to a place without hearing bad language and seeing the rough stuff displayed by the disrespectable members of the race who make it hard for the whole race on account of their conduct in such places"; closed for 30 days (1947) for serving minor.

Hi Spot Cocktail Lounge 166 West Kinney Street (at West Street). Owned by lawyer Meyer Maurer and Julius (Youdy) Ravin (late 1930s); no entertainment initially, but reportedly waiter had "specialty dance" he pulled on "mellow nights that was a scream"; band music led by Bennie (Red) Robinson from center of bar (early 1940s).

Hotel Sheraton 15 Hill Street. Featured Nacki Sacki Fats and Jackie (1949); better known as Douglas Hotel.

Howard Bar and Grill   64 Market Street. Featured Ray-O-Vacs, Four Clefs, and Three Chucks and a Chick (1949); Togge Smythe, Meltones, Frank (Red) Brown, and girl drummer Dolly Gordon (1951); Arthur Terry emcee for Monday jams (1951).

Howdy Club   400 Washington Street. Jimmy Clark, bartender; catered (1943) to "all the oldtimers," offering "good service and a congenial atmosphere"; featured Charlie (Brother) Kelly on drums, Gene Kee on piano, and Jabbo Smith on trumpet (early 1940s); impromptu jams (1946); Teddy Brannon Trio with vocalist Joyce Jackson (1949).

Hydeaway Bar   335 Halsey Street. Dinky bar in front with tiny room in back offering live entertainment; opened July 4, 1942; "100 percent colored-owned and operated" by Frank Tucker and ? Simmons; Robert (Spider) Williams, bartender; featured entertainers (early 1940s) Anna May Lundy Lewis and Milton Pittman.

J & B Tavern   no address. Featured Ted Saunders and His Knights of Rhythm (1938).

Johnson's Cafe   296–98 Plane Street (now University Avenue). Downtown white spot where Willie (The Lion) Smith held sway (1920s) before becoming one of Harlem's leading exponents of stride piano; restaurant adjoined cafe.

Key Club   Originated on West Street (1930s) by Walter Dawkins' uncle; inherited by Dawkins, who moved it to corner of William and Halsey streets, its final location; Newark's premier jazz venue (1950s–mid 1970s); gave start to organists Rhoda Scott and Jimmy McGriff; bandstand inside oval bar; guitarist George Benson another regular; impromptu appearances by Sarah Vaughan (1970s); became flea market after deaths of Dawkins and his wife, Jean, who ran it solo for many years.

Kinney Club   36 Arlington Street (at Augusta Street). Top nightclub in city's tenderloin district; mecca of sporting life; in early part of century known as Kinney Hall, serving as venue for black traveling show auditions; stayed open all night; upstairs floor shows (1930s–40s).

Kit Kat   1 Peshine Avenue at Waverly Avenue. Offered rollicking floor shows (late 1930s); under new management became Picadilly (1941); octagon-shaped barroom with sky blue interior and floodlighting effects; spacious bar surrounded by Venetian blinds.

Krueger's Auditorium   Charlton Street and Belmont Avenue. Hall where formal dances catering to older crowd were staged by civic and social groups, including Lucky Thirteens; appearance by Ethel Waters at Newark Eagles' dance (1938); headlined big bands, including Jay McShann, Les Hite, and Lucky Millinder (1940s).

Laurel Garden   457 Springfield Avenue. Attracted top bands and singers of Swing Era—Basie, Ellington, etc.; staged band battles attended by throngs of jitterbuggers (1940s).

Little Dodger's   Court and Prince streets.

Little Johnny's Tavern   47 Montgomery Street. John Johnson, owner; jumping jam sessions (1939–45); Lawrence Miller a favorite.

Lloyd's Manor   42–48 Beacon Street. Drew big-name bands and artists (late 1940s), like Billy Eckstine (1946), Dizzy Gillespie (1947), and Lionel Hampton (1949); became Penguin Club.

Lyric Bar   89 Springfield Avenue. Former Hi-De-Ho Club; featured Bunker Hill Bob on drums (1951).

Marble Rail   44 North Fifth Street. Formerly Diamond Jim's; featured Togge Smythe's Musical Four and former Earl Hines vocalist Jesse Perry (1947).

Masonic Temple   *See* Graham Auditorium.

Melody Club   Morton and West streets. Operated by Emory Hall; Snag and Homer, managers; featured Madhatters (1945) and Gus Young's Band (1946).

Miner's Theater   265 Washington Street. Vaudeville venue owned by Henry Clay Miner where all-black shows such as *7-11* were staged (1920s); black and white revues presented (1940s) when theater became burlesque house and was renamed Empire.

Musicians' Club   on Springfield Avenue. Early 1930s hiring hall.

Willie Johnson: "If a job paid four fifty, you gave the Musicians' Club a dollar and a half."

Nankin Garden Restaurant 26 Branford Place. Upstairs Chinese restaurant, next to Shubert Theater; featured jazz music (1920s).

Nest Club 241 Warren Street. Formerly Cabin La Blanche; bought by Eurlee Reeves (1937); closed (late 1950s); for 2 decades staged floor shows featuring local talent like musicians Joe Crump and Gus Young, emcees Charlie Matthews and Arthur Terry, singers Elsie Paige and Mae Darling, dancers Anna May Hall, Myrtle Hutchinson, Sadie Matthews, and Gertrude Turman.

95 Prince Street Upstairs speakeasy over H. Leibowitz's dry goods store, where trumpeter Hal Mitchell played with stride piano legend Donald Lambert (early 1930s); owned by Clarence, whose nickname was "Little Baby Doll."

Nitecap 1027 Broad Street. Supposedly staged first *Sepia Night Club Revue* on city's main artery (1951); *Cavalcade of Stars* featuring Billy Ford and His TV Orchestra, Two Zephyrs, Hart Sisters, Apache dancers, and "Newark's own Gracie Smith"; offered piano player Lew Nash and 2 shows nightly on weekends.

Omega Bar and Grill Ninth Avenue and Spruce Street, Roselle, N.J. Popular Union County watering hole owned by Wes Saunders, once partner of Ma and Pa Frazier's at Dodger's; formerly (1939) Alpha Bar; offered "jams for all" on Monday nights; favorite spot of singers Miss Rhapsody, Celeste Jones, Henry Polite, and Nate Wilson, backed by trio called Three Blue Notes (early 1940s).

Orange Armory Orange, N.J. Staged dances that attracted thousands of jitterbuggers (1940s); headlined stars including Benny Carter (1944), Lionel Hampton and Dinah Washington (1945), Luis Russell (1946), and Nat King Cole (1951).

Orpheum Theater 385 Washington Street (at Baldwin Street). One of key stops on black theater circuit; featured top acts on way in or out of Apollo Theater in New York (1920s–1930s), including Bill (Bojangles) Robinson, Miller and Lyles, and Jack Johnson.

Palace Lucille Market and Plane streets. Early Newark night spot (1918 or before), along with Radio Inn and Kinney Hall; blues singer Hattie Dukes often performed there (1920s).

Panda Room no address. Al Short, owner; featured Deek Watson's Brown Dots (1946).

Paradise Club 8 Bedford Street. Early 1930s club where Miss Rhapsody sang; became Dodger's Bar and Grill.

Paramount Theater 193–95 Market St. Built in 1896 by Henry Clay Miner; from 1920s on, managed by Adams family; originally vaudeville house; also featured legitimate theater; remodeled (1916), converted to movie house, and renamed Paramount; when it closed (1980s), was oldest theater in Newark.

Pasadena Club Fourteenth and Orange streets. Where musicians who were nucleus of Savoy Sultans, then Rhythm Dons, played early in their careers (mid 1930s); Los Caballeros' first spring dance (1936); upstairs hall; still downstairs tavern.

Perkins downtown, no address. Gambling den where drinks were sold; backroom used for dancing to live music; like Palace Lucille, one of oldest spots in city offering "entertainment for blacks."

Charles Sowell: "I used to go there right after I came to Newark—around 1918. It was right across from the Palace Lucille at Plane [now University Avenue] and Market streets."

Pete's Spruce Street. Where Sid Watson's 5-piece band played for dancing (late 1930s); hot dog stand (1940s).

Picadilly 3 Peshine Avenue. Previously Kit Kat Club (1941); run by Georgie Haber and Roddy Rodberg; Frankie Young, manager (1943); home of Picadilly Pipers: Clem Moorman, Al Henderson, Ernie Ransome, and Melba (Bonnie Davis) Smith; nightly entertainment and matinees on Sundays 4 P.M.–7 (early 1940s); Bill Goode at piano in

Tahitian Room. Its motto was "If You Click at the Pic, You'll Click With the World."

Radio Inn and Dancing Academy 278 Halsey Street (between Hill and Pearl streets). Early Newark nightclub (1920s); owner, civic leader Alfred C. Gibson, father of drummer Danny Gibson and uncle of promoter Tiny Prince; band led by Rosie Jones; Emma Hawkins and Miss Rhapsody among regular performers.

Radio Record Shop 58 Market Street. Owned by Herman Lubinsky, founder of Savoy Records; had booths where patrons could listen to records; catered to customers including young members of Hot Club of Newark; "steals" for collectors in 19-cent bins (late 1930s–40s).

Rainbow Inn 257 Union Place, Rahway, N.J. Henry White, owner; "back of the woods" spot where Milton Pittman introduced jam sessions (1938); Stella (Estelle) Bailey, Anne White, Lawrence Miller, Buddy Turman, Sadie and Mandy Matthews, and Arthur Terry featured on first bill.

Reiff's Bar and Grill 94 South Orange Avenue. Fanny Reiff, owner; featured Old Man Mose and His Swingsters (1938) and Quallo and His Swingsters (1939).

Rin Tin Inn 179 Orange Street. William Osgood, who was shot to death by his wife, proprietor; Eddie Osgood, manager; blues singer Grace Smith, mainstay (1938).

Rocky's 104 Barclay Street. Sausage and hot dog joint where Pancho Diggs, Leon Eason, and other musicians used to hang out, "digging some of the hot music on the jukebox."

Roscoe's Poolroom no address. Hangout for musicians looking for work and youngsters who wanted to dance in back room.

Royal Ballroom 373 Bloomfield Avenue. Hall where Tiny Robinson and His Orchestra played New Year's Eve dance (1944).

Saul's Tavern 60 Waverly Avenue. Saul Unger, proprietor; presented amateur hours on Tuesday nights (1939) with Matty Alston as emcee; regular entertainers included Mousie and His Cats, Arthur (Prince) Hall, and John (Smoky) Jones and His Swingsters.

Savoy Ballroom Springfield and Belmont avenues. Barnlike dance hall over furniture store; home of Savoy Dictators, whose musical backdrop was mural created by Al Madison and Danford (Larue) Jordan.

Savoy Palace 252 Court Street (at Belmont and Springfield). Opening act (1942) Corporal Brady Hodge and His Orchestra in the Terrace Room; home to Ernie Phipps (1943); offered amateur hours with cash prizes every Sunday night 11–midnight; Billie Holiday on bill (Jan. 1944).

Savoy Theater Springfield Avenue. Began new policy of offering big-time vaudeville acts (white and colored), popular stage band, and entertainers like Chappie Chapelle, oldtime favorite booked out of Harlem (Aug. 1943).

Shady Rest Country Club Scotch Plains, N.J. Watering hole of black elite where Barons of Rhythm got their start (late 1930s).

Silver Saddle 272 Clinton Avenue. Formerly Blue Mirror; recording star Florence Wright, Princess Margo, Nacki Sacki Jackie (Mandeville), emcee, and Gus Young's Band on initial bill (1951).

Skateland Montgomery Street. Home to thousands of jitterbuggers (late 1930s) who reveled to Pancho Diggs Orchestra and Emzey Waters singing "Swanee River"; featured Savoy Sultans regularly (1942–43); site of International Sweethearts of Rhythm's Newark debut (1943); converted into tractor trailer factory (1945).

Steve's Tavern 92–94 West Street. Butch and John Savarese, owners; Andrew Bailey and Louie (The Stick) Bryant, bartenders; jam wars on Mondays and Wednesdays (1939).

Teddy Powell's Holiday Inn 149–53 Meeker Avenue. Former Downbeat Club; reopened in 1950, offering big-name acts including Savannah Churchill, Little Jimmy Scott, Pearl Bailey, Wynonie Harris, Timmie Rogers, Redd Foxx, Ruth Brown, and Joe Turner; Billie Holiday a 1951 attraction.

Terrace Ballroom 1020 Broad Street. Part of Mosque theater complex; scene of dances, fashion shows, and big-name entertainment (late 1940s); featured attractions including Duke Ellington (1947), Sarah Vaughan (1948), and Count Basie (1951).

Three Deuces former Twinlite, 53 Rankin Street. Featured vocalists Bill Goode (1946), bassist Slam Stewart and Myra Johnson (1947), and Lil Green (1947).

Three Towers Belle Meade, near Somerville, N.J. Joseph Hazy, proprietor; featured Newark entertainers like Billy Moore and His Trio with Belle Powell, vocals (1946), and Miss Rhapsody (1946).

Twinlite Tavern 53 Rankin Street. James Rhett, owner; floor shows in Tempo Room featuring mix of local talent including Charlie (Brother) Kelly (1944) and Danford (Larue) Jordan (1945); name acts including (former Ink Spot) Deek Watson and Brown Dots; closed (1946) because of financial losses.

Tyler's Chicken Shack Avenel, N.J. Owned by former baseball magnate Charlie Tyler, who was shot to death (1944) by sniper, patron who confessed he and Tyler had argued over price of drink; gave Union County its first glimpse of jam sessions hosted by Milton Pittman (1938); grand opening (1941) of new bar and grill room attended by 800 people; featured quintet led by trumpeter Wilbur (Dud) Bascomb in which saxophonists Lou Donaldson and Ike Quebec played (c1950).

Victoria Hall North Fifth Street and Davenport Avenue. Barker and Hayes, owners, promoted jitterbug dances featuring Gus Young (1941).

Villa Maurice 375 Washington Street (near Court opposite old First Police Precinct). Nathan Williams, owner; Angeline Williams and Charlotte (Chezzy) Williams, hostesses; featured "a galaxy of girls and music" (1937); South Seas decorations; floor shows (1938) featuring bands led by Roosevelt Durham, Milton Pittman, and Charlie (Brother) Kelly and singers Leatha McCraw and Sadie and Mandy Matthews.

Washington Cafe 415 Washington Street. Featured Billy Harris and His Super Four (1951).

Waverly Tavern 205 Waverly Avenue (at Lillie Street). Louie (The Stick) Bryant, bartender; grand opening (July 1939) featuring Billie Sermond, Lawrence Miller, and Sterling Jump Quartette; dancing and nightly entertainment with two floor shows Thursday–Sunday; became Blue Palace (1951).

Wideway Ballroom Broad and Hill streets. Booked by beauty shop owners and other organizations for dances, often employing Johnny Jackson Orchestra (late 1940s); featured Andy Kirk's Clouds of Rhythm (1951).

References

Unless otherwise noted in the text, newspaper quotes are from the *New Jersey Afro-American* (1941–87) and the *New Jersey Herald News* (1938–43).

Introduction

Baraka, Amiri. *The Autobiography of Leroi Jones/Amiri Baraka*, p. 4. New York: Freundlich Books, 1984.

Cunningham, John. *Newark*, pp. 53–56, 172–82, and 274–82. Newark: New Jersey Historical Society, 1966.

Nanry, Charles, with Edward Berger. *The Jazz Text*. New York: Van Nostrand Reinhold, 1979.

Newark Directory. Newark: Price and Lee, 1938.

Sowell, Charles. Interview. East Orange, N.J., Feb. 7, 1988.

Stearns, Marshall. *The Story of Jazz*. New York: Oxford University Press, 1956.

Stellhorn, Paul Anthony. "Depression and Decline, Newark, New Jersey: 1929–1941." Ph.D. dissertation, Rutgers University, New Brunswick, N.J., 1982.

Woodruff, Constance (Williams). Interview. Atlantic City, N.J., Dec. 10, 1990.

Chapter 1
A Jazzy Age

Bernhardt, Clyde. Interview. Newark, Sept. 18, 1985.

Chilton, John. *Sidney Bechet: The Wizard of Jazz*. New York: Oxford University Press, 1987.

Clark, Jimmy. Interview. Irvington, N.J., Sept. 28, 1985.

Cunningham, John. *Newark*, pp. 172–73. Newark: New Jersey Historical Society, 1966.

Eason, Leon. Interview. East Orange, N.J., Dec. 4, 1985.

Henderson, Al. Interview. Newark, Oct. 14, 1985.

Johnson, William (Willie). Interview. Irvington, N.J., Oct. 5, 1985.

Matthews, Charlie. Interviews. Newark, Dec. 23, 1985 and Jan. 3, 1986.

McIntyre, Florence (Hall). Interview. Newark, Nov. 24, 1985.

Newark News. "Demolition Saddens Music Lover: Opera House Making Way for Renewal Project." Aug. 13, 1963.

———. Entertainment pages. 1925–30.

Star-Eagle. Entertainment pages. 1925–30.

Van Vechten, Carl. "Negro 'Blues' Singers." *Vanity Fair*, pp. 67, 106, and 108. March 1926.

Williams, Bobby. Telephone interview. New York, June 14, 1983.

Chapter 2
Pigsfeet and Beer

Anderson, Howard (Duke). Interview. Belleville, N.J., April 7, 1985.

Clark, Jimmy. Interview. Irvington, N.J., Sept. 28, 1985.

Henderson, Al. Interview. Newark, Oct. 14, 1985.

Johnson, William (Willie). Interview. Irvington, N.J., Oct. 5, 1985.

Jones, Alice. Telephone interview. East Orange, N.J., Oct. 20, 1990.

Lang, Floyd. Interview. Newark, Jan. 22, 1986.

Levering, David Lewis. *When Harlem Was in Vogue*, pp. 107 and 108. New York: Vintage Books, 1982.

Matthews, Sadie. Interview. Newark, Oct. 18, 1985.

Moorman, Clem. Interview. Passaic, N.J., Jan. 20, 1986.

Roberts, Bill. Interview. Newark, Nov. 30, 1985.

Chapter 3
The Kid and Miss Corprew

Carner, Gary. "Conversations with Hal Mitchell: Jazz Patriarch of Newark." *Black Perspective in Music* 17 (1989): 135.

Columbus, Chris. Telephone interview. Atlantic City, N.J., Oct. 18, 1990.

Gillespie, Dizzy, with Al Fraser. *To Be or Not to Bop*, p. 85. Garden City, N.Y.: Doubleday, 1979.

Mitchell, Harold (Hal). Interview. Newark, Dec. 7, 1985.

Chapter 4
The Lion and the Lamb

Bernhardt, Clyde. Interview. Newark, Sept. 18, 1985.

Clark, Jimmy. Interview. Irvington, N.J., Sept. 28, 1985.

Cole, Donald Reuben (Jay). Interview. Passaic, N.J., Dec. 14, 1974.

Dance, Stanley. *The World of Duke Ellington*, p. 127. New York: Scribner's, 1970.

Dexter, Dave, Jr. *The Jazz Story: From the '90s to the '60s*, pp. 56 and 57. Englewood Cliffs, N.J.: Prentice-Hall, 1964.

Ellington, Duke. *Music Is My Mistress*, p. 92. Garden City, N.Y.: Doubleday, 1973.

Kirkeby, Ed. *Ain't Misbehavin': The Story of Fats Waller*, p. 42. New York: Dodd, Mead, 1966.

Moorman, Clem. Interview. Passaic, N.J., Jan. 20, 1986.

Morgenstern, Dan. "Newport: News and Blues." *Jazz Journal*, Sept. 1960, pp. 12 and 13.

Newark News. "Orange Jazzman Shuns Spotlight." July 17, 1960.

Queen, Bob. Telephone interview. Philadelphia, Dec. 28, 1985.

Rose, Al. *Eubie Blake*, p. 147. New York: Schirmer Books, 1979.

Smith, Ted (Big Ted). Telephone interview. East Orange, N.J., Nov. 7, 1985.

Smith, Willie (The Lion), with George Hoefer. *Music on My Mind*, pp. 5–7, 29, and 31–37. New York: Doubleday, 1974.

Wallace, Frank R. Interview. East Orange, N.J., Dec. 15, 1990.

Wells, Viola (Miss Rhapsody). Interview. Passaic, N.J., Sept. 4, 1974.

Chapter 5
Tales of a Runaway

Anderson, Howard (Duke). Belleville, N.J. Interviews. April 7, 10, and 17, 1985.

Chapter 6
Ballads and Blues

Bernhardt, Clyde. Interview. Newark, Sept. 18, 1985.

Brown, Gertrude (Turman). Interview. Newark, Oct. 15, 1985.

Hall, Billie (Sermond). Interview. Newark, Oct. 5, 1985.

Henderson, Al. Interview. Newark, Oct. 14, 1985.

Howard, Thad (Chuck). Telephone interview. Latham, N.Y., Oct. 24, 1985.

Jones, Audrey (Celeste). Interview. East Orange, N.J., Oct. 20, 1985.

Roberts, Bill. Interview. Newark, Nov. 30, 1985.

Smith, Grace. Interview. Newark, Oct. 17, 1985.

Woodruff, Connie (Williams). Interview. Passaic, N.J., Sept. 8, 1990.

Chapter 7
Miss Rhapsody

Durham, Eddie. Telephone interview. New York, March 9, 1981.

Norfolk Journal and Guide. "It's Wrong to Type Blues Singers as Vulgar, Cheap, Cussing Pistol Packing Mamas, Says Miss Rhapsody." Calvin News Service, Dec. 16, 1944.

Roberts, Bill. Interview. Newark, Nov. 30, 1985.

Shaw, Arnold. *Honkers and Shouters: The Golden Years of Rhythm and Blues*, p. 46. New York: Macmillan, 1979.

Stewart-Baxter, Derrick. *Ma Rainey and the Classic Blues Singers*, pp. 100–2. London: November Books, 1970.

Variety. "Variety Bills—Week of June 11." June 8, 1943.

Wells, Viola (Miss Rhapsody). Interview. Passaic, N.J., Sept. 4, 1974.

Chapter 8
The Comics

Basie, Count, as told to Albert Murray. *Good Morning Blues: The Autobiography of Count Basie*, p. 91. New York: Random House, 1986.

Bernhardt, Clyde. Interview. Newark, Sept. 18, 1985.

Eason, Leon. Interview. East Orange, N.J., Dec. 4, 1985.

Gregory, Joe. Interview. East Orange, N.J., Nov. 6, 1985.

Howard, Thad (Chuck). Telephone interview. Latham, N.Y., Oct. 24, 1985.

Jennings, Inez. Telephone interview. Newark, Dec. 19, 1985.

Jones, Audrey (Celeste). Interview. East Orange, N.J., Oct. 20, 1985.

Moorman, Clem. Interview. Passaic, N.J., Jan. 20, 1986.

Null, Gary. *Black Hollywood: The Black Performer in Motion Pictures*, p. 109. Secaucus, N.J.: Citadel Press, 1975.

Roberts, Bill. Interview. Newark, Nov. 30, 1985.

Thomas, Flo. Interview. East Orange, N.J., Nov. 16, 1985.

Woodruff, Connie (Williams). Interview. West Orange, N.J., April 20, 1989.

Chapter 9
Joe Gregory

Gregory, Joe. Interviews. East Orange, N.J., Oct. 29 and Nov. 6, 1985.

White, Melvin (Slappy). Telephone interview. Las Vegas, Dec. 4, 1990.

Chapter 10
The Dancers

Amsterdam News. "The Elks Rendezvous." March 2, 1946.

Bradley, Doryce. Interview. Newark, Jan. 1, 1986.

Brown, Gertrude (Turman). Interview. Newark, Oct. 15, 1985.

Gregory, Joe. Interview. East Orange, N.J., Nov. 6, 1985.

Howard, Thad (Chuck). Telephone interview. Latham, N.Y., Oct. 24, 1985.

Matthews, Sadie. Interview. Newark, Oct. 18, 1985.

Morton, Lucille (Dorsey). Interview. Newark, Oct. 19, 1985.

Roberts, Bill. Interview. Newark, Nov. 30, 1985.

Washington Afro-American. "Spotting Capital Nite Spots." Feb. 18, 1945.

Woodruff, Connie (Williams). Interview. Passaic, N.J., Sept. 8, 1990.

Chapter 11
Dancing

Brinson, Carl (Tiny Prince). Telephone interview. Newark, Nov. 26, 1985.

Gillespie, Dizzy, with Al Fraser. *To Be or Not to Bop*, p. 85. Garden City, N.Y.: Doubleday, 1979.

Henderson, Al. Interview. Newark, Oct. 14, 1985.

Kanzler, George. "Basie Band Comes Out Swinging." *Star-Ledger*, Jan. 25, 1991, p. 65.

McQueen, Jackson (Flap). Telephone interview. Jersey City, N.J., Nov. 23, 1985.

Pavlow, Al. *The R & B Book: A Disc History of Rhythm & Blues*, pp. 28, 31, and 34. Providence, R.I.: Music Publishing House, 1983.

Queen, Bob. Telephone interview. Philadelphia, Dec. 28, 1985.

Chapter 12
Newark's Finest

Bradley, Herman. Telephone interview. Brooklyn, N.Y., Jan. 4, 1986.

Brinson, Carl (Tiny Prince). Telephone interview. Newark, Nov. 26, 1985.

Henderson, Al. Interview. Newark, Oct. 14, 1985.

Kelly, George. Interview. New York, Sept. 23, 1990.

Mitchell, Harold (Hal). Interview. Newark, Dec. 7, 1985.

Moncur, Grachan (Brother). Interview. Miami, Fla., March 3, 1987.

Chapter 13
Teen Sensations

Basie, Count, as told to Albert Murray. *Good Morning Blues: The Autobiography of Count Basie*, pp. 211–12. New York: Random House, 1986.

Eason, Leon. Interview. East Orange, N.J., Dec. 4, 1985.

Jones, Jimmy (Chops). Interview. Newark, Dec. 8, 1985.

Salley, Leo. Interview. East Orange, N.J., Oct. 29, 1985.

Stanford, Jimmy. Telephone interview. Mechanicsburg, Pa., March 28, 1986.

Swangin, Thomas O. (T. O.) Interview. East Orange, N.J., Dec. 17, 1985.

Chapter 14
The Kinney Club

Bernhardt, Clyde. Interview. Newark, Sept. 18, 1985.

Clark, Wesley. Interview. Newark, Oct. 22, 1985.

Eason, Leon. Telephone interview. East Orange, N.J., Jan. 22, 1991.

Hall, Billie (Sermond). Interview. Newark, Oct. 5, 1985.

Hurt, (Uncle) Willie. Interview. Newark, Oct. 5, 1985.

Kukla, Frederick H. (Fred). Telephone interview. Lyndhurst, N.J., Jan. 13, 1991.

Morton, Lucille (Dorsey). Interview. Newark, Oct. 19, 1985.

Thomas, Flo. Interview. East Orange, N.J., Nov. 16, 1985.

Chapter 15
Son Berry and the Boston Plaza

Berry, Earline. Telephone interview. Irvington, N.J., Dec. 11, 1990.

Jones, Audrey (Celeste). Interview. East Orange, N.J., Oct. 20, 1985.

Roberts, Bill. Interview. Newark, Nov. 30, 1985.

Chapter 16
Mrs. Reeves and the Nest Club

Coleman, Lander. Interview. Passaic, N.J., Oct. 4, 1985.

Gregory, Joe. Interview. East Orange, N.J., Nov. 6, 1985.

Howard, Thad (Chuck). Telephone interview. Latham, N.Y., Oct. 24, 1985.

Matthews, Sadie. Interview. Newark, Oct. 19, 1985.

Reeves. Eurlee. Interviews. Newark and Carolina, P.R., Jan. 2, 1986 and June 14, 1986.

Chapter 17
Pop Durham's Alcazar

Coleman, Lander. Interview. Newark, Oct. 4, 1985.

Eason, Leon. Interview. East Orange, N.J., Dec. 4, 1985.

Gregory, Joe. Interview. East Orange, N.J., Nov. 6, 1985.

Henderson, Al. Interview. Newark, Oct. 14, 1985.

Henderson, Florence (Williams). Interview. Plainfield, N.J., Jan. 13, 1991.

Johnson, William (Willie). Interviews. Irvington, N.J. and Newark, Oct. 5, 1985 and Jan. 14, 1991.

Moorman, Clem. Interview. Passaic, N.J., Jan. 20, 1986.

Smith, Cladys (Jabbo). Telephone interview. New York, Dec. 20, 1985.

Woodruff, Connie (Williams). Interview. West Orange, N.J., April 20, 1989.

Chapter 18
The Pipers

Henderson, Al. Interview. Newark, Oct. 14, 1985.

Moorman, Clem. Interview. Passaic, N.J., Jan. 20, 1986.

Patterson, Neal. Interview. Newark, Dec. 7, 1990.

Woodruff, Connie (Williams). Interview. Passaic, N.J., Sept. 8, 1990.

Chapter 19
Dodger's Bar and Grill

Anderson, Howard (Duke). Interview. Belleville, N.J., April 17, 1986.

Clark, Wesley. Interview. Newark, Oct. 22, 1985.

Jones, Audrey (Celeste). Interview. East Orange, N.J., Oct. 20, 1985.

Matthews, Charlie. Interview. Newark, Dec. 23, 1985.

Scott, Jimmy (Little Jimmy). Telephone interview. East Orange, N.J., Dec. 12, 1990.

Wells, Viola (Miss Rhapsody). Interview. Passaic, N.J., Sept. 24, 1974.

Chapter 20
The Coleman Hotel

Coleman, Lander. Interviews. Newark and Passaic, N.J., Oct. 4 and 12, 1985.

Coleman, Rev. Russell. Interview. Newark, Oct. 4, 1985.

Chapter 21
Herman Lubinsky and Savoy Records

Bernhardt, Clyde. Interview. Newark, Sept. 18, 1985.

Brinson, Carl (Tiny Prince). Telephone interview. Newark, Nov. 26, 1985.

Brown, Nate. Interview. Atlantic City, N.J., Nov. 14, 1985.

Eason, Leon. Interview. East Orange, N.J., Dec. 4, 1985.

Grossberg, Bruce. Interview. Hackensack, N.J., May 4, 1986.

Grossberg, Lois. Telephone interview. Mahwah, N.J., May 11, 1986.

Henderson, Al. Interview. Newark, Oct. 14, 1985.

McQueen, Jackson (Flap). Telephone interview. Jersey City, N.J., Nov. 21, 1985.

Mendelsohn, Fred. Telephone interview. Lake Worth, Fla., May 13, 1986.

Mitchell, Harold (Hal). Interview. Newark, Dec. 7, 1985.

Shaw, Arnold. *Honkers and Shouters: The Golden Years of Rhythm and Blues*, pp. 343–53. New York: Macmillan, 1979.

Wright, Edward (Eddie). Interview. East Orange, N.J., April 14, 1986.

Chapter 22
Ike Quebec

Clark, Wesley. Interview. Newark, Oct. 22, 1985.

Cuscuna, Michael. Liner notes. *The Complete Blue Note Forties Recordings of Ike Quebec and John Hardee*. New York, April 1984.

Eason, Leon. Telephone interview. East Orange, N.J., Jan. 22, 1991.

Feather, Leonard. *The Encyclopedia of Jazz*. New York: Bonanza Books, 1960.

Jones, Jimmy (Chops). Telephone interview. Newark, Jan. 22, 1991.

Lang, Floyd. Interview. Newark, Jan. 22, 1986.

Matthews, Sadie. Interview. Newark, Oct. 19, 1985.

Mitchell, Harold (Hal). Interview. Newark, Dec. 7, 1985.

Woodruff, Connie (Williams). Interview. Passaic, N.J., Jan. 21, 1991.

Chapter 23
Sarah's Gonna Sing

Brooks, Phyllis. Interview. Newark, Feb. 25, 1988.

Greene, Evelyn. Telephone interview. Newark, Feb. 26, 1988.

Howard, Chuck (Thad). Telephone interview. Latham, N.Y., Oct. 24, 1985.

McIntyre, Carl. Interview. Newark, Nov. 24, 1985.

Wells, Viola (Miss Rhapsody). Interview. Passaic, N.J., Oct. 8, 1974.

Chapter 24
Bopping at the Manor

Anderson, Howard (Duke). Interview. Belleville, N.J., April 10, 1986.

Brown, Nate. Interview. Atlantic City, N.J., Nov. 14, 1985.

Carr, Roy, Brian Case, and Fred Dellar. *The Hip: Hipsters, Jazz and the Beat Generation*, p. 24. London: Faber and Faber, 1986.

Gitler, Ira. *Swing to Bop: An Oral History of the Transition in Jazz in the 1940s*, p. 230. New York: Oxford University Press, 1985.

Gonzales, Babs. *I Paid My Dues: Good Times . . . No Bread*. East Orange, N.J.: Expubidence Publishing, 1967.

———. *Movin' on Down de Line*. Newark: Expubidence Publishing, 1975.

Gregory, Joe. Interview. East Orange, N.J., Nov. 6, 1985.

Lester, Connie. Interview. Secaucus, N.J., Nov. 7, 1986.

Moody, James. Interview. Secaucus, N.J., Oct. 31, 1986.

Roberts, Bill. Interview. Newark, Nov. 30, 1985.

Wilmer, Valerie. *Jazz People*, pp. 93–99. London: Allison and Bushby, 1970.

Chapter 25
The Dawning Of Rhythm and Blues

Leiter, Robert D. *The Musicians and Petrillo*, pp. 132–69. New York: Bookman Associates, 1953.

Queen, Bob. "Nocturne Revue." *New Jersey Afro-American*, Oct. 25, 1947.

Woodruff, Connie (Williams). Interview. Passaic, N.J., Sept. 8, 1990.

Appendixes

The sources listed are in addition to all interview and most book citations given above.

Anderson, James (Billy). Interview. East Orange, N.J., Nov. 16, 1985.

Bailey, Estelle. Telephone interview. Albany, N.Y., Oct. 26, 1985.

Bell, Sanford. Telephone interview. Bloomfield, N.J., May 11, 1986.

Bernhardt, Clyde, as told to Sheldon Harris. *I Remember: Eighty Years of Black Entertainment, Big Bands, and the Blues*. Philadelphia: University of Pennsylvania Press, 1986.

Bogar, Nancy. Telephone interview. Union Township (Vauxhall), N.J., Jan. 15, 1991.

Brannon, Humphrey (Teddy). Telephone interview. Newark, March 4, 1986.

Cameron, Mary Pitts Jones. Interview. Spotswood, N.J., Nov. 2, 1985.

Chilton, John. *Billie's Blues.* New York: Stein and Day, 1975.

———. *Who's Who of Jazz.* New York: Time-Life Records, 1978.

Costello, Rita. Telephone interview. New York, Nov. 28, 1985.

Dance, Stanley. *Jazz Era: The Forties*, p. 105. London: Macgibbon and Kee, 1961.

———. *The World of Swing*, p. 167. New York: Scribner's, 1974.

Driggs, Frank, and Harris Lewine. *Black Beauty, White Heat: A Pictorial History of Classic Jazz.* New York: William Morrow, 1982.

Freidwald, Will. *Jazz Singing.* New York: Scribner's, 1990.

Gibson, Danny. Telephone interview. Newark, Feb. 8, 1986.

Gordon, Meredith. Interview. East Orange, N.J., Dec. 16, 1985.

Handy, D. Antoinette. *Black Women in American Bands and Orchestras.* Metuchen, N.J.: Scarecrow Press, 1981.

———. *The International Sweethearts of Rhythm.* Metuchen, N.J.: Scarecrow Press, 1980.

Harris, Sheldon. *Blues Who's Who: A Biographical Dictionary of Blues Singers.* New Rochelle, N.Y.: Arlington House, 1979.

Hughes, Langston, and Milton Meltzer. *Black Magic: A History of Black Entertainers in America.* New York: Bonanza Books, 1967.

Jones, Frank. Interview. Montclair, N.J., Jan. 8, 1987.

Kernfeld, Barry, editor. *The New Grove Dictionary of Jazz.* 2 vols. London: Macmillan, 1988.

Latta, Dorothy. Telephone interview. Newark, Nov. 9, 1985.

McCarthy, Albert. *Big Band Jazz.* London: Royce, 1983.

———. *The Jazz Bands.* London: Spring Books, 1974.

Meeker, David. *Jazz in the Movies: A Guide to Jazz Musicians, 1917–1977.* New Rochelle, N.Y.: Arlington House, 1977.

Newsweek. "Lucky and Lucius." Sept. 7, 1942, p. 72.

Outcalt, James (Chippie). Telephone interview. Detroit, Jan. 17, 1987.

Phipps, Gene, Sr. Interview. Newark, Nov. 8, 1985.

Pittman, Jean. Interview. Montclair, N.J., Oct. 14, 1985.

Pittman, Milton, Jr. Interview. Newark, Nov. 8, 1985.

Plater, Ala Mae (Miller). Telephone interview. Newark, Jan. 17, 1986.

Plater, Alma. Interview. Newark, Jan. 13, 1987.

Powell, Napoleon (Teddy). Interview. Newark, Jan. 24, 1987.

Rollins, Harold (Pop Pop). Telephone interview. Lakewood, N.J., Feb. 16, 1986.

Rust, Brian. *Jazz Records, 1897–1942.* 2 vols. New York: International Publications Service, 1970.

Simmons, Hattie. Interview. Newark, Jan. 13, 1987.

Simon, George. *The Big Bands.* New York: Macmillan, 1967.

Smythe, Togge. Telephone interview. Willingboro, N.J., Dec. 13, 1985.

Toler, Freddie. Telephone interview. Orleta, Calif., May 29, 1986.

Wilcox, Cecilia. Interview. Bloomfield, N.J., Jan. 9, 1987.

Willis, Luther (Gates). Telephone interview. Las Vegas, Feb. 9, 1986.

Winslow, Erma (Ethridge). Telephone interview. Sharon Hill, Pa., Dec. 17, 1985.

Background Works

In addition to the sources cited above, the following works have been helpful.

Albertson, Chris. *Bessie.* New York: Stein and Day, 1974.

Anderson, Jervis. *Harlem: The Great Black Way, 1900–1950.* London: Orbis Publishing, 1982.

Brown, Scott. *James P. Johnson: A Case of Mistaken Identity.* Metuchen, N.J.: Scarecrow Press, 1982.

Chilton, John. *A Jazz Nursery.* London: Bloomsbury Book Shop, 1980.

Collier, James Lincoln. *Duke Ellington.* New York: Oxford University Press, 1987.

Dance, Stanley. *The World of Earl Hines.* New York: Scribner's, 1967.

Ellington, Mercer, with Stanley Dance. *Duke Ellington: An Intimate Memoir.* Boston: Houghton Mifflin, 1978.

Fox, Ted. *Showtime at the Apollo.* New York: Holt, Rinehart and Winston, 1983.

George, Don. *Sweet Man: The Real Duke Ellington.* New York: G. P. Putnam's Sons, 1981.

Gitler, Ira. *Jazz Masters of the Forties.* New York: Collier Books, 1966.

Green, Stanley. *Ring Bells! Sing Songs! Broadway Musicals of the 1930s*. New York: Galahad Books, 1971.

Jones, Leroi. *Blues People*. New York: William Morrow, 1963.

Morgenstern, Dan. "Jersey Jazz: Still Stomping After All These Years." *Rutgers Magazine*. Jan./Feb. 1988, pp. 21–27.

Shaw, Arnold. *The Street That Never Slept*. New York: Coward and Geoghagen, 1971.

Smith, Jay, and Len Guttridge. *Jack Teagarden: The Story of a Jazz Maverick*. London: Cassel, 1960.

Southern, Eileen. *The Music of Black Americans: A History*. New York: Norton, 1971.

Index